ECHOES FROM A
VANISHED WORLD

ECHOES
FROM A
VANISHED
WORLD

M. BURNETT

Copyright © 2024 M.Burnett

The moral right of the author has been asserted.

Apart from any fair dealing for the purposes of research or private study, or criticism or review, as permitted under the Copyright, Designs and Patents Act 1988, this publication may only be reproduced, stored or transmitted, in any form or by any means, with the prior permission in writing of the publishers, or in the case of reprographic reproduction in accordance with the terms of licences issued by the Copyright Licensing Agency. Enquiries concerning reproduction outside those terms should be sent to the publishers.

Troubador Publishing Ltd
Unit E2 Airfield Business Park
Harrison Road, Market Harborough
Leicestershire LE16 7UL
Tel: 0116 279 2299
Email: books@troubador.co.uk
Web: www.troubador.co.uk

ISBN 978 1 83628 030 9

British Library Cataloguing in Publication Data.
A catalogue record for this book is available from the British Library.

Printed and bound by CPI Group (UK) Ltd, Croydon, CR0 4YY
Typeset in 11pt Minion Pro by Troubador Publishing Ltd, Leicester, UK

For my husband and all my Spanish family.

Contents

A Desolate Destination	1
A World Unto Itself	9
Distant Conflicts	18
Blighted Childhood	27
Starting Anew	42
A City at War	58
A Broken Country	77
Limited Lives	94
Emigrating	112
Returning	125
Another Time, Another Place	140
A Very Spanish Institution	144
Beyond Perfection	157
The Rich and the Poor	167
Vestiges of the Past	179
The Transition	193
Violence Against Change	201
Going Crazy	213
Being a Foreigner	227

For Better or for Worse	238
Getting By	249
The Passing Years	260
The Wrong Children	265
The Endless Plains	280
A Threat to Peace	294
Boom and Crash	306
Dying	321
Remembering	333
Spain Today	341
Epilogue	353

A DESOLATE DESTINATION

July, one of the hottest months of the year, was not a good time to arrive, I realize that now. Yet maybe I can be forgiven for not knowing. I was young, I lived from day-to-day.

I travelled, loaded down with a lifetime of possessions crammed into old suitcases. Deeper and deeper south into the unknown, through the mountains, the endless forests and occasional little towns, then slowly on into central Spain, bleached by the sun, the vast emptiness only broken by small villages of adobe and a couple of towns. Packed and chaotic, the train carried a mix of Spanish society through the interminable plateau. As the day wore on, mothers pulled out vast amounts of bread, cheese, chorizo and fruit which they handed round to anyone who happened to be there. The small compartment grew hotter, smellier and noisier, I became thirstier, more tired and confused until, after what seemed an eternity, we finally arrived in Madrid.

On I went. From the north of the city, already booming, through the old centre and across the River Manzanares, reduced to a trickle with the summer drought. Endless blocks of flats sprawled across each side of the river, along the busy road out to the south-west with its shaded side streets. The area had something impermanent about it as if it was only for fleeting residence since surely no-one could truly belong in such soulless blocks constructed in the barrenness. Each flat had an open balcony, originally intended for people to sit out in summer and enjoy the night air but more often used to keep bicycles, bits and bobs and bright orange bottles of gas, giving the whole area a chaotic look. Sitting out looking across wasteland or busy roads was never very appealing anyway.

There were few trees and only sparse vegetation struggling to survive. It was always windy, wastepaper blowing around, everything shimmering with heat. I could see nothing of beauty. It was concrete, plaster, aluminium, tawdry and tired, a desolate, modern urban landscape although something of the old did remain. There were 19th century apartment blocks with a mishmash of small shops lining the road now darkened with pollution from the incessant traffic, dejected and sad, their former glory gone.

This is my first memory of Spain: the makeshift, the dusty and forsaken.

If I had expectations they were not of this, but looking back I think I had none. Foreign lands in the 1970s, long before cheap travel and the Internet, were more unknown and unknowable. Now that news is beamed in 24/7, the world has shrunk. We relate to every tin-pot regime, we know the details of tragedies in distant lands. True or not, it's all laid out for everyone to see, virtually impossible to avoid. Back then, it was more hidden and unavoidably more selective. I knew, of course, that Franco[1] had died. I remember the news splashed across a news-stand one miserable November day, yet it meant little to me in a leafy suburb in middle England. If I was unsure about the details of Franco's regime, I knew that any dictatorship was definitely wrong, after all, I was a child of the sixties and although the heady days of the 1968 revolution were long gone, they had left a fading trail of idealism, left-wing politics mixed with flower power, hippies and "make love not war". In those distant times, I could reduce everything to a common denominator, to black and white, right or wrong. It is always simpler for the young to enthusiastically cheer causes before they become tangled with the passing years.

Apart from the wrongs of the dictatorship my knowledge of Spain was sketchy: a little of its long-past glories in the 16th century, of conquests, empires and treasures followed by empty centuries until the outbreak of the Spanish Civil War in 1936. I had seen a propaganda film made for the Republican cause which opened with scenes of peasants before the Civil War trudging through fields with horses and carts in a rural tableau from a by-gone age. Fighting followed, death, air-raids, *Guernica*[2], the collapse of the Republic and to finish, scenes of peasants trudging to work, looking suspiciously like

---

[1] A dictator who ruled Spain from 1939 to his death in 1975.
[2] The city bombed by German and Italian planes during the Civil War and immortalized in a painting by Picasso.

those at the beginning. A grainy, black-and-white film but the message was clear: in spite of the Civil War, of the destruction, of the death and injury and a society riven apart, nothing had changed in the harsh, dreary existence of the Spanish people.

In the late seventies Spain was no longer a land of peasants and political repression: it had opened up as a holiday destination, with sun, plastic donkeys, cheap plonk and whirling dancers. Family friends had refused to visit while Franco's dictatorship lasted, and in my family it was not considered to be a suitable destination for holidays, whether for the plastic donkeys or the political repression I'm not sure but, as I had neither been nor intended to go, it remained a blur of war, oppression and sun. That was all to change.

My new life was about to start in one of those anonymous modern blocks. Like many flats at that time, it felt as if it was built only for the summer. In those first months with sleepless nights and uncomfortable days this seemed like a good idea, but as they say Madrid has "*9 meses de invierno y 3 de infierno*"[3]. When winter suddenly arrived, the stone floors were cold. The heating, which was expensive and inefficient, was appropriately called "black" heating as it left a huge black mark up the wall. It was as if they were still not quite used to building flats for a modern age, as if they wanted to believe they had left behind the cold and discomfort of the past and from now on it would always be warm and sunny.

---

3   9 months of winter and 3 of hell.

There was no lift, the hoi polloi walked up stairs, lugging everything up with them: children, pushchairs, shopping. It was normal then, people were tougher. With their cheap aluminium windows and flimsy tiles the flats were utilitarian. Each had the same layout, the same stone tiles on the floor and almost the same furniture. This was sparse, no rugs or carpets, a synthetic leather sofa which stuck to your legs in summer and was cold and slippery in winter. The neighbours' conversations could be heard through the thin walls while a faint odour of drains pervaded the whole flat. The bathroom and kitchen looked onto a central well where even in August, as lunch time approached, the hiss of pressure cookers could be heard and the block filled with a smell of cooking beans and chickpeas.

The area was closed and self-sufficient. The private and public spaces merged into one as if they were still living in a village rather than the suburbs of a big city. Perhaps, it was what they needed at the time: togetherness and stability in contrast to the shifting world around them. I heard families chatting as they walked arm in arm in the street in the evening, the generations sitting on benches together, and I wanted to believe this was something I could easily be part of. After all, wasn't I about to join one of these big, happy families?

It was only a short walk to where my future family-in-law lived. At that time all good sons and daughters would live as near to their parents as possible. When I went to meet them for the first time it was early evening, I remember the sultry heat, the excitement and the blue sundress I wore, my best to impress. Their ground floor flat was a strange place with plastic flamenco dancers, tapestry pictures, uncoordinated and sombre. I was unsure whether the thick, net curtains were there to keep out the light or the prying eyes of the neighbours but it meant no sunlight entered, ever, and it was never particularly hot. That was how I thought of the interior of Spanish flats for years: dark, cool, suspended in time.

I sat down on another sticky sofa and was offered drinks but there was no welcome. It was not what I had hoped for, but then nothing in Spain ever was which is why it took me so very long to understand it, why I hated the country in those first years, not with a passion but with bitter resignation.

Spain was remote for me in every way: the time, the place, all Spanish people had lived through, all they believed. Mine was a life of financial security, democracy, new cars and washing machines, a clear-cut future if I had wanted it. I grew up with all the accoutrements of a life in an industrialized country, symbols of progress and a testimony to education. Intimate records of the family were lovingly collected, souvenirs of happy moments: fashionable holidays on the Côte d'Azur in the twenties, Weetabix-style cycling holidays in the thirties, letters from friends in pre-war Germany, yellowing maps of Norway and Sweden. My past was preserved in books handed down through generations, in autograph albums with copperplate script and water colours, photographs of a large Victorian family on trips, formal photos in studios with refined backdrops, records that they had succeeded in life.

Wars brought untold suffering but they were fought in other places and by the time I was growing up they were dissolving into the background, leaving only memories of victory and the lingering vanity of Empire. Britain back then still believed in itself. Change was always forward, sweeping on inexorably towards a better future: jobs, houses, cars but above all security.

Spain shared none of this, neither the progress nor the certainty. Until relatively recently, possibly more than most other countries in Europe, it was bound inexorably to its land and climate. Travelling through the country was to journey back through the ages. The roots of Spain lie in its majestic mountains, the sweeping plains, the desolate moors, the small villages where even the nearest provincial town is distant.

In spite of the heat and the endless bright sunlight, those early months will always be etched on my mind as the darkness of Spain. Although ignorant of so much I realized this vaguely, for even then I saw Spain as a place of contrasts. It is light: the brilliant light of Madrid, the mellow glow of the setting sun on the endless plains of Castile, the fading light on the small, stone villages. Against so much brightness and light it is hard to perceive the darkness of its history but it was there. The family I was about to join knew this only too well.

I never realized what lay ahead. How could I have done? How could I have known when I was blissfully unaware of the realities of life in a country fitfully emerging from a brutal regime into contemporary Europe? For, behind the cosmetic face of modernity it presented to the world, Spain remained firmly anchored in the past. Unlike my family, none of the older generation was born into the benefits and safety of democracy nor were they ever given the opportunity to improve their lives. The family's roots lay in an unchanging rural world, almost untouched by reforms for generations until finally, they were to be dragged, unprepared into an uncertain future.

A WORLD UNTO ITSELF

For centuries the family lived in a small village in the Gredos Mountains which, like so much of Spain, are in turn bountiful and harsh. Theirs was one of the many thousands of villages scattered throughout the sierras, the mountainous regions of Spain. Their lives rolled on through the centuries without dramatic change, more often than not isolated from Spain's unsettled history. Momentous events took place on the great plateau of central Spain or the medieval cities, not in hidden mountain villages.

Any student of Spanish history will have heard of the Renaissance splendours of Toledo, the Roman ruins of Segovia, and other great cities which played an important role in 15th and 16th century Spain. They will know of the ports of La Coruña on the Atlantic coast, Valencia and Barcelona on the Mediterranean and the magnificent cities of Cordoba, Seville and Granada in the south, but they will have heard far less of the wind-swept moors, the rugged mountains making up 60% of Spain's land mass where many small villages and hamlets were isolated by the rough terrain. Until very recently the winter snows left them inaccessible to the outside world for many months before the searing heat of summer arrived, leaving these regions with the sole option of subsistence agriculture. This was a rural world barely touched by any modernization until well into the twentieth century.

If it is not the Spain which has drawn historians, neither is it the Spain of many people's dreams: the olive and citrus groves of the Mediterranean, the beaches and white-washed villages. The inhabitants of the sierras are not the friendly, sparkling people of Andalusia, they rarely dance and sing. They are tough and stoical, hardened through centuries of living in the mountains and subsisting in these hostile lands.

The village where the family had lived from time immemorial nestles at the end of the Valle del Tiétar, surrounded by mountains, its stone houses creep up between the crags, trickling through the scrubby holm oak trees and clinging onto the slopes of the mountain. It is an organic structure growing around the mountains, with houses springing up where they can and sometimes falling into ruins to be reabsorbed by the land.

Only about 70 miles to the southwest of Madrid, the village is now within easy reach of the capital but a mere seventy years ago it was still isolated and self-sufficient, a world unto itself with most things provided in the village or the nearest small town. Had anyone taken the journey from the village to Madrid along the rough, winding roads they would have found little more than a small, provincial city, although for centuries, people and, in particular the poor, rarely travelled far if they could avoid it.

Their ancestors were all born in the same or nearby villages and nothing suggested that those born in the late

19th century would ever abandon it despite the poverty. It was a place of stability where they would continue to live just as their parents, grandparents and ancestors had done, leaving only when they could be sure their travels would afford them something better. Even in the 1980s there were elderly people who had never set foot in the capital, who had never seen the sea and who never envisaged life beyond the mountains.

The family was more fortunate than the inhabitants of other sierras as the valley of the Tiétar is blessed with a great abundance of natural resources. Nevertheless, for centuries, life was about survival, marked out by the seasons and ruled by the weather. They eked out a living from small patches of land seized from the mountain side but, unlike the poor peasants working the *latifundios*, the large estates in Andalusia and Extremadura, they usually owned the land, although here as well the poorest had to work as *jornaleros,* or agricultural labourers. Life was not easy but for all its harshness there was enough to eat and moreover it is an area of great beauty.

Spring is bountiful, the summer heat ripens fruits, autumn is mellow, a time to harvest the last the land has to offer; then comes the bitterly cold winter bringing frost and snow. For many people, Spain symbolizes sun and warmth but it is the cold which leaves a lasting impression. From the account of his experiences in the Civil War, Laurie Lee seems to have suffered far more from the effects of the cold than from the fighting[4].

---

4   *As I walked out one Midsummer morning.* Laurie Lee

A log fire was always lit in the huge stone fireplace for warmth in winter and for curing ham and chorizo in the autumn and, when necessary, the rest of the year for cooking. In the seventies, wool-filled mattresses still provided insulation against the freezing nights, while rough, homespun blankets covered the beds. The former were extremely lumpy, the latter heavy and prickly as I found out from experience but they did provide much needed warmth. The city dweller's romantic notions of country life would have left the villagers perplexed.

This area tucked away in the mountains may lack the immediate appeal of the Mediterranean coast but as part of the history of the Spanish people it is also the story of the family. Tracing a family tree is complex in a country where illiteracy was widespread for many centuries, and family records, often unreliable, can only be found in churches. Moreover, a great number of documents have been destroyed in the many conflicts which have taken place on Spanish soil and those remaining are poorly archived. Dates and names, however, matter little, since family and village are synonymous. It made them what they are, shaped how they behave and what they believe. Unfortunately, due to the scarcity of written records, narrating the history of the village meets with much the same obstacles as research into family history. Nevertheless, it can be pieced together from the history of Spain, the region and architectural remains.

Its remote origins are shrouded in mystery, but we know that a settlement has existed on the site of the village for centuries with evidence of a prehistoric community. Then in 218 BC Romans arrived in the peninsula. When their empire collapsed as it did in the rest of Europe, the Visigoths settled. In 711 it was the Moors who invaded Iberia conquering all but the northwest of the territory.

Did the Arabs settle in the village? Probably, as they swept up through the whole country, but lacking concrete evidence either in documents or in the buildings this can only be conjecture. The Moors were finally expelled from the country in 1610, although in practice there is ample evidence that many of them remained. Considering that the Moorish city dwellers who had converted either willingly or forcibly could remain after 1610 it is highly unlikely the inhabitants of small mountain villages were expelled. During the re-conquest, as it was called, when the Arabs were being driven out little by little, at least officially, the valley was often on the shifting border of re-conquered lands so, in order to secure the area against invasion, Christians from the north were brought in to repopulate the region.

If the history of the region strongly suggests that the family's ancestors were at least partly Moors, their appearance supports this theory for they are dark skinned, with black hair and large dark eyes. In fact, even today they have sometimes been taken for Arabs by Arabs themselves.

Although a continued Arab presence in the village is merely supposition it would have been a good place to stay. Although ill-suited to intensive farming, the land teemed with wildlife. In later centuries it became a place where the rich went for hunting and falconry, appearing in *El Libro de la Montería*[5] written by King Alfonso XI in the mid-fourteenth century, which described the Hispanic woods and mountains as well as the breeds of dogs and the prey to be found in each area. Generously endowed by nature, it was indeed a hunter's paradise: game, wolves, bears and wild boar roamed the forests, a variety of birds soared above the mountains while pike, barbel and other fish were plentiful in the rivers.

By medieval times, many prospering villages and hamlets peopled by descendants of the waves of invasion, occupation and immigration were strung along the valley. A mayor and other officials were elected allowing each village to be self-governing and disputes with neighbouring villages, usually over land, would be settled in local courts.

A wide range of products was on offer at fairs and markets held in a nearby town. Cooking utensils, arms, other hunting tools, skins and livestock were sold but the range of goods was not limited to essential wares as it was also possible to purchase luxury items, such as cloth from Italy and the Netherlands, lands under Spanish control. Even serfs were offered for sale. All kinds of fruits pears, apples, peaches, figs as well as vegetables were traded and there was wine either from the valley or imported from abroad. Whatever else was needed could be produced by the village itself.

Religion was an essential part of Spanish life and the little church was the focal point of the village for

---

5 The book of hunting arts.

both religious and secular matters. Council meetings were held in the porch outside, but the church was first and foremost the place where they attended mass and were christened, married and buried. Death was a constant companion, and many desperate prayers must have echoed around the church's walls as they begged for salvation. Spain suffered the scourge of the plague particularly in the 17th century, and with the perennial problems of excessive rain or drought and cruel winters, agricultural production was always at the mercy of the climate. Unlike Britain, no agricultural revolution took place in the 18th century. Machinery was introduced at a very late date and in any case, it would have been of little use on the small patches of land on the mountain slopes where it was rarely used until well into the 20th century.

It wasn't until the early 19th century that events beyond the valley encroached on their lives, bringing war and conflict that lasted for some years. Before that the valley had remained almost untouched by the increasingly bitter political wrangling and the growing unrest in the cities. In 1808 Spain joined the war against Napoleon in a conflict which gave rise to the word *guerrilla*, an idea that has been somewhat romanticized as many of these fighters were probably merely bandits or outcasts. The craggy Gredos mountains with their densely forested slopes provided a perfect place to hide out waiting to ambush the French troops and exact revenge. When the French were finally driven out they left a devastated country about to face more than a century of unrest, political assassinations and the Carlist wars[6], which were to kill proportionally more people than that of 1936 to 1939.

Spain until relatively recently has been a hard country to govern. Not as Franco claimed because the Spanish needed a father to control them but because it is so diverse. The most mountainous country in Europe after Switzerland, the various sierras break up the country, making communications and the transportation of people and goods extremely complicated, unlike Britain where industrial regions, ports and cities were easily connected by a canal and later rail network.

The economy, however, was not the only problem: in the late 19th century a deepening rift existed between the rural and urban society. The former, far more traditional, wanted to conserve the old social order and was unreceptive to new ideas whereas the latter believed that social and economic progress through innovation and change should be imposed at any cost.

Interestingly, despite being city dwellers themselves, writers and intellectuals looked to the rural world to find the quintessence of "Spanishness". In Pérez Galdós's[7] novel *Doña Perfecta*, Pepe Rey, an engineer goes to a small provincial town to marry his cousin, Rosario, the daughter of Doña Perfecta. While he is a liberal, convinced of the

---

6   The Carlist wars were a series of civil wars which took place in the 19th century.

7   Pérez Galdós (1843-1920), who wrote about the common people, was a key figure in Spanish literature. His works include novels, plays and reports on social and political issues.

need to remedy the backwardness of rural Spain, Doña Perfecta is determined to preserve traditional society, in other words all that was considered to be "Spanish", particularly religion. The clash between these two opposing characters does not end well; a warning of the risks inherent in forcing reform on a society which has lived by its own rules for centuries.

The Spanish countryside in the 19th century must have been an exceptionally harsh environment to inhabit. Foreign writers and painters including many Britons arrived looking for the exotic, the uncivilized, wildness and colour. They produced works of art generally glorifying what they saw and which were only occasionally tinged with criticism of the Catholic Church. But surely only adventurers from distant lands could find romanticism in 19th century Spain. Theirs was a vision not many villagers would recognise, but then they did not often paint the mountain inhabitants with their homespun clothes and rough ways, and if they found little to delight them in the villages of the mountain valley, the wary villagers in turn would have been reluctant to welcome these strange people from another land.

For centuries, the family followed the same traditional path almost completely unaffected by events in their own country, let alone by world politics. Ironically, when the outside world irredeemably impacted on their lives, it was through neither national politics nor a positive sign of progress, but a crisis in a far off place that would have seemed exotic even for sophisticated city dwellers: the Caribbean Island of Cuba.

DISTANT CONFLICTS

The loss of its last overseas territories, Cuba, Puerto Rico and the Philippines in the 1890s, brought to a close a catastrophic century for Spain marked by rebellion and unrest at home as well as conflicts abroad. Inevitably, not only would news of Spain's despair seep through to the smallest, most isolated hamlet but it would touch the lives of some of the inhabitants.

Rebellion in South America had begun in 1812, influenced by the ideas of the Enlightenment, the French Revolution and the American war of independence. Taking advantage of Spain's weakness during the Peninsular War, the rebels, led by Simon Bolivar, rose up to throw off Spanish control and set up independent states. By the end of the 19th century, Cuba and the Philippines were the only territories remaining from Spain's once vast overseas Empire. Both were lost after disastrous campaigns which inflicted great suffering on the troops. It was, however, the loss of Cuba which struck the deepest blow, marking as it did the death of the once great empire and symbolizing the decline of Spanish power and prestige.

The USA, which had become an important player on the international stage by the end of the 19th century, was interested in the Philippines in the Pacific, and Cuba in the Caribbean, while the Spanish government felt bound to do whatever it could to prevent the loss of both islands. Influenced by an aggressive press campaign, the North American public was eager for control of Cuba to be taken. Finance was provided for groups on the island opposing Spanish rule. Then, in 1898 the explosion of an American boat, the *Maine,* in the bay of Cuba, provided the perfect excuse for the USA to go to war. Spanish troops were needed for the defence of the island, and so, for the first time in many years but unfortunately not the last, men throughout the country were required to fight a foreign war. It was one which they surely felt had little to do with them, and what was worse, one that would have no benefits for them whatsoever. It is highly unlikely that they were aware of political affairs in such a distant place before being called up.

By this time no-one, not even those in a small mountain village could escape the power of the increasingly centralized Spanish state. Some of the recruits were sent to the Philippines, others to Cuba, *The Pearl in the Caribbean,* an island where many fortunes had been made with slavery and the production of sugar and tobacco. This Caribbean island was to be the destination for Isidro, my husband's great grandfather, who was born in the village in the 1870s.

Unsurprisingly, as hardly anyone was keen to fight anywhere never mind in far off lands, a compulsory three-year military service was introduced in 1885 in order to maintain a supply of fresh troops in the face of the high death toll in foreign wars. Conditions in Cuba were horrific even for those used to the poverty and hardship of city slums, harsh mountains or the vast plains of Spain. These men, unprepared for the extreme conditions, had to face all the dangers of the sweltering jungles: tropical diseases from insect bites, sudden changes of temperature, high humidity, torrential rains and huge rodents. Fatalities were high although few died on the battlefield. The ill-equipped, badly prepared troops soon began to fall at an alarming rate with far more losses through sickness and injury than through planned military action which was, in fact, limited since they were fighting an elusive enemy who relied on ambushes and surprise attacks in a terrain they knew well.

Escape from this grim destiny was possible through a payment to ensure a posting in Spain and hence release from the obligation to serve abroad. Needless to say, this option was only open to the wealthy who had the resources to pay, therefore, it was the poor who went, leaving behind the sons of the rich, the politicians, the military commanders and those with influence in a country where influence was everything. Not only did this cause resentment, it also meant that those commanding had never been in Cuba so knew little about the conditions there and probably many of them cared even less. What mattered was victory. It was not to be.

The war ended in a humiliating disaster and caused what became known as the *crisis del fin de siglo*[8]. More

---

8 The crisis at the closing of the century.

than anything else the effects were psychological, dealing a serious blow to the prestige of politicians, plunging intellectuals into a state of crisis while causing a loss of face for Spain internationally. What did this defeat actually signify for the general population? The answer is probably that, with the exception of those who actually had to fight, it did not affect them overly, their lives continued much as they had done before.

Although we know that Isidro went, we know nothing of his reaction. Most likely he talked little about it and definitely would not have written about it. It is highly probable that he was illiterate like 60% of the population at the time, a reason why there are so few accounts of the experiences of the poor soldiers in these conflicts. What we do know is that he was one of the lucky ones who returned to their village to take up life where it had been abandoned.

The village was not only his home; it was, much more than the nation, the place which formed his identity. It was where he felt at ease, he knew the customs, the folklore and the food. He was surrounded by his family and his ancestors. Poets and writers coined the term "*patria chica*", the little homeland, to describe it but for country folk like him it was simply a sentiment, something which shaped their lives but which they would never have been able to define.

He settled down with his wife and his first son, Ramón, born in 1901. That same year Gregorio was born to another family and, despite the disaster of Cuba which loomed so large in political circles, life for these two baby boys was little different from that of their ancestors and, like the generations before them, they had no reason to believe it would ever change. The houses, the streets, the work, the farm implements were all the same, but gradually with greater contact with the outside world came the realization that perhaps life could be better.

There is a romantic notion that all the villagers were equal, but this was not so. The village was ruled by a strict social hierarchy which ensured everyone was acutely aware of precisely where they stood in a system which had remained largely unchanged for centuries. The vast majority knew perfectly well they had little chance of moving up the social scale.

Respect was paid to a very few prestigious professions which bestowed the right to oversee every aspect of local life: spiritual, political and economic. The key figure was the priest who knew the village secrets, said masses, provided moral control and was kept busy with christenings, marriages and funerals. In some of the larger villages there might be a doctor, but usually medical professionals travelled around from one place to another and were only called upon in cases of extreme gravity.

In general, local matters could be dealt with by these two professionals, while a trip to the nearest big town, Talavera, was necessary for weightier legal business such as drawing up wills and property transactions. There they would visit the notaries, lawyers or registrars all notable, not to mention well-paid, figures of provincial life. Although some looked up to them, others resented the ease with which they had entered their professions and their influence. The seeds of discontent which were to burst out later in the century were already planted, although perhaps not so deeply in villages where many had their own land as among the landless agriculture workers who predominated on the latifundios, particularly in the south.

Most lucrative professions were firmly closed to anyone who lacked the right connections, even supposing any villagers could have afforded the long, costly education required to pass the state entry examinations, leaving many families with few prospects for change. Gregorio's family had small plots carved out of the mountain slopes which provided sufficient food for the family and Ramón's family were the village builders, masters of constructing the solid, grey stone houses. But although both families had enough to get by neither generated the excess money needed to pay for a good education in the nearby towns, the best route out of the village.

From the mid 19th century all villages had a school with a teacher who was lower down the social scale than other professionals. The rudimentary education system was designed solely to provide a very basic knowledge of the three "Rs", nothing more was considered necessary for village children. Once compulsory education was completed at the age of nine, most children were expected to assist their parents with tasks at home or in the fields.

Despite the lack of opportunity, Ramón and Gregorio's early years would have been uneventful. Whatever news filtered through to their tiny mountain village, hardly affected their lives. In the first part of the century politicians and intellectuals still harboured a faint hope that Spain's problems would be solved peaceably although such expectations were fading as the years rolled by. Social and economic progress in the late 19th and early 20th century was at a far slower pace than in other European countries, and although WWI provided opportunities for development, the benefits were patchy. The few changes to land ownership had little effect on the small holdings in their village.

Once again, it was a war that impinged on the lives of the new generation, one nearer home but in an equally hostile territory.

By remaining neutral, Spain avoided the bloodshed of WWI, the most catastrophic of European events in the early 20th century, although at the time it had already embarked on another foreign war. It had controlled Ceuta and Melilla, in North Africa for centuries when, in 1909, tribes from the Rif, a mountainous area in North Africa, attacked Spanish iron ore mines leading to the decision to send in troops. After the initial assault there was a lull in fighting until 1919 when the offensive was resumed. The objective was to take full control, expanding Spanish authority into the hinterlands of the two enclaves.

Luckily for Ramón he had married María in the little village church and their first child was born in 1921. He was now the sole breadwinner in the family and as such could request exemption from military service. Gregorio, wiry and resilient with a wry sense of humour and most importantly still single, was not so fortunate. Like the men in the generation before him, he was sent to fight in a foreign land he would have known little about.

This North African colony brought few advantages to the Spanish state and even fewer to those who were sent to fight there. If the conditions in Cuba had made life hard for the soldiers, in Morocco things were little better. They controlled, or rather tried to control a poor, mountainous area inhabited by tribes used to fighting in the rough terrain of their own territory. As well as the disorganization and general chaos, corruption was rife in the Spanish army. By 1921, when Gregorio was there, the rebel forces had reorganized themselves under an able commander, and at the bloody battle of Annual the Spanish were totally defeated with heavy losses. Once again, defeat in a foreign war did nothing to improve the delicate political situation within the country.

When, unlike many others, Gregorio came back home he could have foreseen nothing of what was to come. He did what was expected of him, following tradition by marrying his fiancée Vicenta. Their second child, Cecilia, was born in 1928.

These two lads, Gregorio and Ramón, had been born at the dawn of a new century, one which heralded deepening despair rather than a brighter future. No-one, not even the inhabitants of the most remote mountain village could escape the convulsions that were about to rock the country. If they followed disparate paths, neither they nor their children could avoid the disasters which would overwhelm the country for most of the 20th century. Theirs is the story of an ordinary family, but no less dramatic for that. They were the ones at the bottom who decided little but suffered greatly, caught up unwillingly and often unknowingly in the tragedy which was to engulf Spain.

BLIGHTED CHILDHOOD

In spite of being born into a country no less unstable than that of her parents and grandparents, Cecilia's early years were spent in an ambience of continuity and relative calmness far from the turmoil of distant events in Madrid. Nonetheless, her childhood was to be blighted by tragedy caused not by the deteriorating political situation but by circumstances that were all too common in rural Spain.

She always remembered these years in the village as idyllic and in a certain way they probably were. The world she knew was a far cry from life in the northern cities of Britain in the thirties with their industry and trade activities where my own parents grew up. These English cities were dirty, often dark and nearly always damp; the winters brought dense fog, washing left out in the backyards was marked by soot.

In the 1930s Castilian[9] villages still remained virtually untouched by industrialization or profound modernization. It is true that in the 1920s the village enjoyed certain improvements introduced into cities long before. Electricity was brought to the village although not

---

9   Castille is an area in central Spain.

to every house, and a main road was built from the capital to the valley, opening it up to visitors and trade. Whilst this was positive for some, it actually turned any village it bypassed, like hers, into a backwater.

As Cecilia recalls none of these changes had much effect on the village which remained a traditional, unchanging place resonant of fairy-tales, of the dark forests of Russia or Poland, distant lands in mystical times. Wolves still roamed the mountains. Once, when she was walking to the nearby river she turned to find a wolf trotting behind her, fortunately not a hungry one as it was summer when there was plentiful prey.

During the cold winter months, with deep snow on the mountains the wolves would come down to the village, driven by hunger to steal the sheep in pens near the house. It is easy to imagine: a freezing night, the moon highlighting the mountain peaks against the dark blue sky, a pack of hungry wolves emerging from the shadows. The enormous dogs protected by spiked collars crouched waiting. Then the attack. She would hear teeth clashing, snarling, and the desperate bleating of the sheep. The next morning the blooded body of a wolf, a dog or perhaps both would be found, a testimony to the viciousness of the fight. Sometimes, if the dogs had failed and a sheep was killed, this would mean less food for the family in the bleak winter months.

Nature could be cruel but the fertility of the soil in this region meant they were better off than many others living in rural Spain in the late twenties and thirties. Deprivation, of course, existed in Britain but it was the product of industrialization, a new phenomenon discussed and analysed if not solved by progressive thinkers. It was the inspiration for Marx and the concern of socialists like the Webbs, whereas the desperation of the backward regions of Spain were hidden away or ignored for centuries.

Those born in the thirties, forties or even fifties and sixties in these little villages have told me tales of the hardship and struggles of their early lives. In the 1950s, in Extremadura, one of the poorest regions of Spain, María Carmen's family had no choice but to send her to work as a servant for a family in the nearest city of Badajoz when she was only eight years old. There she was expected to look after children older than she was. She finally taught herself to read and write but only when she was an adult. Antonia, a neighbour from Trujillo also in Extremadura, was sent to deliver the bread her widowed mother baked, as soon as she could walk. This must have been in the early thirties.

Many accounts of the pre-war years in Spain speak of the poverty in Andalusia, in Extremadura, in the centre of Spain, Galicia, Cantabria and Asturias in the north. Accounts written by Spanish people about their early years, or descriptions from foreigners who came to the country intrigued by its distinctness for, at a distance, even poverty holds a strange attraction.

Not all records are written: itinerant photographers, again many foreign, travelled around rural Spain in the late 19th and early 20th centuries capturing the hardships of life in the villages as well as the simple delights. Some are photos of joyful local festivals which are such a feature of Spain, other are timeless testimonies of suffering, photos of a population in dire straits. The dilapidated houses, unpaved streets, ragged children, poor peasant farmers working on the impoverished land are there in a depiction of all that poverty brings: suffering, hopelessness and especially untimely death, omnipresent in city and country life.

Unlike the posed photos of the Victorian and Edwardian era, of people who understood cameras and images and expected them to reflect their status, these people were unconcerned about being portrayed in the best light, oblivious to the power of the image. Yet, it was photos and films rather than novels which proved to be an effective tool for shining a light on the suffering of communities which had lived unseen for centuries when they revealed the state of abandonment of Las Hurdes, a remote mountain area in the far west of Spain near the Portuguese border, once again in Extremadura.

Few had been aware of the privations suffered by the inhabitants of this region but one of them was Gregorio Marañón, a doctor concerned with public health and with enough standing to persuade the king, Alfonso XIII that he, personally, should see what their lives were like. Travelling on foot or horseback as there were no roads, the royal expedition set out in June 1922. The king visited tiny hamlets where stone hovels perched on the steep slopes of the mountains among the Spanish oak trees, the heather and rock rose. The inhabitants did their best to welcome their king in a fitting fashion but the photos and footage clearly show the state of the population marked by alarming levels of cretinism due to the poor diet while malaria, typhoid and other infectious diseases were common. Illiteracy rates were high and apparently moral standards were sadly low. The latter appears to have been a particularly worrying problem in Catholic Spain and when potential solutions to the afflictions of the area were presented they included more churches and priests, which I'm not sure would have helped greatly to improve their lives. As usual, much was promised but little was done. In 1933, five years after Cecilia was born, in a mountainous area not far away, Luis Buñuel made a film about Las Hurdes called *"Tierra sin pan"*[10] showing nothing had changed. To a certain extent this is understandable: by this time the political and economic situation of Spain were deteriorating rapidly and only three years before the Civil War it was unlikely anything could be done. In fact, it would be many years before the inhabitants of Las Hurdes saw any improvements in their lives.

Fortunately, life in Cecilia's village was not so bad. Looking back at these records of village life, it seems to us that life was harsh, the labour unrelenting but as she knew nothing else, she accepted and was happy. She shared with many country folk, a stoical attitude to life nurtured over centuries. Nonetheless, if in later life she looked back on those halcyon days of childhood with nostalgia, she did sometimes let slip that village life was not always as perfect as she liked to make out. Although unambitious and generally contented with their lot, the family could not but be conscious that they were somewhere far down in the pecking order.

---

10 Land without bread.

Gregorio might have had enough land to keep the family fed, yet it was not enough for little Cecilia to be friends with the daughter of a wealthier landowner. She told me that the close childhood friendship with this girl was vetoed by the parents. Distinctions of wealth mattered greatly. Everyone knew their station in life and was expected to stay there. Like the generation of her parents, education offered her little hope for improvement.

If education was still rudimentary for children as a whole, it was worse for girls like Cecilia of a lower social status. An inkling of knowledge was quite sufficient for their role of wife and mother. Indeed, for the Catholic Church an educated woman was a dangerous thing which meant that, although Cecilia could read, she rarely did so in later life; just one of very many women who were denied the opportunity to learn, thus restricting their lives for years to come.

She never expressed any regrets about her lack of education or the path mapped out for her early in life. Besides, in the early 1930s she was still too young to know that far away in Madrid a few dauntless women were fighting against the odds to improve the fate of Spanish women. It is unlikely that Vicenta, her mother, was aware that momentous changes were about to take place since there was no radio and with a scant education, reading a newspaper was an arduous task even supposing she had had the time. It was almost exclusively women in large cities who were involved in the reform movement and even there they were few.

Three of these women fighting for change, Clara Campoamor, Margarita Nelken and Victoria Kent were the only female deputies in the new socialist parliament which came to power in the first elections of the 2nd Republic in 1931. These educated women with ambitions to improve the fate of women in Spain were the first to win seats in the Spanish parliament. Unusually for the time in Europe but even more so in Spain, they had received a good education and therefore were well-equipped to take on the powerful patriarchy. Ironically, even though they were considered capable of representing their voters and participating in important decision making procedures, as women, they were considered incapable of voting for the members of that very same parliament. In their struggle they faced opposition not only from many sectors of political and civil society but above all from the Church. If the fight for the vote in Britain was bitter with fierce opposition from many people, in Spain it must have often felt like a hopeless battle when the omnipresent Catholic Church held sway especially in the rural areas.

Furthermore, despite sharing feminist views, there was a deep rift between these three deputies. While Clara Campoamor defended women's rights to vote, Victoria Kent and Margarita Nelken did not, believing that women would only follow the dictates of their husbands or the church thus giving the victory to a right-wing government. The press had a field day: only three women in parliament and they could not agree between themselves.

Women were finally given the vote in 1931 which, while relatively late, was earlier than in other European countries such as France where women weren't allowed to vote until 1944. For many years the right to vote was to be of little consequence for Spanish women. They could vote in the elections in 1933 and then in 1936 immediately before the country plunged into war. After Franco's victory there were to be no more free elections until 1977.

The short-lived suffrage changed little in the lives of women like Vicenta. Her path had already been charted out; she had a role to play, her own cares and worries. In general women busied themselves with domestic chores as they had been brought up to do, letting the men get on with the politics. With the set back of the dictatorship, gaining some equality in other spheres was to take much longer down an arduous road. Having met many women of the next generation over the years I can see that, with little education and a lifetime of oppression, they were simply unable to deal with the issues of feminism which is not to say they were weak, most were, in fact, incredibly strong and resourceful. Later, given the right environment and encouragement Spanish women would take up the fight for equality as determinedly as anywhere else.

We will never know if Vicenta did vote but I doubt it. Neither she nor Cecilia's father, Gregorio, took any interest in politics. He would be out all day cultivating the land and tending the animals, she would be at home, working hard to make the most of the food they could produce, cleaning and sewing clothes for the family. Their lives were wholly centred on the village and what went on there. Apart from the time when Gregorio was forced to go to war in North Africa, no doubt unwillingly, they hardly ever ventured far.

Now that the family's memories are fading, reduced to snippets from another world, to annotations of births, marriages and deaths in church records, there remains just one photo of Vicenta with her young daughter Cecilia, probably taken by an itinerant photographer around 1935, shortly before the outbreak of the Civil War.

This image does not draw me any closer to them. This mother and her child gazing out from the photo come from such a faraway time and place that I realize their lives are much more remote for me than the years that separate us would suggest. Only in her thirties, it shows a woman old before her time, lines prematurely etched on her face, her skin weathered to dark brown by years working outside.

Cecilia was the second of their children, she was followed by another son and then in 1939, as the Civil War drew to a close, Vicenta fell pregnant again this time with twins. This was always a dangerous situation for country women when medical care in the rural environment was inadequate. Poorer members of the community could count on the help of the local midwife, women with plenty of experience but little medical knowledge and no drugs or equipment.

In consequence, deaths in childbirth were quite common and tragically, only a few days after the birth of the twins, Vicenta died of septicemia leaving newborn twins as well as the three older children. The odds on these two small babies surviving were not favourable and as expected, shortly after the birth, one of them died. The surviving twin had to be cared for by relatives for the time being. Cecilia told me that half of the children born in spring were already dead by the end of winter, probably many of pneumonia or other respiratory diseases. This was the case of the remaining baby who died before he reached his first birthday.

There is no record of these two infants even though photographs were taken of dead children. It seems a macabre practice for us now but it is a testimony to the parents' unwillingness to accept the ephemeralness of life despite the frequency of untimely deaths in rural Spain. Not only did Cecilia's siblings die too quickly even for photographs but their mother, who would have drawn the most comfort from them, was also dead.

Gregorio, with a young family to look after, could not afford the luxury of grieving. Life went on and while he had to be out in the fields all day, the family needed someone to care for them. The solution to this situation was never in question: Cecilia. Only 11 at the time, she would have to take over her mother's role. This was considered quite normal as, at her age, her education was over.

First, she was sent to an aunt's house in the village in order to learn everything about running a household. In the rural world, support from the family was essential, with so much death and illness and no state provisions it was the only way anyone could survive. When she had learnt enough to cope, she returned home to take over the management of the domestic sphere, already at such a tender age the undisputed ruler of her own realm.

In a household of males she would make all the decisions about everyday matters: what to buy in the village shop, what to eat and what to keep back from the summer bounty for later in the year. There were no modern amenities. No electricity supply in the homes meant no electrical appliances to ease the daily chores, no running water meant it had to be carried from the village wells or springs and kept in pots on a stand in the entrance to be used frugally.

Everything was done as it had been for centuries. Food preparation took up a large part of her day. Goats' milk was used to make cheese especially in spring. Autumn was a busy time when food had to be stored in readiness for use in the lean winter months. Figs, grapes and plums were dried and olives were cured. Sometimes a rabbit caught in traps would be a welcome addition to the diet and the family kept chickens for meat and eggs. The beginning of the colder weather was marked by the killing of a pig.

In England slaughtering a pig, as in Hardy's *Jude the Obscure,* was a symbol of the dying rural world in the 19th century. In Spain, even in the 1990s, I spent time in villages where pigs were still being killed in autumn, when the whole village would busy themselves preparing the food that would keep the family going for many months. Now, as then, every little bit of the carcass was used. Chorizo and *morcilla*, a type of blood sausage, were made with the meat, blood, fat and seasoning stuffed into skins made from the intestines. Other parts were cured and the bones were kept for stews. Most of these products would be added to other dishes with lentils and beans or for *cocido,* a popular dish all over Castilla y León, made with chickpeas and pork-products and guaranteed to keep out the cold in winter months.

Clothes were washed in a large communal basin set up by one of the village fountains or on the flat land by the river, some distance away from the village. It is a pretty river, sweet and refreshing in summer but turning bare hands raw red in winter. The clothes were thrown over stones to be scrubbed and then wrung and laid out to dry, back breaking work although it gave the women a chance to get together, gossip and exchange points of view, household tips and share their problems. At the end of the day everything would have to be carried back to the village.

These must all have been demanding tasks for a young girl but Cecilia was never a rebel, quite the contrary, throughout her whole life she preferred to accept the rules of tradition which had brought her recognition from an early age. She didn't question her role then and she never would. She had the fatalism of country folk, an unquestioning acceptance of her destiny and the map of life drawn out for her. Hardened through adversity, by death, toughened by the weather and work, defenceless then in the face of society and even the law, she readily accepted the hard work. From the moment she took charge of the household she would hold sway with an iron fist in her own domestic kingdom of earthenware pots, log fires, brooms and washing tubs, tending the *cocido* on the dying embers and gossiping with the neighbours. From these early years she kept an uncompromising, unyielding hold on power within the family as well as an unshakeable faith that she would always enjoy its full support. She took comfort from the reassurance offered by the predictability of village life marked by the seasons and overseen by the ceremonies of an all-pervasive church.

She was never an ardent believer, she knew nothing of dogma nor cared for the outward show of piety but for many years it was the mainstay of her existence. Even though the rules made by the hierarchy of the church, the bishops in the cathedral cities, the cardinals or the Pope in Rome filtered down to the rural areas through the country priests, what predominated in the villages was the religion of tradition. It had helped people like Cecilia survive times of hardship; it was a guide for life, governing birth, marriage and death. It would not be entirely true to say she continued to believe but neither would she ignore God completely just in case. Outright rejection of the church would have meant relinquishing everything that had regulated and propped up her early life: a blind belief in some omnipotent power, the festivals and chanting meaningless prayers. Moreover, no passage of life could be complete without the church's blessing. Through the celebration of births, marriages and deaths, the priest supervised the villagers in this world as well as in the next.

The omnipresence of the church was felt in the *fiestas* which marked out the year. If for the church these celebrations were an accommodation to local festivals from the mists of time, for the villagers it was an opportunity for social interaction rather than for religious observation. That it is not to say there was not a strong feeling of devotion but it was to their shrine and to their tradition and above all to their particular Virgin Mary.

Throughout Spain, May is the month when the faithful beseech the Virgin for her intercession in worldly life and the first of this month is still the date the village pays homage to their Virgin. The festivities begin in a suitably sober fashion on April 30th when the villagers gather outside the church to chant canticles. The following day a band marches around the streets playing traditional tunes before a mass is held in the church. The Virgin is then carried out of the church to the edge of the village to sing a Hail Mary before carrying her in a procession back to the shrine where a fountain provides cool water. Anyone drinking it can ask a favour of the Virgin or simply quench their thirst for already in May it can be quite warm at midday. Back in the village everyone enjoys a communal paella which goes on until late in the day.

Many of these celebrations were rituals to ensure abundance during the agricultural year. In September it is the turn of the Virgin of the Olives. At nine o'clock at night old furniture and junk are carried out of the houses to be set alight, then at midnight "rondas" or rounds of popular songs are sung in honour of the Virgin. In the past, livestock fairs were held but today crafts and local products have taken the place of the animals.

There are old photos recording these festivals with everyone decked out in their best clothes in front of their ramshackle houses, for they were held in almost all villages, even those in the most remote corners. Today they continue to bind people to their village as they will return each year to come together with childhood friends and family despite being born in the cities.

In May, if she could, Cecilia would always return to the village which had shaped her life more than anything else. If these visits became more sporadic as she grew older, her creed for life was based on the best of rural life: the continuity and simplicity. Not everyone would agree: Ramón, born at the turn of the century and María, his wife, spent their early married life in the village before deciding they would be better off elsewhere. As they set out on their new venture, little did they know that this decision would drag them into the very heart of the struggle which was to mark Spain for 40 long years.

STARTING ANEW

MADRID

While some villagers, like Gregorio and Vicenta, were willing to accept the hand they had been dealt, others were well aware that something better was available elsewhere. For Ramón and María the call of the city was hard to resist once the seeds of discontent were sown. During their early married life they remained in the village and, as was expected, quickly produced a string of children, all nine of them surviving which was unusual in the twenties and thirties. The fourth, born in 1928, the same year as Cecilia, was named Juan. After paying for clothes and food, there was little to spare from Ramón's wages as a builder and stonemason, and with no land of their own to cultivate life was precarious. Over time, they realized that, by escaping the confines of the village, they could better their position, casting off the status preordained by God.

Unrest was spreading throughout Spain: from the south among the destitute Andalusian peasants working in the latifundios, to the north among industrial workers. All of them had their grievances which showed no sign of being redressed. As disaffection with the government spread and resentment against the power and wealth of the church and landowners grew, so did the appeal of left-wing politics and anarchist groups. These political groups were centred in major cities such as Madrid as well as in the northeast around Barcelona, in the Basque country, and in Asturias where coal, essential for early industrial development was mined.

A glimmer of hope came in the twenties with the successful uprising led by Primo de Rivera[11]. Unusually for a dictator, he was considered acceptable by almost all the key players in politics at the time: most significantly by the army but also by monarchists, leading politicians and, albeit grudgingly, socialists. A populist leader, he brought high expectations that a stable government could finally be established. Furthermore, he aimed to rid the country of corruption and, in general, offered solutions to the many social and political problems besetting the country. In particular he promised to end the system of *caciques*, local landowners who used their authority and wealth to influence local politics in an unjust and arbitrary fashion.

It was during this dictatorship that Ramón decided to try his luck far from the village. The family set off for Madrid, the capital, a place of dreams, a gathering point for people from all over Spain who were arriving from the impoverished countryside full of hope. Like all cities as it grew and evolved, it was destroyed and rebuilt with the passing years. It was a silent witness to everything that had gone on through the centuries, reflecting innovations

---

11 A dictator in the 1920s.

along with all that should have changed but somehow never did, for, just like Spain itself, through the 19th and early 20th centuries, Madrid was always yearning for something better which was just beyond its grasp.

When the city was first established as the capital in 1561, at the time of Spain's great empire, those who walked its narrow, cobbled streets were proud to be part of a country which ruled the world. In the 16th and 17th centuries, days of glory when Spain was still a powerful state, building took place in the gracious district of "los Austrias": the majestic Plaza Mayor, the alleys and doorways, places of intrigue and secrets, the haunts of the hidalgos and of the great playwrights and novelists: Lope de Vega, Calderón de la Barca, Quevedo and, of course, Cervantes. Still today, nuns live there in closed orders shut away down dark echoing corridors in their own 16th-century world. To buy the sweetmeats they sell, a bell magically opens a small door leading to a long, low corridor redolent with the mysteries of religion. At the end, a Hail Mary must be recited in a small windowless room before a disembodied voice from beyond requests the order. Payment is placed on a rotating tray to disappear into the darkness of another age from whence appear the boxes of traditional sweets, marzipans, nougats and little cakes.

In later centuries, as the centre of government, Madrid continued to expand but slowly in a higgledy-piggledy fashion. As Spain's power waned, it remained a small, provincial city well into the 19th century. The winding streets which seem so romantic nowadays were places of overcrowding, disease and death. Throughout the 19th century frequent uprisings, which had hardly touched village life, took place on these streets, and if the remote mountains areas had felt the presence of the Napoleon's armies during the Peninsular War, it was here in Madrid that the fight against the French had some of its bloodiest manifestations recorded for posterity by Goya in his paintings of *The second of May in Madrid*, and later in his series on *The disasters of War*.

As the 19th century progressed, efforts were made to expand in an orderly fashion. In 1870 the Queen abdicated, and in 1873 the First Republic was proclaimed. Political exiles, returning from France as circumstances became more propitious, brought with them schemes for a better, less chaotic city modeled on the ones they had seen, in particular the Paris and Bordeaux of Hausmann. What is more, they wanted a new capital in keeping with what they hoped would be the new progressive status of the country. When ambitious plans were drawn up with good intentions the old had to be torn down to make way for the new. Sadly, this included the old city walls. At the time, other Spanish cities, Avila and Lugo among them, could not even afford to demolish their walls which have remained to this day, bringing in revenue as tourist attractions.

The city was to be divided into "*barrios*", or districts, each with a specific purpose: residential, small trades or industry. No doubt it was intentional that a certain "class" was to be allocated to a specific area. The rich would have the residential district of Salamanca, while the extremely wealthy built their palaces along what is today the Paseo de la Castellana, now fittingly occupied by banks and insurance companies. The artisans, tradesmen and lower middle classes had their district to the west of the city and the industrial areas were to be around the Atocha station and along the Calle Toledo, leading south out of the city.

As usual things did not work out quite as planned, although at least the plan lasted longer than the republic which ended in 1874. When the price of land within a designated area soared, people began building further afield in areas without any regulations, while plots within the city lay empty. If inventiveness was never lacking with innovative ideas such as the Ciudad Lineal of Arturo Soria, only so much could be done in times of political unrest and uncertainty, and many projects came to a halt. One scheme that did go through was the emblematic Gran Vía which was constructed by cutting through the old centre at the beginning of the 20th century, changing the shape of the city for ever.

Against this background of thwarted modernisation, a shifting world of surviving however possible, of intrigue and of wheeling and dealing continued to swirl beneath the city. Nobody captured this as well as Pérez Galdós whose novels portray a society where petty snobbery abounded, for, whatever they might like to believe, in the towns just as in the villages the Spanish were never too keen on mixing social classes.

While the many poor huddled around Atocha station and towards the river, cramming into what was the old part of the city, only a stone's throw away, there was another world where the rich had their residences along the Paseo de la Castellana and around the Retiro, in the elegant district of Salamanca. The wealthy came from all over Spain, leaving behind not poverty, but their country estates in the care of servants. They built themselves palatial dwellings in the capital surrounded by gardens which have been gradually engulfed by the city until only the buildings remain. They came in order to be seen, to participate in government, to enjoy the entertainment and to be at the heart of events. Whereas Barcelona was developing as an industrial city, Madrid was the seat of the government. For the intellectuals there were scientific institutions, art galleries and concert halls while for the merely frivolous it was the centre of fashion, theatres and music.

If there was much to entice the rich, what exactly did Madrid offer to María and Ramón and the many poor immigrants who had been flooding into the city since the second part of the 19th century? At first sight, it is hard to see its appeal. The city to which the family immigrated in the twenties was still a small town by the standards of other major cities at the time with a population of fewer than a million. Nothing about it could compare with other European capitals: it was not a great industrial city like London, it did not have the glamour of Parisian cultural life or the sparkle of pre-war Vienna. Never having had the glory, it could not even match the desperate decadence of a once-glorious city like Berlin.

Nonetheless, in spite of all it lacked, it was the capital of Spain and one of the few places where better prospects for a growing family were to be found. Even with the instability of governments, the city had experienced considerable industrial and commercial growth since the time of World War I thus creating a demand for labour. Under Primo de Rivera expansive public works were carried out, improving transport throughout the country while industrial production increased, and the supply network grew. The railway network in particular was expanding, with Madrid as the hub of a national rail system, and it was in this sector that Ramón found a job. This improved the standard of living not only for him and María but above all for their children who could benefit from the facilities available in the city.

If education in the villages was deficient and educational standards extremely low, progressive ideas were slowly filtering into the cities from abroad. New schools were established in order to prevent the next generation of children growing up in ignorance like their parents. Hopefully, when the time came, they would have the opportunity to enter professions denied to all except the chosen few. From 1931, the Republican government had ambitious plans to expand the school building programme to ensure every child could benefit from state education. Schools run by religious orders had always been available and accepted poor children who they felt had potential. No doubt they offered a better education than the village schools, but rote learning was still the order of the day. Juan, a bright child, was selected to spend some time studying in one of these religious institutions, but in later life he spoke disparagingly of the education he received, or perhaps his objections were more to do with the strict discipline he suffered at the hands of the monks, not to mention the indoctrination which would have been unacceptable for a boy from an anti-religious household.

As well as education, the city gave some hope to the sick with modern medicine. If their children were not to die like Cecilia's twin brothers, then María and Ramón had to look beyond the simple medical care available in the village. When Juan was spending some time in the village as they often did in the summer, he became seriously ill. A local doctor was called and mercury injections were prescribed which, perhaps not unsurprisingly, led to a rapid deterioration. His condition was so grave that the family decided to use some of their scant resources to send him to the hospital in Madrid where doctors told his parents he was being poisoned and treatment should be stopped immediately. Without the injections he made a full recovery.

It is not surprising that city life with its opportunities for work, better education and medical care proved so attractive. Even so, arriving in Madrid for the first time must have been an overwhelming experience after life in their small mountain village. No matter that it was little more than a provincial town, it would have seemed magnificent if not somewhat daunting to the new arrivals, full of excitement for a family used to the tranquility and predictability of the countryside. The whole city was imbued not only with ceaseless activity but with a unique character which was not quite European, a romantic otherness which appealed greatly to travellers such as George Borrow in the 19th century or Laurie Lee in the 20th.

Juan and his older brothers and sisters, like any children from a small isolated village, found Madrid to be a thrilling place with so much to see and enjoy. The buildings would have appeared enormous to anyone used only to the squat, stone houses in the village. Everywhere there were places for work and for fun, cafés where one could sit and plot for better things in this world, the churches to pray for better things in the next.

There were also the parks and squares. The Plaza Mayor is the typical large square found in many cities throughout Spain and parts of South America. These old, picturesque squares surrounded by a covered walkway with shops were where important civic events as well as markets, particularly at Christmas, still take place. The nerve centre of Madrid was moved to the Puerta del Sol in the 19th century and at the time of the family's arrival, was the busiest place.

Trams, the cheapest way of getting around, could be dangerous and were certainly extremely noisy. There was also the metro, donkeys and carts, as well as a few cars, not to mention people shouting as they went about their everyday activities. It was a city where everyone could and did live a large part of their time outside. The concierges took chairs outside to enjoy the sun, gossip and pass the time of day with the neighbours. With few cars it was safe for children to escape the cramped apartments and play outside in the streets. There were the street sellers for every season. The arrival of old women roasting chestnuts in the street showed it was time to get out scarf and coats, the melon sellers that the summer heat was truly here to stay.

The outdoors was also a place for organized entertainment. The family was never very interested in the popular bullfighting, but the hot summer months were also a perfect time for outdoor parties or *verbenas* as they were called. In the cooler months there was indoor entertainment: imposing theatres with classical plays or music hall acts. Some of it was reserved for the well-off, but the popular cinema was affordable for most people. Gaiety pervaded the city, and nowhere more than in the south.

All this, the entertainment, the hustle-and-bustle was to be part of their lives once the practicalities had been sorted out: first they needed a place to live. With the influx of poor immigrants from the latter part of the 19th century, cheap housing was difficult to come by. Shacks cobbled together with any available material sprung up near the centre, which had become an area of disease and death appropriately called Insula, an island of wretched poverty and insalubrious conditions amid the exuberance of city life. Ramón and his family were luckier than the poor souls forced to live in these conditions, as his stable job allowed them to rent a flat in a slightly better area. They finally settled in the southern area of the city populated mainly by working class people where cheaper rents were to be found. The districts to the south of the Plaza Mayor, La Latina and Lavapiés had always had their own special character, "*castizo*". This lighthearted term used to describe what is typical about the area and its people is something akin to cockney, giving an idea of cheerfulness and the picaresque with a suggestion of fun and fiestas, solidarity and shared ideas.

In this part of the city, the streets were lined with all kinds of dwellings for, unlike the new housing on the outskirts of the city, the buildings in the centre were mainly 19th century or older. In the early 20th century most had long been abandoned leaving them dilapidated and uncared for, the perfect place for large families of immigrants. With recent renovation, they have now been returned to their original elegance with their facades painted in sugar-icing colours highlighting the intricate plaster work and ornate balconies.

Old noble residences had often been left derelict and when they were finally demolished, blocks of dwellings specifically designed to meet the increasing demand for housing were built on the plots. The "*corralas*", a sort of tenement, were vertical slums erected in the late 19th century which housed the stream of immigrants flooding into the city to work in the tobacco factories, the slaughter houses and other new industries springing up in the south. Entry to these blocks was through a large front hallway which led to a central patio or "*corral*", often with its own well which was used to wash and dry clothes, chat or more likely argue with the neighbours. Staircases led up to each floor where balconies running along the sides of the central courtyard provided access to each small apartment often only about 30 square metres (322.9 square feet) with a communal toilet at the end. It was no wonder that for whole families packed into these cramped, dark blocks, life outdoors was an attractive option.

The flat Ramón and María moved into was a cut above the *corralas* but would have been crowded with so many children. Sharing rooms had always been normal and even in the 1980s I met families that lived in one-bedroom flats, the parents sleeping on a sofa bed in the living room which was tidied away during the day. It wouldn't have bothered Juan and his siblings who were used to living in close-quarter, and anyway it was a minor inconvenience with all that was going on. As long as they had enough to eat, children arriving in the city were happy but whereas they lived only in the moment as children do, the parents' illusions of a happy life were far more brittle.

Beneath the façade of merriment all was not well in the mid-twenties. Ramón, an intelligent man and his feisty wife must have known this and no doubt their hopes for a new life were tinged with concern for the turn of events throughout Spain. It is not known if Ramón and María had a deep interest in politics before they settled in Madrid for it is usually in cities that new ideas develop. The city reflected all that Spain had been struggling to become for over a century. Now that people were streaming in from all over the peninsula to work in industry, on the railways and increasingly in offices, they could meet other people and exchange ideas which helped spread discontent with the governors and a yearning for change.

Ramón met his fellow workers daily and the railway sector was known to be particularly radical. The fact that María did not go out to work did not mean she was not involved in the community. She met women from all Spain: women from the industrial and coal mining areas in the North, women from the poor South who had come to work in the domestic sector and women who had always lived in the city. They met in the wash houses, on the stairs of the flats and in the markets. Without fridges, it was necessary to go shopping everyday especially in summer, and nearby was a typical wrought iron market with a profusion of products brought in daily from all over Spain.

In the cities they would also have easier access to news. Newspapers were bought and passed round. If someone in the block had a radio everyone could gather round to listen and share their points of view. Café culture played an important role in Madrid life. Intellectuals gathered to debate cultural, political and philosophical ideas and in the poorer areas, like La Latina, small cafés brought people together: bars for artists, poets and writers, not to mention revolutionaries, smoked-filled rooms to solve the problems of the world.

Ramón never said much about anything. By the time I knew him he was large, toothless and taciturn but many years before he must have had more initiative or at least María did. I never met her, as she died in her early sixties long before I arrived in Spain. No photos of her exist; in fact there is no material evidence of her at all although I feel her strong character in her children. Resilience not delicacy was the quality she most likely learnt through life, ,and, as they say, when the going gets tough the tough get going.

Small players in a game with no winners, Ramón and his family were to be swept along on the tide of expectation until their world plunged into despair. Intellectuals such as Ortega y Gasset in 1919 had seen the path Spain was taking, and probably by the time the family arrived in Madrid it was already too late to prevent the brewing storm which would engulf the country.

Primo de Rivera may have had good intentions but as usual he was unsuccessful. By the late 1920s it was clear that his promised government reforms and the control of *caciquismo*[12] had come to nothing. Moreover, the problems of nationalism and public order persisted while the Moroccan war rumbled on in the background. Spain had experienced growth with increased industrialisation and an improvement in the infrastructures of the country, then came the crash of 1929. Its effects were not, in fact, as catastrophic as in other countries but the Spanish economy had never been very stable anyway. Unusually for a dictator, in 1930 when Primo Rivera realized his position was untenable, he left, a broken man, to die not long after in Paris. In spite of his ambitions to remedy many of the historic ills of Spanish society, the situation he left behind was worsening day by day.

In the municipal election of April 1931, for the first time in Spanish history the republican parties won. King Alfonso XIII who had reigned since 1885, the last years alongside the dictator, was becoming increasingly unpopular and had no choice but to abdicate leading to the proclamation of a republic, the second in Spanish history. Such a joyous occasion, especially for the south of the city where support for the republican cause was

---

12 A system in which a powerful landlord dominated local government, usually through fear.

strong, called for a fitting celebration, therefore a parade was planned departing from the Plaza de Cibeles Square. So great was the crowd that it took them 2 hours to travel the short distance from the square down the Calle de Alcalá, a distance which would normally take merely 20 minutes.

The victory parade ended not in the Plaza Mayor, the old centre of the city, but symbolically in the Puerta de Sol, the spacious square built to be the modern heart of a more progressive Spain. It is the centre of Spain, kilometre 0 from which all distances are calculated and where today people gather to celebrate the New Year as the big clock chimes twelve. Nobody ever knows what the New Year will bring, but it is unlikely that hopes for the future will end in a tragedy like the one looming over Spain in the early 1930s.

No doubt the square was scruffier in those days, the buildings run down after years of neglect. Nevertheless, it was still a proud, symbolic site, the hub of communications with trams clattering through and entrances to the few metro lines, a place of shopping and meeting friends; all in all a fitting place for Spain to celebrate this historic victory. Photographers were in the square to capture the moment the leader of the socialist party, Largo Caballero and the republican Miguel Maura received the congratulations from the people of Madrid. Hindsight lends poignancy to these black and white photos capturing a fleeting moment of joy as the procession arrived in the square.

Juan`s family were surely there. It was an occasion that could not be missed. Only three years old, he was carried along on his father's shoulders above the enormous crowds in the square, through the swarms of people thronging the nearby streets. The district where they lived voted overwhelmingly for the new socialist party. On June 28 of that same year, the socialist party won another historic victory, this time in the general parliamentary election. María was not allowed to vote, something she and many other women must have found particularly galling on such a momentous occasion although no doubt she took part in the campaign, arguing, cajoling and joining together with the many women who were fighting for a new society.

The city had turned into something more than merely a place of better opportunities for the present, it promised, not for the first time, a better future for Spain and the fulfillment of political ambitions. More somberly it was becoming a city of growing contrasts. If it offered hope, it also gave rise to despair, if it was a place of wealth, it was one of poverty, if it was carefree and fun, it was creating unrest, uncertainty and fear. It is easy to see why they chose to leave behind the village and seek their fortune elsewhere. Nevertheless, if they could have made their decision with the advantage of hindsight, I wonder whether they would have chosen to go or not.

A CITY AT WAR

Anyone taking part in the celebrations who truly believed that the new socialist government could transform the country was deluded. Indeed some intellectuals considered it already too late to solve the entrenched problems and heal the deep rifts in society. Did ordinary people realize that the task facing the new government was insuperable even as they celebrated? Sadly, the joy this historic triumph brought for those supporting the left was to be short-lived.

Attempts by the socialist government to introduce drastic reforms did nothing to calm the revolutionary zeal of the discontented but served to heighten concerns among influential groups in society. The church was opposed to the proposed separation of church and state, conservative groups including many women did not approve of the vote for women, factory owners were unwilling to cooperate to improve their workers' situation, while landowners opposed any attempts to legislate on the thorny question of land ownership. Added to all this was the insolvable issue of autonomy for certain regions which continues today. Thus, conflicts raged over every aspect of society: the economy, ideology, religion and the unity of Spain.

Almost immediately groups on the left, emboldened by the socialist victory, carried out violent attacks on their enemies, landowners and above all the church, which they considered responsible for the dire situation. Not everyone on the left was anti-Catholic but many were, including María and Ramón. Their quarrel was not particularly about dogma. They saw it as the embodiment of all they rejected: tradition, authority and the status quo. The triumph of a left-wing government stoked this anti-clericalism, so it is unsurprising that ecclesiastical institutions and buildings became one of the prime targets for the pent-up anger. Church buildings were burnt and artifacts destroyed. In May 1931, only one month after the elections, a Jesuit School near the Gran Vía, in the very heart of Madrid, was burnt and 90,000 valuable books lost. In this case no-one was killed but elsewhere members of religious communities were less fortunate. Nuns and monks were dragged out of convents and monasteries, priests and bishops were taken from their homes or churches to be brutally murdered while any cleric or member of a religious order was well-advised to go into hiding. These uncontrolled attacks served to increase the ire of the Catholic factions in society of which there were many.

In addition to the grievances against the institutions and authorities, there were plenty of reasons for discontent. Suffering was widespread. In his book "*The face of Spain*", Gerald Brennan describes the crushing poverty of the agricultural workers in the latifundios in Andalusia where many attacks against landowners took place but industrial workers were no better off with low wages, few rights and no social services. Numerous strikes, uprisings and demonstrations were brutally crushed in the early 1930s. Nevertheless, the actions by groups on the left were often extreme and, as always with mob violence, frequently unjustified and unfair.

With the situation deteriorating rapidly and the government proving incapable of resolving the complex problems, elections were held once again in 1933 and for the first time in Spanish history women were allowed to vote. The victory for a coalition of right wing parties gave credence to Victoria Kent's prediction that, unfortunately, women would follow the dictates of their priest or husband. It may be true that the majority of middle and upper-class women and perhaps some in villages did indeed vote for the right but no doubt intellectuals and working class women, like María, especially those living in big cities would have seized the chance to keep the left in power. Nevertheless, there were other factors which helped the right to win: disappointment among the middle classes that the socialist government had not provided the promised solutions and, to make matters worse, a call for abstention from the anarchists causing the loss of a considerable number of votes for the left.

Given the Herculean task it faced, it was hardly surprising that the new right-wing government had no more success than its predecessor, and in 1936 elections were called yet again, this time with marginally more seats for the left. A coalition of left wing parties, the Popular Front, was formed including not only moderate socialists but more extreme left wing parties that hoped for nothing less than revolution. Despite the growing schism in politics, the majority of deputies on neither the left nor the right were themselves extreme but both factions included elements which were.

With each new day came worsening news. In view of the growing agitation among right-wing sectors, certain generals had been plotting an uprising for some time. The plans were incomplete and some among them, including a certain General Franco, were unenthusiastic about going ahead, until two events triggered a surge in their support. On July 12, 1936 José Castillo, a left-wing military officer, was murdered. Later the same day Calvo Sotelo, a monarchist deputy, was kidnapped and shot in revenge. In spite of it being generally known that the perpetrators of the second assassination were members of the public order forces, the government did nothing to find the culprits and so the downward spiral continued irremediably. The city waited tensely. Used as they were to unrest and uncertainty, all the population could do was to get on with life as best they could.

The uprising that would lead to the tragedy of Spain in the 20th century began not in the capital but far away in Melilla, one of the Spanish enclaves on the North African coast near to where Gregorio had fought many years before. On July 17, 1936, troops rebelled against the elected government under the leadership of the officer who had at first been reluctant to go ahead: Francisco Franco. In the weeks leading up to the uprising he was stationed in the Canary Islands which were yet further away from the centre of power than Melilla. Such was his hesitancy to join that the leaders of the rebellion, fed-up with his dithering nicknamed him "Miss Canary Islands", implying that in taking such a long time to make up his mind he was behaving like a woman. A hurtful insult indeed for a right-wing general!

Once he had assented to join the plot he urgently needed to get to the Spanish territories in North Africa where he had commanded troops during the wars and, as a highly respected leader, was sure he could rely on the support of both Moroccan and Spanish soldiers. Fortunately for him and his fellow conspirators, a group of British supporters were prepared to help by providing a Dragon Rapide, a type of plane made by the British and on this occasion piloted by a British man. In this way the British played a vital role in the incipient movement although, of course, this was a private initiative and had nothing whatsoever to do with the British government.

From this point on events escalated rapidly. Troops were sent from North Africa to Andalusia: some were flown over with the assistance of Italian and German planes provided by Mussolini and Hitler, others were taken by boat despite the blockade by the navy which had remained loyal to the elected government. Most of Andalusia was quickly subjugated allowing the rebel troops to move north towards Madrid on August 3. Talavera, the nearest town to Cecilia's village, was taken on September 3. At the outbreak of war, the village had been in the hands of the Republicans falling soon after into rebels hands thereby avoiding the destruction suffered in other villages. The church was partially burnt in 1936 but the houses were virtually undamaged since the village remained under the rebels' control for the rest of the war. In general, small villages were not destroyed and avoided the worst of the fighting unless they were caught in zones of combat or, like the village of Belchite, were bombed. Many larger cities, on the other hand, were destined to face almost three years of conflict. This did not mean that smaller towns and villages escaped the murders and reprisals between the supporters of the two factions. At the end of the war thousands of bodies buried in unmarked ditches throughout the country were to remain unacknowledged officially for almost 60 years.

As there was no further fighting in the valley, Vicenta, who lived until the end of the war in 1939, Gregorio and their children could live more or less as they had always done. Reading about the war, it is easy to believe everyone was for or against the Popular Front government but their family, like many others, did not take an active interest in politics and simply wanted to get on with their lives in peace. Not joining the troops of one faction or the other either willingly or unwillingly was virtually impossible for young men, but when war broke out Cecilia and her brothers were too young to participate and their parents, in their mid-thirties, were too old, and besides they had family responsibilities. As the conflict intensified and spread, their voices and those of many moderates were drowned out. All they could do was look on in horror as their country was laid to waste.

News of the uprising reached Madrid on July 18 but since few people owned a radio, it was not until midday that it began to spread around the city. At first it had little effect on the lives of the people, inured as they were to rebellion and unrest. The elderly had lived through similar revolts, and in the past most military uprisings had been fleeting, perhaps installing a new government but in general changing little else in their lives. Neither did the government take the uprising seriously enough during the first few weeks, feeling sure it could be quelled without too much difficulty. Nonetheless, the army was put on alert. The Republic had the loyalty of large numbers in the armed forces as well as the advantage of controlling the country's finances. Soon however, when the gravity of the threat became clear, the decision to enter into action, delayed for too long, was a question of utmost urgency.

In Madrid and throughout Spain it was a time to take sides. Those who remained loyal to the government were the Republicans, while those in favour of the rebellion chose their name astutely, the "Nationals", a term with undertones of patriotism. Both brought together multifarious factions. The Nationals or Nationalists as they are often called had the support of the church and of most, if not all Catholics as well as the monarchists, who obviously supported the return of the king, and the Falangists, admirers of the ideology of Mussolini and Hitler. The Republicans were even more diverse, ranging from anarchists to socialists, intellectuals, illiterate peasants and industrial workers. Both sides were joined by some of the military leaders and sections of the Guardia

Civil, a militarized security force. For Ramón and María the decision was simple: they would do all they could to help the cause of socialism and defend their ideals. Not everyone found the choice so straightforward. People changed sides and any National supporters caught in Madrid prudently feigned support for the Republic to keep themselves safe, hiding as well as they could within the city. If everyone experienced the war in their own way, deepening dread was shared by almost all.

As the conflict spread, for the first time Spanish women, like women in the rest of Europe in 1914, were being offered the opportunity to assume roles outside the home. With their men folk fighting on the front they were required to take on jobs that had always been the reserve of men and they did so willingly. No doubt Maria's stubbornness and combativeness served a purpose at such times, for she was keen to make the most of this unique opportunity to play an active role for something she believed in rather than merely looking after her numerous brood. This did not mean she could neglect the home. By the beginning of the war, there were nine children in the family. Those born in the early 1920s were in their late teens and could take part in the fighting but the younger children had to be cared for as well as possible. Despite the raging war, women still sat outside sewing and would wash clothes in the communal fountains as well as providing food in straitened circumstances.

Their contribution was indispensable when, after almost three months of tense waiting, the attack on Madrid began in October. Madrid, as the capital city and the seat of government, was vital for controlling the country and had to be defended at all costs. Since the areas that now sprawl out to the north had not yet been built, the city was centred on the main thoroughfare of Gran Vía and the Puerta del Sol where buildings were converted into military headquarters. Barricades had to be built and trenches dug around the city, tasks which required help from women and children. Everyone had to be involved, and when the seriousness of the situation became clear, arms were handed out to the population somewhat reluctantly.

The first major battle for Madrid was in the cold month of November, four months after the uprising in Melilla. The defense of the city from November 7 to the 13 became known as the Heroic Week of Madrid when it suffered carpet bombing, a new type of warfare which would soon become tragically common throughout Europe. Thanks to foreign reporters and above all Picasso's painting, the whole world would soon know about the bombing of Guernica on April 26, 1937 but prior to that, the people of Madrid heard sirens wailing from 9 at night to 2 o'clock the following afternoon. These air-raids, along with canon shots, devastated large parts of the city. After the first horrifying November of war, the conflict continued for another two and a half years with a constant deterioration of conditions. When the city came under attack, most members of the Popular Front government fled the city for Valencia, claiming this was necessary to ensure the continued functioning of the administration.

The enemy was not only outside, an undercover war was being waged within the city by Nationals who had left it too late to escape or who had stayed to spy or fight. Snipers killed people out searching for food, using fast moving vehicles to shoot at them before making a quick get-away, while others fired on any passerby from windows. Road blocks set up to catch them were often manned by fanatics who weren't in the habit of asking many questions: any suspect was shot on the spot especially during the curfew hours from 11 at night to 6 in the morning. Anyone could be the enemy, without even summary justice, executions were arbitrary. Lives were cheap. People were hauled out of their homes and businesses to be shot or taken out to an area of land near to the recently constructed airport, a place of no return like many others in Spain during those years.

In the besieged city, the fighting was not the only cause of hardship. Despite organizations setting up a system of emergency aid, after an initial moment of confusion, everything was in short supply and prices were rising. With the city blockaded by Franco's troops there was a dearth of all food stuffs, and, as the war dragged on even the most basic products were lacking, with rationing being introduced virtually at the very beginning of the conflict. Communal canteens were opened to provide food for the soldiers and their families. Everyone received a ration of meat, *tocino*[13], fruit, potatoes and green vegetables but by the end of the war everything was scarce: products like

---

13 Salted belly pork.

milk were only for little children, leaving the population badly undernourished. If help hadn't been provided by the Red Cross and international organizations, the situation would have been dire. Amenities, never good before the war, worsened as the siege continued. Although local committees were now organizing supplies of water and electricity, buildings frequently had only one tap or one toilet for the whole block.

In 1936, with about a million inhabitants, Madrid was not a big city by European standards but new arrivals swelled the numbers, exacerbating the problems. As the fighting intensified and the Nationals closed in, refugees fleeing from the surrounding countryside and villages flooded into the capital where they were joined by the International Brigades, volunteers from Europe and the USA who had come to the aid of Republican Spain: a growing number of mouths to be fed from the meager supplies.

For the Republicans in the city, enduring these conditions was a price they were willing to pay for victory. Their lives might have been fraught with danger, but it was those suspected of being National supporters who had the most to fear throughout the years of war in the city. At that orderless time, merely owning a shop was "proof" of being a capitalist. I met a man who as a child saw his father dragged out of his shop and shot on the pavement. A friend's uncles, arrested after they were denounced by the concierge, were taken out of the city and shot. I knew a mother who spent the war years in prison as a young girl never knowing what would happen next. These are the stories of Madrid but in other cities under the control of the Nationals the stories of cruelty and revenge are exactly the same, leaving an indelible scar for years to come.

A civil war cannot have the appeal to glory and patriotism or the imperative of national defense that other wars may have; it does not draw people together but thrusts them apart. Anyone and everyone is a spy or a traitor. War and conflict unleash petty spitefulness once the restraints of peace and order are taken away. This should not be forgotten. In a British documentary about Nazi Germany some years ago, it was claimed that the Nazis worked at a grassroots level, that ordinary people were involved in the persecution. No doubt they were but an unscrupulous dictatorship provides the perfect opportunity to settle scores and wreak vengeance. Perhaps this is not so obvious in Britain where urbanization has split up societies and where there has been no bloody civil war or revolution for many years, but it is so in any dictatorship or internecine conflict when justice flies out of the window. Neighbour betrays neighbour, brother fights brother while rancour, petty grievances and jealousies which have simmered on for years in tight-knit urban or rural communities and in small provincial towns bubble to the surface.

This division did not die at the end of the war, it festered in people's hearts and minds, and their stories have been passed down through the years. Eighty years later few of the people who experienced the war are alive but for those who are and for their children, the feelings of loss have persisted, perhaps fading with time but ever present in the background. For Republicans the pain and suffering had to be concealed during the regime when any talk of the war was unadvisable. In later years Juan and Cecilia's families only rarely spoke of it in depth. This was partly because it hardly affected Cecilia and her family in the village, partly because those involved preferred to forget, yet, as time went by, comments and anecdotes slipped into conversations.

Juan was only eight when war broke out, but children are always involved in war however young and he would have felt the effects on his family knowing that his older brothers were away fighting. He only ever gave away small snippets of his life in Madrid in the war years, recollections that were half-joking and jovial, but he must have seen death and injury, he would have known gnawing hunger, and although he might not have realized it at the time, the lack of stability and education would stay with him for the rest of his life. Informal schools were organized in the besieged city so that children could receive a modicum of education. These were often set up in flats by teachers who would later pay the price for their "participation" in the war effort with a prison sentence or in some cases with their lives.

Certain of his memories seem more mythical than real, glorified days compared with the humdrum life of his later years, the disappointments of city life which had once offered so much. The companionship and neighbourly assistance he recounted were probably true, after all they lived cheek by jowl, nearly everything was communal, and the women worked together. What I found hard to believe in a city of rations and starvation were his tales of Christmas when doors were open and everyone was invited in to share bottles of *cava*, Spanish champagne, and a seasonal feast.

More convincing are his memories of the flashes of the bombs against the night sky, the sound of gunfire, the ruined buildings and playing in the rubble. Perhaps he did run around in the corridors of a nearby seminary, oblivious to what was going on around him or, like so many other people, he preferred to discard much of what he had seen and heard leaving only a child's memory with the horrors blocked out. Rather bizarrely, he recalls dancing in a theatre which could in fact be true as theatres were still open and plays were put on to boost morale.

I have said that before arriving in Spain my knowledge of the country was sketchy. I had read the "usuals" like *Homage to Catalonia* and Laurie Lee, but over the years not only have I heard numerous first-hand stories of the war, I have also come to know other writers less well known outside Spain. Some are factual, other fictionalized accounts based on experiences. Books have been written by Republicans in exile, for example Max Aub, priests and national supporters such as José María Gironella. Naturally, all these narratives vary vastly in accordance with the authors' political views, but what they all have in common is the horror of the Civil War and the devastation and bitterness it caused to the country.

These accounts have filled in details that I could never have gained from the family or foreign combatants whose stories do not always reflect the complexity of Spain. One I have read recently, Elena Fortún's novel *Celia en la Revolución*, is based on her own experiences in the war years. A supporter of the Republic cause like the writer and journalist Barea[14], she could not but be horrified by what she saw of the arbitrary power wielded by the forces in Madrid. The book might be fiction, the accounts it holds are not: the starvation and eating rats were things she would have experienced, but worse of all are her descriptions of the *paseíllos*. These were the "short walk" when anyone suspected of supporting the nationalist cause was taken out from their home to the nearest wall or park. Shots would ring out though the night while everyone cowered at home knowing they must wait until daybreak to discover the bodies lying in the street, to see if it was a friend, family member or acquaintance who had paid the price for mere suspicions without a trial or a chance of defense. Next day, they would pass by the corpse wondering who had betrayed them before hurrying on: showing too much concern for a traitor was not a good idea when the price of dissent was so high.

In his account of the war, Barea vividly describes a city torn apart by carpet bombing, scenes which were soon to become common in WWII: houses ripped open to reveal the details of a private life inside as if they were dolls' houses on display, people's secrets violated with every detail revealed: the wallpaper so carefully chosen, the pictures on the walls of intimate family occasions. Everything mercilessly revealed to the world. Were the people destroyed as well as the houses?

---

14 Arturo Barea (1897 – 1957) wrote *The Forging of a Rebel* a trilogy covering his early life and the war years. He was exiled in England after the war.

Most books on the war were printed after it had ended but already at the time journalists, Martha Gellhorn, Hemingway, Saint-Exupéry and many others were sending their first-hand accounts around Europe and the rest of the world. With growing concern about Communist Russia, Fascism in Italy and National Socialism in Germany, the bloody Civil War was the focus of attention across the globe.

Nowadays, fascination with the war has grown with a wealth of material available until it sometimes seems to be the only event that ever mattered in Spain. During the regime, information was censored in Spain itself but since Franco died it has figured largely in Spanish history, events preserved not only in history books but also in films, novels and poems. It was only in the late-seventies in Spain that exhibitions, documentaries and films on the Civil War tentatively appeared. The first one I remember was an exhibition in the Retiro Park, displaying posters reflecting the ideologies of each of the opposing forces. Printed in the large cities, many were produced by well-known artists and graphic designers. Those of the Republic featured symbols of communism and international workers' movements: a hammer and sickle, industrial artifacts and the international five-pointed star. The Nationals aimed to send a message of power, authority and victory with the Falangist symbols of a yoke and arrows, the swastika and an eagle. All were a powerful call to defend their cause.

In stark contrast to these posters on the idealism of war, photos show the brutal realism. Just like writers and journalists, foreign and Spanish photographers recorded the war from its beginnings of hope and excitement to its end in defeat or triumph: Agustí Centelles captured the early years of euphoria, Lluís Companys[15] entering into Barcelona - his moment of glory all the more poignant as we know how it ended: he was shot in 1940. Photos of defeat, refugees trudging into the city at the outbreak of war, then leaving again on the road to Valencia hoping to escape at the end of the war. Most never did.

At a time when photos of war are all too commonplace, these yellowing photos of the Civil War have taken on a new dimension for me because I know the places and perhaps even the people. Viewing the photos with hindsight takes away the political and leaves only pathos and poignancy. For all their strangeness they are no longer distant people in a strange city but are part of the present. Devoid of their partisan identity they become people who could have been alive when I arrived. The enthusiastic soldiers are the ragged refugees crossing the Pyrenees facing years of exile only to return on Franco's death, the fiery revolutionaries without their cause once again become poor, ragged peasants, growing old in villages. The scraggy half-dressed children are now respectable grandparents; the haggard, haunted people moving furniture might finally have prospered. Whatever happened to them they are people I could have met in other guises.

The city itself has been transformed and would seem to have forgotten its recent past. The ruined streets to the west of

---

15 A Catalan leader who was executed after the war.

the city are now leafy boulevards. Most of the city is new with massive building projects carried out from the mid-fifties. Today, it is a modern city, hectic and noisy but for anyone who believed they could forget, the scars of war were not only left on people but on cities throughout Spain. Many still bear the marks of conflict, a subtle reminder of what happened if any is needed. In the eighties a block of flats caved in. Apparently, it had taken a direct hit during the war and although the structure had been weakened, it had managed to hold up for forty years before finally collapsing. Streets of elegant 18th century buildings are marred by ugly concrete blocks hastily constructed in the sixties, not to enhance the neighbourhood but simply to fill the gaps left by the bombing.

Battlefields are now parks. New districts of modern apartments have been built where some of the worst fighting took place. The Cuartel de la Montaña, now a peaceful place for Sunday walks and early morning runners was once a scene of bloody fighting. On Sundays we walk to the Parque del Oeste, the West Park where the old bunkers, still visible among the trees, are surrounded by daffodils in spring. Strolling there brings tranquility, away from the hustle and bustle of city life, but it is also a moment to wish that things could have been different, that the city could have developed in peace without the slaughter and suffering. But peace and democracy were never part of Franco's plans.

He could have taken control of Madrid much earlier but before mounting the final attack on the city he wanted the whole country to be defeated to ensure no opposition whatsoever remained. In the last polar winter of the war, from 1938 to 1939, the final desperate battles were fought in the coldest part of Spain around Teruel and the River Ebro. With the defeat of the Republican troops, any delusions of possible victory evaporated. Only a miracle could avoid the inevitable collapse. There was none.

By the end of the war most people were beyond politics: life was about surviving the cold, the starvation and the lack of just about everything. With the end looming, the in-fighting among the factions in Madrid was becoming just as brutal as the war raging outside: the more moderates on the Republic side were willing to negotiate a peace while the hardliners preferred to struggle on to the bitter end. On March 28, 1939 the nationalist troops finally marched into the city. The tide had turned dramatically. Those who had been on the "right" side found themselves on the "wrong" side, the hunters were the hunted. For some the time had come to admit what they genuinely believed but had been obliged to conceal.

Franco, who had taken on the role of supreme leader, issued a communiqué: "The war is over". Except it wasn't. He would make sure of that.

Much had happened for Ramón and María since they left the monotony of their village in search of a better life. They had enjoyed better economic prospects and participated at the centre of political life. María was part of the first generation of village women who had glimpsed the chance to improve their position in society. They had been at the momentous proclamation of the second Republic and then defended it with all their strength. Now came the hardest part of all: facing defeat and all that it would bring.

A BROKEN COUNTRY

The war had ended, taking with it the promises for a brighter future for the family and the hopes of Republican women.

On Thursday March 28, 1939 another triumphant parade took place in Puerta del Sol. Like the celebration for the proclamation of the 2nd Republic eight years earlier in 1931, it marked a new beginning but there was little else these two events had in common. If the first was an occasion of almost spontaneous joy, the second was a well-organized, military parade bringing a deepening sense of foreboding for many. If the first was a celebration for the left, the second was for the extreme right but far worse for Ramón and María it marked the beginning of a dictatorship which, unlike the unstable Republic, was not to be short-lived but would last for nearly 40 interminable years.

Juan had been too young to have any memories of the first celebration in Sol, yet neither did he have any of the second simply because he was not there. This time his family did not join the crowds cheering for a future which they knew would be wretched and most likely would not include them in any positive way.

The second Republic had already divided society, but the divisions now were far starker, enshrined as they were in the philosophy of the new regime. It was no longer simply the rich and the poor, the Catholics and the anti-Catholics, but more significantly the victors and the vanquished, the right and the wrong, and those who could hold their heads up proudly against those who were forced to bear the bitterness of defeat. Whatever he may have claimed, this schism served Franco's purpose: let the defeated never forget, let all opposition be crushed or exiled. For him and his supporters these were the Years of Triumph, the Years of Victory.

In the spring of 1939, a very short time before the outbreak of World War II, the Nationals could come out of hiding into the bright Madrid light, casting off the fear of discovery, of betrayal by a neighbour, a relative or even by a close family member. They poured onto the streets to welcome Franco's troops with Nazi salutes, safe in the knowledge that better things were ahead. It was their time for restitution of jobs and property. They could worship freely in their churches, show off their wealth if they had any left, for even the middle classes had been sunk into genteel poverty. There would be acknowledgment of their suffering, redress for their grievances; they would be allowed to mourn openly for their murdered relatives. Sons and fathers killed in battle could never be brought back but at least the pain of their deaths would be softened by a belief in their righteousness and recognition from the state.

They knew they were the ones for whom this second victory parade was being held in order that they might momentarily put aside their losses and look forward to a bright future in a fascist state especially as Germany, one of Spain's close allies, was going from strength to strength. Not only did Franco share the ideology of the Axis states but without the logistic support from Mussolini and Hitler who provided troops and armament, the outcome of the Civil War could have been very different. Later Franco would do his utmost to shed any association with these powers but for the moment what could go wrong when Germany, Spain's ally, appeared to be dominating Europe with ease?

Throughout WWII Madrid was overrun with Germans who were more focused on their own interests than those of Spain, but both countries were keen to maintain a fluid relationship which is why Heinrich Himmler, one of the foremost Nazi leaders visited Spain in 1940. This was the apogee of fascist power with the apparent success of the Blitz which had begun in September in London. Himmler arrived in Madrid one particularly rainy day in October to enjoy every possible honour from the new regime. His principal task was to lay the ground work for a meeting between Franco and Hitler which was to take place on the border between France and Spain. There was, however, still time for a programme of visits which included a bullfight and the monastery-palace of San Lorenzo de El Escorial, not to mention sumptuous meals which the starving population could barely have imagined. This was the perfect time for old acquaintances to be renewed with Franco's brother-in-law, Vallejo-Nájera, and Pilar Primo de Rivera, the late dictator's sister, all fervent supporters of National Socialism. Having been honoured guests in Germany, they could now return the favour.

It was not only the authorities who enthusiastically received this illustrious visitor, the people of Madrid turned out in droves to cheer the cavalcade. Flags bearing swastikas and the *Falange* symbol of arrows and a yoke adorned the main streets providing a fitting welcome while helpfully covering up the war damage. The residents were keen to show their support for Germany, the perfect ally to ensure a prosperous future. Like Franco, these same people would one day be keen to forget their fervour and blind support for Hitler once the atrocities of his regime came to light. But that would be later, for the moment the exuberance of the reception on the streets of Madrid driving home the triumph of fascism was another torment for the defeated and a harbinger of what was to come. Yet even for the victorious the ostentation of the visit could only provide a temporary distraction from the ravages of war.

The fabric of Spain had been destroyed; Madrid was in ruins with 10,000 buildings including many residential blocks damaged beyond repair. If this was the promised "New Era" it was not a good start. The dearth of housing meant families were forced to share not one flat but often only one room while others only found shelter from the bitter cold in shacks cobbled together out of any material they could scavenge. Needless to say, the situation was more desperate for Republicans who were sometimes forced to leave their homes which were given to National supporters. To make matters worse, the winters of 1939/40 and 1941/42 were two of the coldest in memory when all Europe was freezing, from the German troops outside Stalingrad to the wretched inhabitants of many Spanish cities.

1942 became known as the Year of Hunger described by Camilo José Cela[16] in his book *The Beehive*, but it was not only food that was in short supply as all the basics of life were impossible to obtain: clothing, heating, medical care or for that matter, any kind of job to earn money. Desperation and starvation stalked the city. Everyone scraped by as best they could. Needless to say, the black market flourished, beggars including children were everywhere and women turned to prostitution to feed their families, while the police had no option but to turn a blind eye. The streets were always free of litter as children gathered up cigarette butts to reuse the tobacco and scraps of paper were all some had to light fires. No petrol meant no motor vehicles and if the wealthy still had cars these ran with a strange appliance which burnt wood and coal: *gasógeno.* Franco himself was forced to use this ungainly system.

If the physical conditions were visible to everyone, mental anguish was the hidden legacy of war. The rate of suicides was high in the post-war period not that the triumphal photos peopled with cheering, wimpled nuns, soldiers in their pristine uniforms and crowds with their fascist salutes and smiles, gave any hint that

---

16 Spanish novelist who won the Nobel Prize for literature in 1989.

this was the case. But then, as in any dictatorship, this was photography for propaganda not truth. Yet there are other images, forbidden glimpses of the grimness of post-war Spain. A gaunt beggar in rags wraps a protective blanket around two young children, the war wounded wandering the streets and men left without arms or legs.

Franco paid lip service to a country for "all" Spaniards, which could not have been further from the truth: revenge was a key tenet of post-war doctrine in Spain. Even among the victors, differences existed but unity was to be imposed, any hint of rebellion crushed, all ideologies except the official one had to be wiped out and the slightest opposition eradicated as drastically as possible. It was to be "*One Spain, Great and Free*"[17] although only the first of the three was ever true.

Along with the consequences of military defeat the losers had to silently bear the sorrow for the loss, or exile of loved ones and injury. One of Ramón and María´s sons who had been involved in the fighting had fled, joining the dejected refugees trailing endlessly through the Pyrenees on their journey to France, many of whom, like him, would spend the rest of their life away from their homeland. For those remaining in the city at the end of April, the time to flee the city and the country had now passed, all they could do was to lie low and await events. The future looked bleak for if these were "The years of Victory", they were also the years of reprisals.

---

17 España una, grande y libre.

Though the fighting was over, the slaughter continued. Ramón and María may not have fought but they were undoubtedly involved in political activity and had done what they could to support the Republican cause. What this was exactly mattered little. Everyone was suspect, no-one was spared: members of left-wing political organizations, union members, nurses and teachers who had worked behind the lines, their relatives, friends or neighbours. When hearsay and rumour became the only evidence needed, simply being in the wrong place at the wrong time was proof enough of guilt, and the south of the city was decidedly the wrong place to be.

Already in 1939 Franco had passed the Law of Political Responsibility listing the most serious crimes which anyone supporting the Republican side would unavoidably have committed since it included membership of illegal parties, whether socialist or the more extreme communists and anarchists groups, as well as merely publically declaring support for the Popular Front which had formed the legally elected government.

It is hard to conceive the horror for a family like theirs which had rejoiced at the declaration of the Republic but was now cowering in fear, their recent hopes and aspirations now in tatters. In addition to their worries about their own perilous situation, they had young children to care for. Despite initial promises of leniency for anyone giving themselves up, everyday hundreds of people were being rounded up to be imprisoned or executed. They knew their turn could come any day.

Many women were imprisoned including the wives and daughters of political leaders, teachers and nurses who had helped behind the lines, and of course, women who had used their newly found freedom to take part in political activities casting off the discrimination of centuries. The time had come for them all to pay the price for having seen a chink of light through the darkness of oppression of a rigid, traditional society. Women had lost so much more than the war. Many had died, and for the survivors, this fleeting moment of new opportunities had been snatched away leaving them with nearly 40 years of draconian restrictions before they could once again fight for their rights. Yet, at that precise moment the loss of rights must have weighed far less than their struggle to simply survive.

Along with many of her comrades, María was sent to one of the women's prisons in Madrid set up throughout the city. The huge number of condemned meant that new prisons were urgently needed. Some were housed in specifically constructed buildings, others in typical buildings to be found in any Spanish city including convents as the Catholic Church was eager to help the new regime in any way it could. I have passed some of these buildings hundreds of times, out shopping or dashing to meet friends unaware of the role they played since they have reverted to their original purpose. Nothing about their outer façade gives away the horrors that went on inside, for the women's prisons were no less harsh than those of the men. Prepared rapidly, conditions in almost all of them were deficient, although no doubt they were considered more than fitting for the defeated. We do not know which one María was sent to, but it is of little import as the problems in all of them were much the same.

She never talked about her time in prison. And why would she? It was better to get on with life than dwell on the past. Nevertheless, she would have had much to forget. The prisons were severely overcrowded, they were given scarcely enough food to keep them alive and the inmates suffered all the afflictions of the poor conditions. In their weakened state they succumbed to tuberculosis and other diseases while everyone had lice and other parasites. Mothers were separated from their children who then received no treatment when they were sick and often died. The inmates helped each other as much as they could, since the prison guards in the system, bent on revenge, were not known for their humanity. The nuns were no exception, convinced as they were that the women had committed the greatest sin of all by rejecting religion. As far as they were concerned, they thoroughly deserved what they got.

Every day names of the unfortunate souls who were to be taken out from the prisons to be executed were called. With no trials, the frequent death sentences reeked more of reprisal and vengeance than justice.

Reluctance to talk about the past means we do not know which prison Ramón was sent to either, but whichever it was he did not remain long as he soon had the opportunity to leave, unfortunately not for freedom but for work on the new war memorial, El Valle de los

Caídos[18], near the town of San Lorenzo de El Escorial. Franco announced the project for this grandiose structure in 1940, only a year after his victory. Intended at first as a commemoration of the "glorious crusade" to save Spain, by the time it was completed 18 years later in 1958 it was to be a memorial to all those who had died on the battlefield, a change designed to appeal to international opinion rather than a change of heart on the merits of the defeated.

Comprising a basilica built into the rocky mountain side, an esplanade, an abbey with a school attached, accommodation for monks and finally a gigantic cross dominating the valley, a considerable amount of labour was required for its construction. Finding sufficient workers was a problem, as much of Spain's infrastructure had been destroyed in the war, and rebuilding work was underway. Therefore, in addition to the pressing problems of feeding many thousands of prisoners in concentration camps and prisons, urgent measures were required to satisfy the demand for labourers. Luckily, the regime had the perfect solution to these two pressing problems: *Redención de Penas por el Trabajo*[19], a chance for the prisoners to work and reduce their sentence.

This system killed two birds, or more, with one stone. It proved to be an excellent strategy, quelling complaints that prisoners were being fed for free, when others had to

---

18 The valley of the fallen recently renamed Valle de Cuelgamuros.

19 Redemption of Sentences through Work.

work for their living, as well as emptying the overflowing prisons. Moreover, while providing an extremely cheap workforce, it gave the prisoners a chance to atone for their sins. Being a builder by trade, Ramón was perfectly suited to the job. Although working on these projects was voluntary, there were incentives. Not only was the commutation of the sentences generous, but the companies had to pay them and provide a reasonable amount of daily food. After a time there was the added benefit of family visits. Once they had completed their sentence, with all the days worked carefully noted on a special card, many decided to stay on working for wages as it was not easy for an ex-prisoner to find jobs in post-war Spain.

Working on El Valle de los Caídos was relatively good compared with jobs on many other building works at that time, yet it was still demanding. Franco himself had found the perfect spot for his personal project in the Guadarrama mountain range to the north-west of Madrid, a magnificent setting but extremely cold in winter and hot in summer. It might have been marginally better than the prisons but it was far from being a cushy option. Along with the gnawing hunger afflicting everyone in Spain, the workers had to contend with the inclement weather, back breaking work and a constant threat of accidents.

If the hardship of imprisonment as well as the grim conditions affected the adult population, children did not escape. Juan's generation, like any children growing up during a war, were victims whichever side their parents supported: they all saw unspeakable things, they were often starving and education was denied to them. But once the war ended it was the children of the defeated who became the "lost" children besmirched by their parents' actions, and left to suffer the consequences, which in many cases would mark them for the rest of their lives.

Numerous children had no-one to care for them. There were orphans from the fighting, the children of political prisoners and children whose parents were executed in the post-war years. Some young children were kept in prison with their mothers, suffering the same harsh conditions. Many died, for although the idea was not to actually kill children, the treatment they received meant this often happened.

Such treatment of children would seem at odds with the Catholic doctrine Franco so fervently espoused, but it is easy for a dictatorship to find a rationale for its policies, and easier still to find supporters eager to justify their actions however reprehensible. In this case a psychiatrist, Doctor Vallejo-Nájera, was the perfect candidate to provide a justification not only for the treatment of children but for all Republican prisoners. Born in 1889, by the outbreak of the Civil War he already had many years of experience behind him and more importantly he was in total agreement with Franco's ideology adding his own version of the Nazi doctrine of racial purity.

"Purity of blood" had been a major concern in Spain for centuries and was a key issue with the expulsion of the Jews and Arabs in the late 15th and early 16th century. Jews, many of whom held high positions as bankers and accountants, mixed more freely with the ruling classes who thus ran the risk of being "tainted" by their blood, while the peasant classes, living in villages away from the centres of power, could be proud of their purity. Literature reflected this concern, becoming a central theme in the works of Calderón, one of the most famous playwrights in Spain's Golden age, a time in the 17th century when the arts and literature but not much else flourished in Spain. Widespread at the time, the idea of good or bad, pure or tainted blood continued to be deeply entrenched in Spanish society in one form or another. The bad, or in other words anything contaminated from outside, had to be eradicated. This belief, which persisted through the centuries, was to be reinforced by 19th-century theories on racial characteristics and was taken up by Vallejo-Nájera.

As a frequent visitor to Germany, his theories of "purity of blood" were well received among Nazi acolytes. It concurred with their idea of an ideal type of person and the undesirability of others, except of course, in Spain, Aryans with blond hair and blue eyes were few and far between. Whilst pointing his finger at Judaism, which would have met with the full approval of the Nazis, his theories differed in that they were based not on genetics but on the effects that upbringing and environment had on the population. He did not believe in a "master" race but rather a degeneration of the nation and this was clearly the fault of the Jews.

Although they had been driven out of Spain in 1492, those who had converted to Christianity were allowed to remain. Vallejo-Nájera argued that these crafty Jews had not been sincere in their conversion and through the ages they had worked towards the degradation of society and the erosion of all the noble characteristics of the aristocracy and Catholicism. This led to a lack of moral responsibility and the destruction of all essential values which, in turn, could be blamed for all the problems arising over the centuries: the uprisings, wars, unrest and, worst of all, Marxism.

To allow him to prove these theories, Franco requested that Vallejo-Nájera study the mentality of the opposition, that is to say the Communists, Marxists, Republicans and anyone else who did not agree with him. For this purpose, he was given full access to prisons and concentration camps. Helpfully, his research led him to the conclusion that they were indeed brutish and cruel people. Thus, the principal problem, according to Vallejo-Nájera, was how to rid society of these noxious elements and develop true "Hispanidad". Once again a policy was rapidly required and once again a convenient solution was quickly found.

Firstly, it was necessary to separate women from men in prisons to guarantee no more children would be born. Secondly, children born to Republican mothers were to be taken away from them. Pregnant mothers condemned to death were given stay of execution until the child was weaned. When the fateful day arrived, the child was wrenched from the mother who knew she was about to be shot and would never see her child again. The babies were given to families who supported the dictatorship; a false birth certificate posed no particular problems for the regime. In this way they would grow up in an environment far more propitious for ensuring the correct evolution of the Hispanic race.

Some were given to "good" Catholic families. Many, some of whom may still be alive, have never known their true origins. One elderly woman had spent years in prison for her political activism during the Civil War. On her release she found that her daughter, like so many other children, had disappeared, and as a woman with a record of political prisoner in Franco's Spain there was no way she could safely look for her. It was only over 40 years later in democracy that a television programme finally offered her the chance to find her. Mother and daughter were finally reunited and spent the last years of the mother's life together, in spite of holding radically different views. For, as was often the case, the daughter had been adopted by a staunchly right-wing Catholic family, whereas her mother continued to believe in the ideas she had fought for. The daughter's political views remained the same, even after the death of her adoptive parents, so at least in this case, perversely proving Vallejo-Nájera was right.

Other children were sent to orphanages run by the Church or by the fascist organization, the Falange, where older children would receive an appropriate education to prepare them to integrate into the new society. Postwar institutions, usually run by nuns, were not happy places, with an emphasis on indoctrination and harsh punishments. Just like their parents, children had to expiate their guilt, in this case for being born in the wrong kind of family.

Why didn't the Catholic Church do more to protect children? How could it allow children to be treated so cruelly? First and foremost it was because it agreed with the principles of the regime and was more than happy to carry out its work in the name of charity. They not only needed each other, they formed a perfect alliance. The church was prepared to take an active role in the re-education programme, providing a valuable service for the autocratic government and at the same time making itself indispensable. There was no place for scruples in the government when the church had truth on its side, a truth shrouded in mystery which could never be challenged. Moreover, the ideology of the prisoners exonerated the church and the regime of any crime or wrongdoing.

If it is only recently that stories of cruelty and discrimination against children are leaking out, it is because anyone who suffered in the early post-war years soon learnt that silence was the best policy. Years of a dictatorship leave their mark. Later, when their stories had more relevance for me, I would meet people whose whole lives had been tainted by their childhood experiences, bringing home how the past echoes down through the ages, leaving scars long after the events that caused them had faded from most people's minds.

At 11 Juan was too young to understand the ins-and-outs of the political situation but he knew that his family was shattered, his world turned up-side-down. Nevertheless, despite his plight, he was more fortunate than others of his generation for he was no longer a small child, and thus avoided the fate of other children in prisons or in orphanages. Even so, Madrid was no longer a good enviroment for him to be in. The war, like any war, had not only wreaked havoc on the city but the regime had turned it into a claustrophobic place with rigid controls, intrigue and spies on every corner. The imprint of the dictatorship was everywhere. When I arrived, streets still bore the names given after the war: Generalísimo (Castellana), Avenida José Antonio (Gran Vía)... Some were well-known, others minor players but all ubiquitous reminders, if any were needed, of who the victors were. Since it was no longer a comfortable place to live, especially for a child, Juan was sent back to the village where his extended family could care for him until, hopefully, his parents would be released. Needless to say, being passed round the family in postwar Spain did little for his education. Few children without economic resources received much of an education in the forties, which left children who were clever, like Juan, without any kind of academic qualification so exacerbating inequalities in society.

1939 marked the end of Juan and Cecilia's childhood. For which of the two had it been harder: for Cecilia, facing the death of her mother and looking after the family or Juan, whose family had been torn apart by war? Still only 11 years old, life for neither had been easy up until now. As the chapter of Juan's life in Madrid closed, Cecilia was beginning her work as the sole carer of the family. Both their families would have to rebuild their lives after the war but they had to do so in a country destroyed by conflict and with Europe on the brink of war. Repression held the country in its grip while sharp division between rural and urban Spain persisted, but at least for the moment life in the countryside would continue much as it had done before the war.

LIMITED LIVES

Once María and Ramón had served their prison terms, they had little choice but to return to their village, their dealings with the city that had begun with such high expectations over for good.

The city they had left behind would begin to change from the fifties with a new Madrid slowly emerging from the wartime ruins, but it was no longer where they wanted to be. Unsurprisingly, something about the grandiose constructions in the city reflects the government's ideas for the nation and I can understand why this was anathema to them. With time, some of the buildings of the era, such as those in the Plaza de España, have become emblematic in the cityscape. I have never particularly liked them although for me it was their past I could not accept, whereas for María and Ramón in the 1950s it was all they signified for the future.

Not only did the capital no longer hold anything of interest for them, it represented everything they had wished for and lost: a relatively secure job with a wage, increasing prosperity, expectations for women's rights. Instead of all this, it had brought war, death, prison and defeat. The outlook for the coming years might not have appeared particularly rosy but at least, once they were freed, they could go back to the rural world of their past and to the extended family that had never knowingly let them down. Even this small comfort was denied to some people whose villages had been totally destroyed in the fighting or, like those in Castellón, which had provided useful target practice for German planes.

During the penurious post-war years it was far easier for María and Ramón to survive in the village than in the city. The family lent a hand and the countryside provided a basic diet which was often lacking in the towns. With the small amount of work available they had enough to scrape by, especially as they had their own home.

Looking back on the lives of Ramón, María and their family, they remind me of the documentary I had seen in Britain back in the seventies before I knew anything of Spain. It might have been made for left-wing propaganda but for them and many others like them it was reality. Life in the villages went on much as it had done before the war with all that was good and bad. It offered no change or improvement but at least it gave them much needed stability and continuity. The rural world which had done so much to shape Spain would continue to do so long after the Civil War was over.

Having survived the forties, no mean feat for socialists, the fifties was a time to look forward, while attempting to forget the unforgettable. They knew that dwelling on the past served no useful purpose, and hopefully, the stigma of being on the "wrong" side would gradually fade. All they could do for the time being was resign themselves to the regime and ignore the world of politics, which, once again was certainly easier in the village than in the city. There were probably only a couple of radios in the village, and I doubt they read any newspapers even if they had the time or the inclination. Most newspapers, now firmly under the auspices of the Catholic Church, happily fulfilled their principal mission of praising the Caudillo[20], as Franco liked to be called.

Obviously, all news was heavily censored, and, while every one of the leader's glorious appearances was reported in detail, the constant dissensions within the government were glossed over. Despite the picture painted in the media, internal conflicts were a constant feature of the regime with the Falange, the Catholic Church and the monarchists all struggling for supremacy. With the defeat of Germany, the influence of the JONS and similar fascist organizations waned, whereas the power of the church increased. Not only did it provide the bedrock of the regime's ideology but it was the only institution allowed to function more or less independently. All this was of little concern for Ramón and María. As well as their aversion to Franco's antics, they had little interest in which faction came out on top as they hated them all. These frictions changed nothing for most of the population and certainly did nothing to help the economic situation.

If Spain had been impoverished by the havoc wreaked during the conflict, the economic policy adopted by the government only made matters far worse. The economy

---

20 A word for a political or military leader.

was subordinated to the interests of the state with the aim of developing a strong military power. Furthermore, the government believed that with a policy of autarky, or in other words self-sufficiency, Spain would no longer be reliant on other countries. They did, in fact, have few alternatives. The governments of France, Britain and the USA were against providing desperately needed financial aid after Spain's support for the Axis powers in WW2, leaving the country totally isolated. The situation was dire and had the Argentinean government under Perón not agreed to send grain there would have been widespread famine. It wasn't until 1952, fourteen years after the end of the Civil War, at a time when the USA was becoming anxious about the growing threat from Communist Russia, that an agreement was finally reached with the USA to allow American military bases on Spanish soil in exchange for aid. In the same year, a Concordat was signed with the Vatican which, whilst barely altering the lives of the population, did confer international recognition on the National Catholic regime. It must have been disheartening for people like María and Ramón who had held on to a glimmer of hope that the government would fail, to hear that the regime was finally receiving acceptance from abroad. What is more, foreign support offered a balsam to the country's disastrous economic situation making the regime's downfall increasingly unlikely.

Fortunately, the Spain of the late forties and early fifties is something I only know of from firsthand accounts and literature mainly about the cities. These paint a picture of monotony and greyness despite the sun, a dreary time of restrictions. The black market flourished and the need for rationing continued for 14 years. In Britain, the last European country to end rationing after World War II, it lasted 9 years. The fifties, like the forties, was a sepia decade, any colour taken out of life, an image far removed from the joyful, happy-go-lucky attitude even the Spanish themselves would like to believe.

For the time being the colourfulness of the folkloric dancers and singers as well as bullfighting could only superficially conceal the hunger and hardship. Along with football, these were harmless ways to expend passion and divert attention from politics while creating a strong feeling of national identity.

None of this, however, greatly affected village life. The family was never interested in football, and bullfighting was not part of the village traditions. They would attend church on Sundays and feast days, and like almost everyone else, they would be very careful about what they did and said. No chink of dissension was allowed to trickle through the state's armour of control for the tentacles of oppression, although far more omnipresent in the cities, still reached into the remotest corner of the smallest hamlet.

Nevertheless, life did improve little by little. By the early fifties, all their children were adults and could make their own way in life. Juan, like most young people from poor families, had to start working in his early teens. For young people of his generation without resources, a higher education was not an option, therefore, despite being intelligent, he followed in his father's footsteps as a builder, learning the trade as he worked alongside him.

At this time, Cecilia, who had been in charge of the household since her mother's death in 1939, continued to look after the family as she had always done. Never having experienced the expectations of women in the thirties, she did not share their bitter disappointment. On the other hand, it must have been especially galling for women like María who had seen, for a few years at least, a tantalizing glimpse of freedom and rights only to be dragged back to a past they had struggled so desperately to change.

The government made it quite clear that one of its principal aims was to undo everything that women had achieved between the formation of the 2nd Republic in 1931 and the end of the war. The *Falange* was responsible for organizing the *Sección Femenina* and *Acción Social*[21], both of which still had considerable influence in the social sphere even though the church was gradually gaining ground politically. Nevertheless, as both *Falange* and the Church believed fervently in the subservience of women this, at least, was a perfect issue for cooperation. Those who had fought most fiercely for their rights were dead, imprisoned, exiled or totally cowed, thus making the task ahead much easier, and this task was to produce the perfect Spanish woman.

In 1939, members of the *Sección Femenina* visited Germany in order to find out more about Nazi policy for women. Like Vallejo-Nájera, their visits to Nazi Germany had provided a valuable insight into how to do this successfully, and they must have been happy to find

---

21 Department for Women's Affairs and Welfare Programme

that the guiding principles of *Kinder, Küche, Kirche* were readily adaptable to the situation in Spain where it become *Iglesia, Cuna, Cocina*[22] with the addition of the cult of the Virgin María, the epitome of Spanish womankind. Like Nazi doctrine, the *Sección Femenina* had nothing whatsoever to do with feminism and very much to do with their definition of femininity: a demure, nurturing woman who would attend church and limit her activities to the domestic sphere.

Most of its rules were intended for young ladies of the victorious side rather than country women like Cecilia; in fact, much that the *Sección Femenina* was proposing would have seemed quite alien to country women. After attending convent schools, girls from reasonably well-off families would participate in the extra classes given by the *Sección Femenina*, then they might take up a position in a women's organization before fulfilling their duty to the state by getting married and producing numerous offspring. These, according to the regime's philosophy, should be the sole aims of every woman and indeed it allowed them few options to do anything else. Married women were not permitted to work but single women, mainly in the towns, were afforded opportunities to take part in public life through the *Acción Católica*.

Despite general agreement within the regime's institutions, there was some dissension even among the stalwarts of the anti-feminist policy. The emphasis the *Sección Femenina* placed on physical education caused

---

22 Church, cot, kitchen.

friction with the church authorities who considered that the clothing required might prove to be too revealing. It did, however, capitulate once reassurance was given that an appropriate dress code would be strictly observed. Furthermore, it was explained that exercise was necessary for healthy mothers to bear healthy babies, although again this would apply more to city than to country dwellers who would have more than enough exercise in their daily lives. Twenty years after the end of the dictatorship, in the 1990s, a staunch Catholic informed me that women didn't need to attend exercise classes as housework was quite enough, another of the Church's theories in the 1940s and 50s, and proof that old beliefs die hard.

Legislation from the Second Republic such as laws on divorce and civil marriage which were intended to liberate women by giving them legal equality was immediately repealed. The Republic had made women "unfeminine" and this had to be remedied, which was best done by bringing state laws into line with ecclesiastical law.

If María was not the kind of woman the regime approved of, Cecilia, who unwittingly satisfied most of its criteria for the ideal woman, most certainly was. Come what may in Madrid, Cecilia's life in the village continued much as before: one long domestic continuum. By the late forties, with years of experience behind her, she was now a competent housekeeper leaving only two requirements to be met: to marry and produce children. A spinster was never an attractive option nor, it must be said, an attractive person. To be left on the shelf was a slur as it meant she had failed in the most essential task, unless of course, she had either decided to dedicate her life to the state as Pilar Primo de Rivera[23] had done, or she had chosen to devote her life to God by becoming a nun.

With many young men dead in the war, finding a husband was a mission to be taken seriously. The church, the radio, magazines and newspapers all insisted on the importance of marriage in what was not so much a campaign as a veritable bombardment. In her book "*Usos amorosos de la postguerra española*", roughly translated as "Customs in love in postwar Spain", Carmen Martín Gaite considers the instructions to help acquire a husband. Young women should be coy and submissive, for no man would want a brazen, know-it-all woman, or at least no good Catholic man would. Men, on the other hand, had to be on their guard against feminine wiles to ensure they were not entrapped by an unsuitable candidate. It goes without saying that pre-marital chastity was a requisite for both. An occasional indiscretion might be permitted for men but certainly not for women, the guardians of the nation's morality.

This philosophy continued throughout a woman's life. A widow was expected to stay that way, as leaping into another marriage bed was seen as infidelity to the sadly departed husband. Even members of the regime could fall foul of this philosophy. Pilar Primo de Rivera, who always appeared frigid and straight-laced, was much preferred

---

23 Pilar Primo de Rivera was the sister of the dictator in the 1920s, Miguel Primo de Rivera who was greatly admired by a section of the government for her work in favour of the regime.

to the more down-to-earth Mercedes Sanz Bachiller: the former remained a spinster devoting her whole life to the *Sección Femenina* while Mercedes, whose first husband, Onésimo Redondo was assassinated at the beginning of the war, remarried a mere three years later in 1939. This was an insult to the memory of a fallen war hero and the condemnation led her to take a step back from public life.

In spite of this message of purity and morality being disseminated throughout Spain, it would have been far more relevant to the upper and middle classes, as it is unlikely that the defeated who were struggling to survive would have worried about the niceties of courtship. In the early 1950s the largest social group was made up of agricultural workers, and clearly life in the countryside was somewhat earthier than the prim and proper dictates of Franco's regime. Notwithstanding, rural inhabitants were as well aware of their place on the social scale as urban dwellers, and understood that a suitable spouse had to be someone with a similar status. With this in mind Cecilia and Juan were well suited.

It was an ideal match. Both wanted stability: Cecilia because she could only envisage her domestic life continuing as it had always done, Juan because it was something he had lacked in his early life. Cecilia was ideal wife material with her proven domestic skills while Juan, with his Rudolf Valentino looks and a job, was a good catch. In 1949, when they were both in their early twenties, the perfect age to settle down, they married in the village church. Yet even under a Catholic regime, life couldn't always be as perfect as one would wish. She was already pregnant. Shotgun weddings, probably more common than anyone cared to admit at the time, were the only solution in this case. It should be said that it was very much the same in Britain although the shame of being a single mother was much greater and persisted far longer in Spain. As late as the eighties I came across a child who was condemned to go through life with the wrong birth date in order to cover up an indiscretion.

The wedding, walking down the aisle, was a girl's moment of triumph, but, in general, instructions stopped there. Indeed once she had achieved her goal, nobody felt the need to teach the rudiments of indissoluble married life. What went on after the wedding was shrouded in mystery for most women, which hardly mattered as they were not considered to be sexual beings. Since the realities of the wedding night were not included in the manuals in order to avoid any hint of salaciousness, the honeymoon must have come as a shock to many young girls who had been fed the airy-fairy fantasies of wedded bliss. Prudery was the order of the day even after the wedding. To save the women's modesty, little buttoned windows were sewn into the front of nightgowns so eliminating the need to undress for the husband. No doubt country women with more practical knowledge of what married life might entail found it far less disconcerting.

For all women whether city or country dwellers, the key to a happy married life was unquestioning obedience and they in turn would be loved, cherished and cared for. In theory division of labour was 50%: she was in charge of all domestic matters while he went out to earn money.

Once again this theory had little relevance for many. Women in the country would have to help with many aspects of producing food while working class women worked hard without the help of electrical appliances and the bevies of servants enjoyed by the wealthy.

According to the regime's philosophy a good woman had neither the desire nor the capacity for study, neither should she bother her pretty head about politics, and it was unbecoming for her to enter into discussions on important issues. Cecilia was more than happy to comply on all counts. She readily accepted Juan's views on politics or any other weighty matter. She didn't question her life or her role. As Victoria Kent feared, she followed the dictates first of her father then her husband although, unlike many village women of her generation, she could read, only doing so when absolutely essential for her daily life.

For years her realm of interest had never extended much further than the boundaries of the village but with the radio the outside world seeped in little by little. The one programme which was popular with many people throughout Spain was Elena Francis's responses to written consultations from listeners. First broadcast in 1947, it was designed to advise women on various aspects of their life and usually dealt with questions of courtship sometimes giving surprisingly perceptive comments, at other times merely suggesting that an appeal to the Virgin Mary would provide the solution to their worries. In addition, common topics included beauty and personal hygiene tips, as it was every woman's duty to be attractive and clean for her husband. Although Cecilia was probably far too busy to sit around listening to the radio, doubtless the opinions expressed would be shared among the village women, and, as the advice dispensed was invariably approved by the government, their ideas on morality and relationships were shaped in accordance with the philosophy of the regime. Such was people's trust in the reassuring words of Elena Francis that it was with some horror that they discovered many years later that the advice was actually written by a man and only read by a woman.

If the rules of courtship and marriage were not particularly relevant to village women, this large sector of Spanish society was of great concern to women's organizations within the regime since both agriculture and improving the health of the population were key factors of its policy. Whereas in the city the *Sección Femenina* organized sports, set up workshops to teach women the necessary skills of sewing, cooking, caring for children and keeping the husband happy, in rural areas they also organized projects to advise on health and other domestic matters.

A time of "social service", the female equivalent of military service, was expected from women. It was rewarded with a certification on completion and was a requirement for obtaining a passport, permits and licences as well as for various jobs. Cecilia's caring role exempted her from this obligation leaving her to continue her life in the village much as it had always done, but with greater recognition and an improved status as a married woman. Her days were simple and mundane although she would work extremely hard to maintain basic living standards: mending and darning, cooking and cleaning, leaving time for village gossip and speculation on family matters but little else.

As Juan worked as a builder, they had no need for agricultural land, instead they were given a small plot to build a house. Squat and solid, it was practical more than anything else with electricity but no running water initially. This had to be fetched from the fountain in the village square using four pots slung over a donkey, which were kept on a wooden stand in the entrance to the house. Water had to be used frugally for only essential washing and cooking. The stand lay abandoned when I first went, left in a corner to fall apart along with the flotsam and jetsam of a bygone rural life.

Compliance with the demand for numerous offspring to replenish the numbers lost in war and exile was unavoidable with a total ban on contraception. Women like Cecilia could never imagine life without children, who not only gave her a purpose in life but were insurance for the future as they had been in rural communities for centuries.

In 1950 when their first child was born, memories of her mother's death only 12 years earlier must have haunted Cecilia, since childbirth in the village remained risky. Any fears were justified as serious problems did indeed put her life at risk. Fortunately, for the next three births, Juan and Cecilia were able to leave the older children with the relatives in the village in order to go to one of the recently built hospitals in Madrid with modern equipment and doctors on hand if anything went wrong.

In many ways bringing up children in the village was easier than it is now, or at least more straightforward. Fortunately, it was also less costly, for while the state encouraged large families, economic help was not forthcoming. The death of a father left widows struggling to fend for themselves often bringing up children in desperate conditions.

As in most rural societies, child-rearing was a skill passed down through the generations and remained untouched by any new-fangled theories, and as long as families stayed in the villages this was quite satisfactory. Children were left to their own devices most of the day when they were not at school, spending their time outside with other children, playing in the fields and around the village. It wasn't a big worry because cars were a rare sight on the road going through the village and everyone kept an eye on the children, which did have its disadvantages as with family and neighbours round every corner ready to report back, it was hard to get away with wayward behaviour.

It might sound wonderful, the perfect place for children to grow up, and in many ways it was, had they not been denied a chance to get on in life. By the time their children were old enough to attend school, education was firmly in the hands of the church which had become far more powerful than the *Falange*. The state funded various activities such as the restoration of churches, priests' salaries and new seminaries to train more priests, but above all it was responsible for almost all education either in private schools or through intervention in state schools. The children destined for success, almost always from among the well-heeled, would be sent to religious schools in nearby towns or perhaps in Madrid. Neither state nor church believed in equality but saw education as the ideal way in which to inculcate the values of National Catholicism.

Each village, even those in the most remote areas, had its own school with the aim of teaching children the basics at a primary level. According to the theory of education at the time, all country children would ever need was a grounding in the 3 "Rs". Academic achievement was not expected of them and few state secondary schools were set up. On account of the disastrous financial situation of the country, facilities for education were often sadly lacking. A successful career woman told me that during the 1950s the pupils in her school in León, in northwest Spain, had their very own heating system. One of the items they took to school in winter was an old tin with holes punched in it and a candle inside so they could warm their fingers enough to write in the coldest months.

Despite the shortage of funding for adequate facilities, enough money could always be found to place a crucifix at the centre of the school room and photos of the *"Generalísimo"*, another of Franco's preferred titles, creating a propitious environment for glorifying the great leader as well as imposing the true religion. Acceptance of Catholicism was not sufficient, everything that was anti-Catholic had to be rejected. Evils seem to have included a large number of "isms", chief among them being Communism and Protestantism as well as Free Masons, who for some reason were particularly dangerous. Naturally, the only correct kind of Christianity was Catholicism, the rest being lumped together in an unholy alliance with Luther as the most heinous character in history according to students from the fifties and sixties. Apart from prayers and religious ceremonies, rote learning and copying were a key feature of education and in many places still are. Rather than the 3 "Rs", education in Spain could be summed up as the 3 "Ps": primers, prayer and propaganda.

This emphasis on religion in every school left little to choose between religious and state schools and having been subjected to a short time in a monastic school, Juan in particular was far from keen on this kind of education for his own children. Besides, watching them imbibe views which his family had fought against and lost was irksome.

In many ways, Juan was more fortunate than others who had been on the "wrong" side in the war. By the end of the fifties the family's economic conditions were easing, and the struggle merely to survive was giving way to the desire for something better for themselves but above all for their children. Juan knew that the education on offer would not stand them in good stead in the future. Moreover, Spain was a stagnant country gripped tightly by church and state. Conformity and total obedience to the rules of Franco, the dictates of the church and last but not least, to the norms and traditions of rural life were the order of the day.

When family members living in exile in France told them how good their new lives were compared to the dreariness of fifties Spain with its limitations, fear and religion they realized only one other option was open to them: emigration. Thirty years earlier, Juan's parents had left the village hoping to find something better in Madrid but now they were not only looking for better working conditions, they needed to escape and to do so they would have to leave Spain.

EMIGRATING

Decisiveness was never a strong point in the family; spontaneity rather than reason guided their lives. I suppose this is partly because events over which they had no control, premature death, unrest and the war had overshadowed their early years, indelibly marking out the course of their lives and providing proof enough that rationality was of limited use in an arbitrary world. What they imagined lay beyond the border was very appealing, and for them that was enough.

Nowadays people dream of coming to Spain perhaps for holidays or to retire but for centuries it was a country people left. Many emigrants didn't or couldn't come back, a few did bringing with them money as well as new ideas on politics and society.

There was a time in the distant past when those leaving were not fleeing but travelling towards an exciting new world with its promise of untold riches. Early adventurers, men like Pizarro and Hernán Cortés, left on voyages of discovery often from the small land-bound villages of Extremadura braving the hazardous sea journey to make their fortunes and to govern their Empire. This was in the 16th and early 17th century when the Spanish travelled to conquer the world, setting up settlements in South America or in the Philippines. Later, when the British were moving around the world, spreading and opening out, Spain was closing in on itself. By the 19th century it was struggling unsuccessfully to keep its empire which finally ended with the defeat in the Philippines and Cuba in 1898, when Britain was ruling over vast territories.

Nevertheless, the Spanish continued to travel abroad, now not drawn by the lure of foreign lands but forced by circumstances at home. Leaving a homeland is all the more grievous for anyone who is fleeing persecution or escaping hunger yet for many it was the only way out.

There was much to flee from in 19th century Spain: the Carlist wars, the military uprisings and especially the poverty. Wave after wave tore themselves away from their homeland, departing from the wind-swept moors of Soria, the mountainous regions of León bordering with Galicia, Galicia itself or from the rocky coastline of Asturias and Cantabria, driven out by the rough land and arduous working conditions which barely allowed them to survive. They left reluctantly for they were closely tied to the land, to their *patria chica* which they were leaving behind forever in many cases. Some, like those in Las Hurdes, the poor region in Extremadura visited by Alfonso XIII in the 1920s, were simply too poor to afford the journey even if they had known what lay across the ocean.

The principal destinations for those seeking their fortune were in South America, in particular Argentina and Venezuela which offered plenty of opportunities for work in the 19th and early 20th century, but only after a long and dangerous sea journey. In 1919 the *Valbanera* sailed from Las Palmas de Gran Canaria, carrying over a thousand people who had embarked from various ports along the Spanish coast on their way to a new life in South America. About half the passengers disembarked in Cuba before it continued on its voyage. Nothing more was heard of the ship until wreckage was spotted two weeks later; all the passengers had drowned along with the crew. They were among the many that never came back.

France not South America was the preferred destination for politicians and intellectuals forced to leave when the political situation became unfavourable but who expected to return to Spain when the winds changed. On their return, they brought fresh ideas not always particularly welcome in conservative Spain.

Not everyone went abroad. Immigrants like Ramón and María flocked to the cities where there was an increasing demand for cheap labour. With the outbreak of war the movement of people increased yet again with soldiers, politicians and refugees moving around the country and abroad. Many children were displaced, often separated from their parents. Those on the Republican side were evacuated not to the countryside as British children but to other countries. Some went to Britain while others were sent to Russia presumably hoping they would return when the Republic won. They never did. Many have died but a few still remain, appearing in interviews with their broken Spanish and regrets. They are clearly not Russian yet they are no longer Spanish either, caught up forever in events of the distant past.

While the war was still raging, a first wave of emigrants was made up mainly of wives, mothers and children who had lost their homes or were looking for relatives who had been in the fighting. They were joined by injured fighters but rarely high-ranking officials or politicians. Then the defeated soldiers followed, among them one of Juan's older brothers. As he was already a teenager, he had taken a more active part in the struggle and now took his place in the desolate processions wearily making their way across the Pyrenees.

The greatest exodus began as the Civil War drew to a close. In the biting January cold, defeated soldiers from the Ebro Front and foreigners from the International Brigades who had volunteered full of zeal to fight against fascism all trekked on foot to the French border along with throngs of Spanish refugees. Barcelona, where many people from other regions had sought refuge, was the last city to fall. Now the inhabitants had no choice but to leave immediately, fleeing with what they wore, joining the stream of humanity heading towards the French border. Half a million Spanish people escaping with the young and the elderly, people in rags trudging through the mountain passes to what they hoped would be safety. They appear hollow-eyed and empty in photographs and film footage, having lost everything they ever had, even the last flicker of hope. They were the defeated, the broken, the homeless, the starving shuffling in masses through the freezing mountains.

They went leaving behind houses and lands and, as exhaustion set in, they discarded the few precious belongings they had managed to bring with them and, in so doing, they relinquished the remnants of their identity.

What they found when they reached the other side of the frontier brought scant comfort. With hindsight it is easy to condemn the lack of willingness to accept these refugees, but it must be remembered that in 1939, before the outbreak of World War Two, the fear of communism all over Europe usually outweighed the wariness of fascism, and these refugees were all considered to be communists or anarchists, though the majority were not. After all, to all intents and purposes Germany was prospering, whereas the spread of Communism from the USSR appeared to pose a far greater threat. To make matters worse, the right-wing government in France at the time had little sympathy with the Spanish republicans, and with Europe on the brink of war it was soon to face its own challenges. It was certainly not the time to accommodate refugees with suspect political ideas.

They were detained in the camps hastily set up by the French government such as that at Argelès where large numbers perished under the grueling conditions. Some joined the forces fighting against the Germans while others who had been politically involved in left-wing organizations continued their work in the French resistance. If caught, with Franco's blessing, they were taken to the concentration camp of Mauthausen where very few survived. Until recently their bravery had gone unrecorded and unacknowledged.

The fortunate managed to continue their journey to North or South America, where the language was no problem and where they could practise their professions. Others like Arturo Barea, the author of *"La Forja de un Rebelde"*, went to Britain. Spain's youth, many trade unionists, writers and politicians were scattered around the globe with little hope of ever returning. No doubt their exile would have been even more painful had they known it would be almost forty years before they could return to Spain as a democratic country.

When I was very young, perhaps only 16 or 17, I met a Spanish man, a friend's father in the small provincial town where I lived. Then I considered him to be extremely old although he was probably only in his early fifties. All I remember now is that he was morose and when he did speak it was with a marked accent. To me he was simply an old man who happened to come from Spain but whose story didn't concern me in the slightest. Nevertheless, there was something about him which touched me which is perhaps why I remember him after so many years but they are memories tinged with romance of distant places and times, not with the realism of exile. He must have felt so lonely in a life he had never chosen, unable to go back. Lately, I have wondered where he came from and what became of him. I imagine he has died now but I wish I had talked to him then and shown him some acceptance as he struggled to adapt to foreign customs and a new language.

It was easier for those in the next wave of emigration in the late forties, fifties and sixties. Yet there were still many reasons to go. Notably in the forties, people wanted to escape the bitter aftertaste of war, of having been on the wrong side, of being the losers, of the gloating, vindictiveness and in many cases retaliation. By the late fifties, the major pull came from Spanish cities which offered employment as well as better living conditions and large numbers of people were leaving the countryside to settle in Madrid, Barcelona, smaller provincial capitals or the coastal area. Here they might have found work but, unlike European cities they did not offer freedom from the regime and living standards were still low.

At the same time, European countries and in particular Britain, France, Germany and Switzerland, rebuilding after the Second World War, were crying out for unskilled labour. With burgeoning industries and massive building projects to replace the destruction of the bombing, as well as the need to provide housing, schools and hospitals for the growing population, work was readily available. Letters arrived from those who had succeeded in their new country bringing snippets of a better life. Juan's older brother was married to a French woman and doing well. Those who were not considered to have committed political crimes visited for holidays with accounts of freer, more prosperous countries. They might have hankered after their beloved village, singing its praises whenever they could, but indubitably in the forties and fifties Spain was a much better place viewed from afar.

The government itself was encouraging people to find work in other countries, setting up the Spanish Institute for Emigration at the end of the fifties. The emigrants would send back foreign currency that was desperately needed by the government. Therefore, by promoting emigration the aims of the government and the interests of many families for once coincided however disparate their motives. With this official stamp of approval, it was altogether a more honourable exit than the flight of the losers in the post-war and Juan and Cecilia could happily follow in the footsteps of earlier generations.

The whole departure seems to have been haphazard. He left, she left and was stopped on the border, and then they tried again a few months later going hither and thither on a whim. At last, on a cold December day in 1961, they were off with the three youngest children in tow joining many others who were about to start a new life. They piled into a train to France, ready to settle in Bordeaux where the authorities welcomed workers to rebuild the country.

The eldest of the children was left with an aunt in a neighbouring village where he was to stay for a year, understandably as taking four young children on such a venture would have been extremely taxing and sacrifice has its limits. Such a decision was not totally in line with Cecilia's staunch views on family unity, a fact which she must have been aware of as various explanations for this decision have been given over time, none of them particularly convincing.

The Spanish and Portuguese formed the bulk of the unskilled workforce in France along with quite a number of North Africans: Moroccans and Algerians of French origin who had been forced to leave their home country after the Algerian War of Independence. The native population of the countries in which these immigrants settled considered them all to be uneducated as well as uncultured and Juan's children remember being called "dirty Spaniards" at school, something which didn't appear to have bothered them overly.

It is true that in many ways they must have appeared strange to their new neighbours even though Spain was in theory part of Europe. In 2006 a film was made in Spain about Spanish immigrants in Switzerland in the sixties: *Un Franco, 14 pesetas*. It relates the hurdles that had to be overcome not only by the Swiss themselves but by the Spaniards, who arrived in a highly organized country from one which, to put it mildly, lagged behind in every way. Nevertheless, there were plenty of opportunities for those who worked hard and work hard they did. Juan and Cecilia were given nothing except the very basic aid for housing and child benefits that French nationals also received.

At first they lived together with a group of Spanish immigrants, managing as best they could until Juan was offered a job which allowed them to move to a better flat. The children started school immediately and did well as children of immigrants often did. The schools must have seemed magnificent compared with the small village school with its crucifixes, photos of the "*Generalísimo*" propaganda and antiquated methods of teaching. In general they were happy yet there were things that they found strange about their new home.

Nowadays, with the ubiquity of modern media, it requires an enormous amount of effort to imagine what it was like for these children who had never before left their small village, who had never seen a television or been to the cinema, who had only had a few books carefully approved by the state and the church, to suddenly be faced with a new world. Everyone they had known so far in their short lives had looked much the same and even now, sixty years later, they remember their surprise at meeting children from other countries for the first time and the fascination at seeing a boy from Africa and a pale redhead. Then, there was the incessant rain and the overcast skies, something they were wholly unused to after the crisp winters in the village.

Despite the initial strangeness, the children have fond memories of these early years in France. At that time it was still safe for them to play outside as they had always done in the village. They could run through a nearby wood, explore a mysterious old house and a vineyard. A favourite game in autumn was dodging the guards to get in among the vines to steal bunches of grapes.

In the mid-sixties two more children were born, which was not too much of a financial burden as already the French state offered help with the rent and extra benefits for the children, something new for them. Life for the family was going well. They had gone to improve their lives and the only way to do this was by being successful in a job so Juan worked hard, leading to promotion which took him as high as any foreigner could go, as the top jobs were reserved for the French.

Cecilia still devoted her time to caring for her family and the home but now ensconced in her modern flat with the latest appliances she would never have had in the village. She happily left the children to their own devices most of the time but always ensured they were well fed and clothed. Her French remained limited, so she preferred to mix with other Spanish or South American families who lived nearby. They had few close French friends, only forming an acquaintance with one fellow French worker. French politics never concerned her in the slightest but then neither had the intrigues and proceedings of government in Spain. Her life was contained in the four walls of her home, the market, the shops, her street, her neighbourhood.

Every summer, they would pile into the car which they could now easily afford and drive down through Spain to the village. France was, at least for the parents, a place to be until the next holiday, until they could go back for the month in August, to the mountains, and the new swimming pool nestled among the rocks and the pine trees. Once back they would spend the evenings sitting outside chatting to anyone strolling past and catching up on the local gossip. And surely they showed off at least a little about their success, their new possessions and the life they were leading. They might have begun to see Spain as some foreigners do: a land of leisure, laid back and relaxed and then they would wish they could stay rather than returning to France.

The two eldest sons married French girls while the family was in France. The first, the daughter of a family friend, was joyfully welcomed into the family, the second absolutely not. The second son met his future wife in Paris on a weekend trip and presented her to the family as a *fait accompli* much to Cecilia's horror. For a casual friend, to spend time with the family was one thing, to introduce a complete stranger and a foreigner to boot as a future wife was quite another. When they returned to Spain, Juan and Cecilia left behind these two married sons who had made their lives in France. With time they have become far more French than Spanish and have always been glad they decided to stay but Cecilia could never quite forgive herself for leaving them. According to her moral code abandoning part of the family was wrong and more than anything else she worried she would be condemned for it. Nonetheless, however guilty she may have felt, it was not enough to make her stay. She was not alone with her unease. For anyone living abroad for many years, life becomes messy. There is always a price to pay on returning: families are split, opportunities are lost.

Of the postwar immigrants, some stayed a short time while others made their home in the new country. They stayed because they had made a good life for themselves or because they had married abroad. If those who had been involved in the Republican struggle could not return during the interminable dictatorship, Juan and Cecilia were free to come and go as they pleased. They had chosen to leave Spain and never had to bear the political refugees' unrequited yearning for their home country.

They never truly felt at home in France. They spoke little of this period spent abroad but it is clear they never intended to make it their whole life and indeed it had little effect on their way of thinking except perhaps nostalgia for their home country and a deepening conviction that everything Spanish was the best. The idea of "Spanishness" was not only fanned by the fanaticism of Franco's followers but also by the rose-tinted memories of the emigrants. Each, in their own way, carried with them a faith in the greatness of Spain.

Sixteen years had gone by, far more than they ever intended to spend in a foreign land, besides by now circumstances had changed and France had its own problems. The boom of the post-war years was turning to recession; unemployment had risen, and then in 1973, came the oil crisis. As often happens, foreigners who had once been welcomed with open arms were no longer needed or indeed wanted. France, like other countries, was keen for them to return to their own lands, offering economic incentives for anyone interested in departing. Juan and Cecilia along with other immigrants were promised a considerable lump sum as well as a guaranteed pension. It was definitely time to go.

RETURNING

The promise of payment was undoubtedly a strong enticement to return. Nonetheless, in the end they returned as they had gone: for no particular reason, with no particular plan. Things simply happened, life sweeping them along. It was because they missed Spain; because life was improving there; because they never intended to stay anyway; because the political situation wasn't quite so bad; because they were no longer afraid; because there were jobs; because they would no longer have to struggle with the language. All in all, because it was their own country and they were not getting any younger.

They joined the many immigrants flooding back for the most part from France, Germany, Switzerland and Belgium. Those who had left the small-mindedness of the village, the poverty and struggle, now returned with money, speaking another language and with a touch of exoticism.

Much of Spain has literally been built on emigrants filtering back or sending money. Traditional villages were soon surrounded by new homes usually constructed without the practical considerations of time-honoured techniques: the wrong roofs for the snow in winter, thin walls and inappropriate styles. Controls were, and still are few. They built showy houses for themselves with little concern for aesthetics, as if the purpose of these large palatial dwellings complete with pillars holding up the majestic entrance was to blight the villages which had caused them years of humiliation.

In some cases the longed-for return was a disappointment. Children born abroad soon realized that Spain was not the paradise their parents had painted or the vision that they had seen on holiday. On a radio phone-in years ago, returning emigrants compared the reality of living back in Spain with their expectations. As children, they had made a yearly pilgrimage back to the village, the sun would shine, Mum and Dad would relax, there were days by the pool, long, slow family lunches and staying out late in the streets with friends. This one idyllic month of the year was a haven of sun, happiness and balmy summer evenings, halcyon days a world away from life in northern cities with their cramped flats, chilly winters and constant rushing. Yet the issues they were to face on returning were much the same, or thornier, than those of the country they were leaving, and even in Spain the sun does not always shine. Some must have wondered what they had come back to as the New Spain had a long way to go before it could compare favourably with the life they had become used to.

It must have seemed static, stagnating and regressive compared with the countries they had left behind. Despite an impression of stability, the world of Pérez Galdós with its wheeling and dealing, getting by and illegality had not completely faded. If you could get away with anything you did. Schools were behind the times, jobs were scarce, while salaries were low and working conditions were often worse than the countries where they had lived. Moreover, the deep wounds left by the war festered on throughout Franco's regime, and during the sixties attempts to modernize were timid and always within the strict dictates of the Catholic Church and the ultra-conservative government.

Despite all this, with a comfortable standard of living, returning was not too bad for Juan and Cecilia. The village might have become a summer refuge for immigrants from abroad like themselves or for urban dwellers escaping the intense heat but it was the same old village even though there was now a swimming pool among the pine trees and bigger cars parked outside the houses. Unlike the coast with the skimpily dressed women with loose morals, theirs was a much more familiar Spain.

Nevertheless, change, whether gradual or sudden, could not be kept at bay for ever and having visited every summer they must have been aware that Spain was nothing like the place they had left sixteen years earlier.

It was fortunate that the economy was no longer solely in the hands of Franco and his most faithful acolytes from the days of the Civil War. Already in the mid-sixties those closest to the dictator noted the first manifestations of his decline. Born in 1892 and by then in his seventies, he had been the head of state since 1939 and was showing signs of weakness as well as a noticeable lack of interest in matters of state.

Inevitably, the disastrous autarky of the late forties had given way to a much more open economy and with the development of industry in the 1960s Spain was finally able to compete in the world capitalist market. The transformation of the economy was in the hands of well-trained men disparagingly referred to as "technocrats" by the old guard of the *Falange*, although needless to say, they were also committed supporters of the regime. Efficient and extremely hard-working, many of them were members of an ultra-Catholic group, the Opus Dei, people from the top echelons of society who could afford a good education and could be relied on to abide by the rules.

In order to improve the economy it was necessary to open up the country to foreign investment which had been severely limited since the beginning of the regime in 1939. Freedom for foreign companies to invest from 1959 aided many industries, among them mining, energy, car manufacturing and of course foodstuffs, important in a country with so much potential for agriculture production. By the early sixties, with the rapid growth of tourism the service sector was fast becoming one of Spain's key industries. I can remember when I was very young the excitement of friends when their families decided to desert Butlins or the chilly, windy coast for exciting package holidays in Spain. Our damp camping trips in the British Isles left me with a vague feeling of superiority as well as a certain amount of envy.

While the increasing flow of foreign currency from tourists was welcome, their pernicious moral standards were definitely not. Their wanton ways and provocative dress were a challenge to the good Spanish boys and girls, but it was a question of grin and bear it, only trusting that good Catholic girls could compete with those from the immoral north in winning a man. Anyway, for the time being only areas around the south and east coasts, the "costas", were affected since very few tourists ventured into central Spain. Moreover, tourism, along with other industries provided much needed jobs to keep people satisfied for, as any dictator knows, a contented population is more likely to be a docile one. Indeed, now that the dreadful forties and fifties were over, people were happier in general or at least resigned to everything the country had become.

If life for earlier generations had been marked by turmoil, for those willing to fall into line with the regime, it could now offer long term security by making everything for life: marriage, the family and work. In the private sector, loyalty to a company and to the boss counted more than efficiency, with companies often providing jobs for the whole family. If father worked in a bank, he would ensure a stable position for his sons and in the later years of the regime for his daughters who could work as secretaries until they married. Entering the public sector then, and even now, meant a job for life with plenty of perks. Franco maintained that anyone relying on the state for their livelihood was unlikely to rebel, and entry exams for any government jobs included a section on the Principles of the National Movement just to check that, at least theoretically, the regime's ideology had been absorbed. With few people able to afford further education, there were not that many candidates for jobs and success at the lower levels was almost guaranteed.

After acquiring a stable job, the next step was buying a property. Again this was encouraged by the regime, as anyone busy working to pay off the debt incurred would think twice before doing anything to risk what they had achieved. Given a pressing demand for housing and with the massive exodus from the countryside, new districts with blocks of anonymous flats mushroomed on the outskirts of big towns and cities. Such housing was a consolation for the masses, a bribe to accept the regime, a sop for defeat and death paid for each month with eternal gratitude to the ruler. These extensive building projects, however, did allow them to own their home in the city, an impossible dream a couple of decades earlier and moreover, they appreciated the comfort after the rambling village houses with few modern conveniences.

This housing was not perfect. Faithful to its ideology, the government left the development of the city in the hands of private enterprises with few limitations, and it showed. The hastily built flats springing up in empty wind-swept places, wastelands on the outskirts of Madrid, appeared half-finished with unpaved roads, no streetlights and littered with piles of bricks in case someone decided to come back one day to finish off. This is what I saw and so intensely disliked when I first arrived. Today, as they have matured, trees have grown and buildings have mellowed, I don't mind them as much or perhaps I have simply got used to them.

It was in one of these districts that Juan and Cecilia bought a flat along with many other families straggling back in the early seventies, the twilight years of Franco's dictatorship. Knowing as they did what a town had to offer they would never have dreamt of going back to live permanently in their old marital home in the village, deciding instead to settle in the capital where their children would have better opportunities. In this way, they joined the multitudes abandoning the old, agricultural world as María and Ramón had done 50 years earlier and, like previous generations, they carried with them part of the rural mentality which had dominated Spain for so long.

Unlike Ramón and María, when they moved to the burgeoning city they were hoping not for change and revolution but for a quiet life. Their new flat was on the outskirts of Madrid, much further south than the crowded centre where Juan's parents had set up home in a rented flat in the 1920s. Flats at that time were unbelievably cheap, especially for returnees, as the exchange rate for the lump sum they had received from France was extremely favourable. It was almost as if they were being given away.

Their new home was on one of the huge estates of low-rise blocks, served only by a market and a few traditional shops and hairdressers. The design was utilitarian, with no lift and only three small bedrooms for the parents and four children but it had a modern kitchen: Cecilia's own realm. Comfortable and easy to clean it was all she ever wanted. These new flats were the ideal place for the perfect Spanish family, and who better to promote this than Franco himself, the benevolent patriarch who liked to be photographed with his grandchildren around him, an example of what family life should be.

In films, which people could increasingly enjoy on their own TV, families were the order of the day; the bigger, the better and happiness was *de rigueur*. There could be many misunderstandings as long as there was a happy ending; our heroine starting out on a life of married bliss ready to churn out numerous children. On the way there was usually quite a bit of singing to create new, wholesome stars for the people. Since this picture of domestic bliss was appealing to almost everyone, whatever their circumstance, it was willingly accepted, so transforming the myths which in turn conditioned reality.

In general, in the late sixties and early seventies the population acquiesced to the dictates of the regime at least outwardly. Some were happy because their lives were improving; some had had any opposition crushed out of them by the oppression of the regime and, aware they had no choice, they had come to the conclusion that, for the time being, defiance was futile. Forbearance would be rewarded when the time came. Others accepted Franco's idea that the population were like children who needed a firm hand, who shouldn't question life too much, and who should be satisfied and happy with the activities provided for them by Franco himself. Bullfighting was promoted and reached its zenith in the sixties with *toreadors* like *El Cordobés* becoming national heroes. Football reigned supreme, encouraged not only to channel passions within the country but also to act as one of Spain's ambassadors abroad: in 1966, Real Madrid won its sixth European Cup without a single foreign player in the team, a great triumph placing Spain firmly on a European footing.

Yet, away from popular entertainment and sport, away from the twee films with the smiles and big, happy families, far from the tourists' vision of cheap wine and food and sun, there was another view of Spain. If some film makers in the 50s and 60s were purveyors of bliss in the regime, others, despite censorship, were increasingly critical. Berlanga, Bardem, Erice and Saura made films portraying urban claustrophobia including coded messages on the repression by the state while singers, poets, intellectuals and artists were increasingly expressing their rejection of the regime.

Opposition was present since the very beginning of the dictatorship, and as time went by, new generations were growing less patient. There was a student rebellion in Madrid University as early as 1956, and with the growth of the economy, the incipient middle classes were unwilling to accept the restrictions imposed by the government. If anyone mentions the Revolution of 1968, a revolution against a wealthy society and the complacency of post-war Europe, it is France and in particular Paris that comes to mind. In Britain it was more benign. I was very young then but the rebellion I remember was with miniskirts, Mary Quant hairstyles, Twiggy and the Beatles. It was fun, unlike 1968 in Spain where students demonstrating along with the unions were risking years in prison if not their lives. Dispensable lives of the undesirables. They died, were tortured and imprisoned all far from the sunny beaches and the cheap seaside restaurants.

By the early 70s it was clear Franco's demise was approaching, leaving questions of the future of the regime hanging in the air. Rather than opening up, increasing dissension was leading to greater repression. In the dying decade of the regime it was, as always, down to the youth, who appreciate neither comfort nor security, to rebel. And they did. Our generation in Spain was that of rebellion with friends and family taking part in the heady days of the late 1960s and early seventies. They have stories to tell of running from the "*grises*", the regime's police force, participating in demonstrations against the government and daily acts of defiance, the general unrest a harbinger of what was to come if things were not handled well. Spain was teetering on the brink, violence simmering under the peaceful surface of social acquiescence.

It was, however, the dramatic events of this period which received international attention more than anything else. In December 1973 Carrero Blanco, Franco's designated successor, was assassinated in a daring attack by ETA. I can't recall hearing of his death at the time, but like so much else that happened in Spain before I arrived, everything was rather vague. Since then, on many occasions I have walked down the quiet, genteel street where it took place, any traces long gone but his death echoes down through the years in documentaries, articles, books and even jokes on Twitter or X as it is called now. It would be impossible now not to know of it or the impact it had at the time.

It was hardly surprising Carrero Blanco was chosen as Franco's successor as they shared the same ideology. Neither was it surprising that this designation was extremely unpopular with many sectors of society, including the

Basque independence group ETA which at this point could perhaps avoid the label of "terrorist" since they were fighting against a dictatorship. The attack was meticulously planned. Carrero, a fervent Catholic, attended mass daily therefore a basement flat was rented on his daily route to church. A group of three men tunnelled from the flat under the road, having told the owners that they were sculptors working with stone which would explain the banging at all hours and the need to remove considerable amounts of rubble.

The explosion was so strong that it blew the car on to the top of a five storey building sending shock waves through Spain and to the governments of other democratic countries, as well as bringing considerable relief in many quarters. Conspiracy theories have abounded since then as they always do. It has been suggested that the Americans must have known something about it, especially as their embassy is just round the corner.

In the aftermath of the assassination it was obvious to everyone, including foreign governments that the situation in Spain had changed irrevocably. It must have brought hope to those fighting for a regime change both within Spain and in exile. Opposition organizations were active just across the border in France, and in 1974 an important meeting of socialists was held in Suresnes in the south of France with Felipe González, a future prime minister, playing a key role. Like him, many returnees as well as others imprisoned in Spain were to become politicians, ministers and union leaders whose names would be familiar to me in my first years in Spain.

If plans for the future of the country were already underway in the early seventies, the regime's opponents would have to bide their time until Franco's death, news of which was eagerly awaited. They would not have long to wait.

November 20, 1975, "*Franco ha muerto*". A sombre day for sombre news, at least for some. A grief stricken Arias Navarro appeared in rigorous mourning to announce to the world that his companion of happier days was gone. They had fought together in the war and shared the victory. However, the man who had died was no longer the Franco of the pitiless cruelty of the post-war years but a decrepit old man with a warbling voice who had long since relinquished the day-to-day running of the country. The following day the news reached the early editions of newspapers where I first noticed it before pushing it to the back of my mind as irrelevant. Fleeting news on the world stage but for the Spanish it was the end of an era. For some it was a time of inconsolable grief, for others a time of rejoicing, their happiness marred only by resentment that it had taken so long. At least the tortured and the imprisoned could find meagre consolation in knowing that he too had suffered in his final, drawn out agony.

If his death marked the official end of a painful period in Spanish history, it plunged the country into unknown territory. Replacing a dictatorship is fraught with difficulties, and once again the country was divided. A wrong step could sound the death toll of democracy before it was established and for various sectors of society this would have been the best outcome. It could hardly be expected that the extreme right which had been blessed with many years of privileges and impunity would vanish overnight. And indeed it didn't. Beneath the surface of tranquillity ran a current of violence and unrest. It might have been possible to return home late at night, to feel safe on the streets but anyone who pushed the limits or dared to think differently was running a risk.

With all this the Spain of Juan and Cecilia's homecoming in the mid-seventies shortly after Franco's death was far more volatile than the one they had left. Surely they realized this yet even if Juan observed events with some concern, if he worried for his children, the political situation was no longer one of his priorities. For Cecilia it never had been. The seventies might have been the start of a new era for them as well as for Spain but if the country's future was in doubt theirs appeared quite placid. They had moved fast forward since the fifties: marriage and children, a job, life abroad and relative prosperity. They were no longer the struggling, young couple who had left their poor mountain village in search of a better life. The restlessness of youth had evanesced and now, despite being only in their late forties, they looked forward to a simple life of ease, gradually fading into a contented old age.

Juan was a father of six who had worked hard and done well. Although still young, having started work at 14, he had already worked for 35 years and by the mid-seventies he had more or less retired except for the occasional odd job. He even refused a lucrative offer of work in North Africa, believing that at 49, he and Cecilia were too old to relocate again. At that time in Spain anyone over 40 was decidedly over the hill.

Anyway, financially there was no pressing need for him to get work. Added to the generous pay-off, he had a French pension for life with another pension for a slight injury at work, as well as a small sum from the Spanish government; altogether not too bad taking into account they weren't particularly ambitious or materialistic. All they wanted was a place to live, luxuries like a new car every few years, electrical appliances to make life that little bit easier and an occasional trip to France to see their sons and grandchildren.

Reunited with their many relatives, in their own country with the customs, traditions and language they had always known, France became a parenthesis in life that hardly touched them. In spite of their time abroad, or perhaps precisely because they had been away, they willingly went along with any political situation, taking any benefits as they drifted into a comfortable old age which was more than they could have ever hoped for in those pitiless years of their youth during the thirties and forties.

It was only a few years after they had settled back into life in Spain, comfortable and complacent, that I was to join them. Their lives could not have been more distinct from my own, nor Britain of the seventies more different from their turbulent country on the brink of a new era. At the time I failed to understand either them or the country. It would take time for, if I already knew that democracy was imperfect, that progress always means discarding things that are cherished, I knew nothing of the pain of their past from which they could never truly escape. While they were to find it hard to accept many of the inevitable changes in the coming years, I had much to learn about their history and all they had been through.

ANOTHER TIME, ANOTHER PLACE

I was aware from the moment I arrived that the past of the family held in this dark flat and a distant mountain village had nothing in common with mine. Those of us born in post-war Britain with its wishy-washy religion and passionless politics were rarely conditioned by dramatic events. As we grew up we took for granted all that was freely offered. Coming as I did from another place and time I must admit that I hardly cared what Spain had been, what it was or what it would become. If their past was largely unknown, I didn't particularly like the present nor did I ever imagine I could ever share their hopes for the future.

What was the hardest to accept was Madrid itself. Still concentrated in a relatively small area, I found it noisy and disorganized: the centre was too dense with a transport system that was aged and obsolete. Not having grown up in a large city, a longing to leave was always there. In those early years we often travelled out of the city, rushing down the dual carriageways, escaping the suffocating heat in summer or the cap of pollution which hangs over it in winter. Back then, these roads with their gaudy hoardings almost obliterating the empty landscape behind were monotonous and uniform. Later, all adverts were banned with a reprieve only for the enormous cut-out effigies of bulls and adverts for a mark of brandy, left in solitary splendour to remind the traveller of another age; brandy and bulls part of their collective memory, not mine.

At least Madrid is conveniently situated at the very centre of Spain, roads spanning out to the four corners of the peninsula. To the east is the Mediterranean coast, the route travelled by families in the sixties and seventies spending innumerable hours driving across the scorching plains in an old 600 Seat to their holidays on the coast in Valencia or Alicante; perhaps to stay at one of the flats in the new resorts or perhaps returning to the village they had left for better life in the city. The houses along the way owned by the wealthy would soon be swallowed up as the road expanded, eating into their gardens as progress encroached on the privileges they had always enjoyed.

The road to the north of the city was the way to freedom, the route to the mountains: majestic and unmarked by all that had gone on around them. Unlike the cities which bear the scars of time, the countryside at first appeared neutral. Only much later, once I had understood the fear that the *maquis*[24] must have felt, could I sense their shadow on the slopes of the mountains, as they hid high up in the forests away from the villages and civilization, still fighting when they should have known all was lost.

---

24 Resistance fighters who remained in Spain after the end of the Civil War.

The road to the southwest had no such feeling of release. This was the route I took on the day of my arrival and my opinion of it barely changed over time. Only much later did I discover it hadn't always been so shabby. Centuries ago, across the river lay the leisure ground of the rich dotted with their palaces and mansions then, in the 19th century, it was taken over by those in need of houses, rapid urbanization encroaching on its gardens and coolness until the traces that remained of its former glory were all but obliterated by the destruction of the war, leaving little except urban sprawl.

Those first months or even years I moved around on a stage against a blank backdrop. I saw the objects and the monuments, observed street names, visited villages and small towns but I didn't appreciate that beyond their quaintness or dilapidation lay not only the history of centuries but also of the fear, joy, expectations and aspirations of their people.

The present of a place without an inkling of the past is unattainable, empty of any meaning. For me the country's recent history and its society were impenetrable, a labyrinth of unrest, strife and violence and above all the Civil War. This one event that defined the country, loomed over life still undigested and unaccepted leaving, even 45 years later, a tangle of loose threads to be tied up. To truly understand the country I would have to look beyond the conflicts to the influences of tradition, of religion, of rural life, all of which have persisted until very recently.

Then it felt as if I had been transported not only to a new place but back to an age with a vague resemblance to Britain in the fifties. Having lived in various places, I firmly believed I could accept anything albeit grudgingly. Many did. For visitors in the late years of the dictatorship and the transition to democracy it was easy to see only the superficial, the fun, the weather, the cheapness and the lively bars. For tourists on the coast that was all there ever was; for people who came to work perhaps for a year or two that was enough. Yet for me, as I had already realized it was to be more than a brief visit, the task was daunting.

If I was to stay I knew that I had to accept the country, lock, stock and barrel. It was for the Spanish to pick and choose the parts they wanted, reinterpreting their past in any way they could, deciding what to keep and what to reject. However, even for them, choices were often complex, the past held too many shadows which could not be easily dispelled, while the future with modernity had its own agenda.

The study of dramatic events attracts attention more than the experiences of normal folk; where they came from, how they think and what has influenced them. Although in the beginning every aspect of their lives was remote, as the years went by their past did indeed grow closer, gradually reshaping the world I lived in and the way I viewed it, but firstly, I needed to acquire knowledge which would provide a map to the present and a key to the future, reaching beyond the myths and the misconceptions. I had no choice but to start with the family.

A VERY SPANISH INSTITUTION

Naturally, I had high hopes for the Spanish family; after all it has always been regarded with admiration and envy. Up until the seventies many families were indeed large, a source of pride to the Spanish themselves as well as being part of their identity. What was, in practice, the product of tradition, the Catholic Church and rural life had become an intrinsic part of some nebulous "Spanishness" rather than a highly functional, albeit imperfect, institution persisting from the past. On the face of it this mattered little to me as I was joining the family in the present. What I saw was all and nothing of what I expected. It was certainly big and noisy but it soon became clear that it was far more complex than simply being fun. If I was to a large extent disappointed it was hardly surprising; with time the Spanish themselves have sometimes admitted that their cherished idea of the family was, in fact, illusionary.

Arriving in summer, at the time of their annual return to their rural origins, it was immediately plain that family and village continued to be as inextricably entwined as they had been for centuries. People might have studied or worked in the big city but in the seventies and early eighties almost all city dwellers continued to travel to their home village to spend their holidays or for local festivals. In Madrid people would inquire if I was going back to my "pueblo" in the summer as if the inhabitants of a city were merely there on a temporary basis; their village or "*patria chica*" was where they truly belonged.

Everything about the family had its roots in a rural world I had never known nor could ever share. Everyone could be identified by a complicated genealogy, a biblical tangle of relatives. On an introduction, they would reel off past generations. "So you are the wife of the son of Juan, the son of María and Ramón" and so on, rambling back into the dawn of time with the family and village merging into one. It would be discovered inevitably that they had distant relatives in common leading to tales of foul deeds, slights, youthful adventures or good times never to be forgotten.

Initially, as they migrated into the city they clung to what they had known, taking a rural mindset with them, recreating something of their country lifestyle in the city. They often chose to live close to each other, in the same neighbourhoods, in the same streets or even in the same blocks of flats. It was expected. I have known families who owned a whole building each with their own flat. An aunt and nephew had long owned homes in a block where I lived, bickering about the boundaries of their estates in some distant village, hating each other but joined forever by their shared origins.

In the cities neighbourhoods informally took on the role of the village. When a serious fire destroyed the interior of a flat along our street, a collection was made among the neighbours to replace the basics since it was rare to have insurance. This was not an organized action of a neighbourhood group but rather a spontaneous gesture. It was a duty to aid those nearby whoever they were. Nevertheless, despite the willingness of the community to help out, it was the nuclear family that usually rallied round when hard times hit.

Until very recently any kind of state support was sadly lacking in Spain, leaving it to the family to offer stability against political upheavals and war, and to assist in times of poverty and need. It provided shelter, employment, childcare, friendship, money and if necessary, food. All this, at least, for the deserving.

Britain had been an increasingly industrialized and urbanized country since the early 19th century with the welfare system gradually developing during this lengthy period. Its implementation was necessary since highly industrialized and urbanized countries are far more unsettled, with people moving from place to place, going away to study or work, and most importantly living however and wherever they want. It was a slow process but over time protection was provided by a state that at least sought to care rather than to merely control. If we in 1960s Britain rejected family life as a bourgeois institution from the stuffy middle-class world of the forties and fifties, it was because we could afford to do so; in Spain, on the other hand, they could not. The Spanish state might have been omnipresent for many matters but welfare was largely left to the family or the church.

Spain's stance on welfare brought home to me how we unconsciously absorb attitudes in our youth, judging others by our own perspectives. Before arriving in Spain, it had never really occurred to me that welfare might not be available in other countries, whereas the Spanish, then and even to a certain extent nowadays, had no understanding that such a system exists elsewhere. I remained unaware of how deep this ignorance ran until I gave an English lesson to a group of lawyers, in which we studied a newspaper article. The objective was to learn the vocabulary and discuss the legal issues of a case involving a woman on benefits. The problem was that although they understood the words, they were unable to grasp the situation. Why was she receiving money as it seemed she had never worked? Why has she had so many children or why wasn't her family helping? The benefit state system was just as bewildering to them as the omnipotent family was to me. From the dreary north it may seem that the Spanish lived a happy-go-lucky life, but it was never so. An easy life is one with economic help and support, a rich land with jobs, not one with sun and fun.

Sociologists have debated whether the strong family tradition in southern European countries obviated the need for a welfare state or whether the welfare states in the north had led to the breaking up of close family ties. In other words did the family only continue to be strong when it is essential? I would say this is the case. The idea of state welfare was alien to many country-folk who relied on the family and village ties. Children with disabilities, old people or anyone that could only have survived precariously found refuge in the family home. Relatives had seen Juan and Cecilia through times of hardship providing support when Cecilia's mother died, sheltering Juan when his parents were in prison, caring for the older children when they first went to France and if it hadn't been for the family it is unlikely they would have ever made the decision to leave Spain.

For the regime the family was vital not only for its role in welfare but also to ensure stability and fulfill the Catholic ideal of large families. Therefore, it was promoted with considerable enthusiasm but little cash. Nevertheless, if this concept of the family was readily accepted at home and abroad, delving deeper uncovered many aspects that I found hard to accept.

Compared with provisions from the state, care within the family is subject to closer scrutiny, and without the need to comply with any standards of decorum it is harsh on occasions. Political correctness is for an easier society, an urban one of ease; Spain in the early days was not for the easily offended. The Spanish called a spade a spade or as they would say they called "bread, bread and wine, wine". If they appeared a little too direct at times it was probably because they were used to mixing in their own narrow environment where familiarity lessened the risk of offence.

The family was their social world, forming a buffer against the isolation of city life. Cecilia and Juan's lives revolved around their family; whereas relatives were everything, friends were peripheral and to a large extent unnecessary. People they met outside the home were casual acquaintances. Men fraternized in the bar, the place for a slap on the back, banter and a hail-fellow-well-met while women would chat in the village street, the shop or the market. They got on with almost everyone, aware that these acquaintances involved no commitment and would never encroach on their closed world. When my children were young in the early nineties, children's parties were primarily for the family and it was only later that large celebrations in hamburger or pizza restaurants became popular. The English man's home might be his castle but for the Spanish in the city it was also their very private reserve, their sanctuary for family, the outside world was for other people.

The Spanish themselves have remarked that even generations younger than Juan and Cecilia are not particularly individualistic, preferring to move in groups. Christenings, communions, marriages and funerals had more to do with socializing and gossiping than with religion, providing the perfect opportunity to get together.

Festivals and celebrations, village days in summer, winter days in Madrid, which marked out the weeks and months were dotted through the year. Many were reserved for the family: birthdays, Christmas and saints' days but above all Sundays, the sacred day which was no longer for the church but for the family, providing food for the body more than for the soul. Sundays spent with the extended family were the best moment of the week for many women whose lives had been forcibly limited to the home, like Cecilia. It was the highlight of her week and failure to attend was frowned on.

During the long-drawn out meal Juan sat at one end of the table, never moving, while Cecilia sat at the other end near the kitchen fetching, carrying and fussing. Coffee after lunch was generally for the men, the women had other things to do with a race for the dustpan and brush, the cloth, the broom, anything to get busy. I could never see the point of so much cleaning, but the Spanish were very house-proud.

Of all family occasions Christmas Eve was the most indispensable, marked by the family being together rather than by the frenzied consumerism of the UK. I can imagine that when they lived in the village it would have been a communal time offering a short respite in the bleakness of winter. A special mass would be held in the chilly church, they would prepare a little more food than usual from the stores from late summer and autumn: cold meats from the slaughtered pig, wine, late grapes, figs and almonds. Family would visit but there would be nothing of tinsels and baubles, plastic and glitter and few activities for the children except carols and religion.

However much it was enjoyed, it didn't afford the older generations many customs to transfer to the city apart from the nativity scene carefully set up each year. In any case they wouldn't have seen the point of today's extravagances. A small, silver tree with a few baubles and a red tablecloth were the only concessions they ever made to this special time. The meal started late. After we would sing carols, *The virgin is combing her hair, The fish in the river drink and drink to see Christ born* or *Giddy up donkey*. Rousing carols owing more to the influence of village life than the rarefied atmosphere of a great cathedral, they are to be sung not sedately but with gusto accompanied by a tambourine and anything else at hand.

Should I spend the festive period in the UK, I'm sure I would hate the senseless consumerism beginning as early as September. On the other hand, I will never give up the deeply-rooted traditions of my childhood: the smell of mandarins and spices, baking cakes and puddings, and collecting pine cones, ivy and mistletoe. That is why it is one time of the year which will always have something alien about it, even the date of celebration.

The "real" Spanish Christmas day, the day for giving presents is January 6, the arrival of the Magi bearing gifts although nowadays many families have adopted the custom of presents on the 24 or 25 December giving children time to play with their new toys before school begins in January. Unaccustomed as she was to any display of lavishness, I don't think Cecilia ever grasped the art of gifts. She used to appear with an array of socks, trinkets and chocolate "brought by the Three Kings" who were presumably short of time as they had left them unwrapped in a plastic carrier bag from the local supermarket.

While celebrations such as Christmas can bring happiness and fun, they can highlight the discontent and loneliness of the rest of the year. The impression of togetherness belied its true nature, for I understood early on that only those who complied unconditionally would be embraced and helped.

The family can be a far harsher censor than the state, threatening not only the withdrawal of resources but ostracism. Anything offered came with obligations, duties and demands. It was no frills, often tough and judgmental. Wayward behaviour brought shame to the whole family and was hard to accept or forgive. Single mothers would usually be given a place in the home but definitely only once and they would be expected to contribute in some way. I could vaguely remember a watered down version of such attitudes from my early childhood which gradually vanished as I matured. When I encountered them again they seemed harsh and outdated yet although they caused heartbreak, they no doubt contributed to a sense of responsibility in society.

After living independently for so long, I found the struggle that young girls faced to gain their freedom hard to comprehend. By law, until 1972 young women were not allowed to leave the parental home without permission, which would be given either when they were delivered into the hands of a suitable husband or if they were entering a convent. Challenging parental authority was the sign of a loose woman up to no good but, with the new freedoms of democracy beckoning, such constraints on their liberty were no longer tolerable for girls born in the fifties and sixties.

No matter how young they still were, women who grew up in the post-war years who had only been allowed to be wives and mothers unapologetically used the power of guilt to control the family. After all, it was their role to guard the moral probity of the family and ensure it presented a wholesome face to the outside world with the family as their showcase.

Shortly after arriving I met a girl in her early twenties who was living with her family but desperately wanted to leave and have a place of her own. Her mother, only in her late forties, swore that she would have a heart attack if her daughter left, which might have been hard to pull off in practice but the message was clear: for a daughter to leave without going to a marital home was a disgrace. The opinion of an array of relatives, the folk back home in the village or the neighbours mattered deeply to them and a defiant daughter equalled a failed mother. This undoubtedly was Cecilia's firmly held view.

Her greatest fear was what other people would say, think or presume, creating a minefield of rumour and secrets where gossip was a key ingredient. The Spanish claim that their worse vice is envy, but I would place gossip at the top of the list. In a rural environment, gossip and scandal were passed down from generation to generation. Family business should never be aired in public but only whispered to a carefully selected audience in the darkness of shop corners or in the safety of the big country kitchen away from the prying eyes of distant relatives and neighbours. Conflicts in marriages, infidelities, separations, (for the moment there was no divorce), financial problems and unwanted pregnancies would all be dealt with within the family. If gossip was a mainstay of village life it continued in the streets of the cities, on the stairs of the block of flats, on buses or in the local shops. The hugely popular Hola, the Spanish version of "Hello" magazine, was first published in 1944 with reports on the lives of famous people all kept within the strict limits of propriety. After all, commenting on this information in the hairdresser or bar was far better than concerning themselves with political issues.

The fear of scandal and shame often occasioned dissension to be hidden away from the outside world. This pretence was something the Spanish family had in common with the Victorian family: cosy and united for the outside world but more problematic within. Perhaps like the Victorian family, unity needed to be preserved precisely at a time when the old rural society was breaking down and people were moving to a predominantly urban environment.

If the reluctance of Juan and Cecilia's generation to accept changes was understandable, it was inevitable that the family would evolve along with urbanization. I wonder how many people in the late seventies and eighties realized how quickly life was evolving when even in the most modern media, the television, the image of the family remained caught in some bygone era. Television series showed families with a working husband, the wife at home, children and a maid with a starched uniform, a cheery soul to add to the comedy. This type of family, no doubt a reflection of the director's own upbringing in the Spain of the fifties and sixties, was fast disappearing. At least in the series there were only two children, a step forward from the happy hoards which peopled many films during the Franco regime. Apart from devout Catholics, some "*gitanos*" and the tail end of families from the fifties and sixties, the majority of families were small but it would be some time before a dysfunctional family dared to appear on the screens.

Nevertheless, when political change arrived abruptly in Spain in 1975, the family had already been imperceptibly and inexorably transforming. Often what they wished for, aspiration, education and a more comfortable life, destroyed part of what they valued. The characteristics of a family shifted from one generation to the next when the child of a simple peasant farmer in the village was finally given a chance to go to university and might become a doctor, a lawyer or an economist. People who for so long had married within the same social circle, now met their partners at university, people from far away with different ideas and a different way of life. The old style family was for women who didn't work, for those living close together and who shared the same education and style of life, not for the outsider.

Before I arrived in Spain I dreamt of meeting them. I conjured up visions of being welcomed into their midst, unquestioningly swept up in their warmth to become part and parcel of the family as a haven against adversities. Before I met them they could be anything I wanted them to be and I wished so hard that they would be the perfect Spanish family. If I imagined belonging, it was to the romanticized family of Franco's films, the happy family on holiday or the noisy family in restaurants not to one of restrictions, tradition, gossip and control.

Early on winter evenings, the lights were switched on before the blinds were closed in their ground floor flat allowing anyone walking past in the dark and cold to see the family sitting together in the warm glow of lamplight. Framed in the window it was a vision of perfection:

people laughing together, chattering children, kindly grandparents, wine and food on the table. It was a scene Cecilia loved but to step inside was to shatter the image. In reality they were part of the darkness and claustrophobia of those early years. Life is always much simpler in a fantasy world.

BEYOND PERFECTION

Unlike haphazard families in this modern world of travel, families in the past were known, chosen from people in the village or the church. If I had simply gone out onto the street and picked on a family at random, it is unlikely we would have had less in common. They claimed they were open, accepting and tolerant but this was far from true.

The first time I visited, on that hot July day, only Cecilia and Juan were there, sitting side by side on the sofa waiting to pass judgment. Whenever I think of them, I always see them in the same flat, in the same room and at the same age, ensconced in their small universe year in year out. Had anyone asked at the time, I would have said I liked Cecilia simply because I thought I should. As the epitome of a woman who had grown up in the prewar in a Castilian village in the mountains, I suppose I idealized her or rather what she represented for me then: a remote, picturesque past.

Often we readily attribute those from other lands with characteristics we wish them to have. We make up our own story for the widow in black and for the tragedy she has suffered. We transform the harsh existence of an old Iranian peasant, a Peruvian Indian, an African wife into something mythical, bestowing an aura of virtue upon them. The mother in the art house film or in the photo exhibition is a figure of stoicism deserving our esteem but it is not always so. To admire from a distance is uncomplicated but it is quite another matter to know them as more than a vague embodiment of an ideology.

Federico García Lorca[25] delved below the romantic perceptions to reveal a cruder reality. In *"House of Bernarda Alba"*, he looks at a group of women, Bernarda Alba and her five daughters at a time of enforced mourning with all the tensions, hypocrisy and moral control of village life. Finished in 1936 shortly before his assassination, the play examines issues which would be relevant for decades to come. These women draped in black of earlier generations than Cecilia's existed in all villages, the anonymity of widow's weeds bestowing uniformity. And they did indeed have much in common: the suffering and the loss of their early lives. Things had changed. Cecilia was the epitome of village womankind of a later generation.

Living in the city had taken away many of the arduous tasks of the village but also the rewards of self-sufficiency. Nevertheless, she carried on with her domestic duties because it was what was expected of her. Wherever she was, she was always the same: in the kitchen in the village, juggling earthenware pots on the open fire, in Madrid with shiny new cookware, boiling, stewing, stirring, padding

---

25 Spanish poet and playwright murdered at the start of the Civil War.

round in slippers, impervious to the cold. When we went back to the village to the house they had kept for weekends or in the summer, she was immediately in her element, easily slipping back to a world of yesteryear.

She didn´t like to be idle and in her free time she would knit and sew, make-do and mend which were all vital tasks when raising a family in the mid-century. Domestic skills were the mainstay of a girl's education during the Franco regime. The nuns, ever diligent when it came to keeping the girls separate from boys, taught children what they needed according to their station in life; for some mending and darning, for others fine embroidery. However, without the benefits of even a basic education and certainly not one in a convent, Cecilia learnt these skills at home.

For much of her life, the art of housekeeping on a small budget, largely lost in Britain, was vital. Brought up in the forties or fifties, Spanish housewives in the eighties were thrifty, providing meals for very little. It was still waste not, want not even though their situation had improved considerably. Everything was used, everything kept. The diet was based on beans, lentils and any cheap part of an animal that could be eaten: brains, sweetbreads, livers, and pigs' trotters and ears. Stale bread was thrown into coffee for breakfast, left-over meat was made into croquettes and bones used for stews and stocks. Preparing meals, however, was much more than economy. She could control through food and if eating the dishes proffered was proof she was appreciated, refusing them was a cruel rejection.

Her home was her kingdom. It was typical among women of her generation to refer to every room and every task in the house with the possessive: "my" kitchen, "my" ironing". An immaculate flat was a sign of a good housewife, for having been denied the opportunity to work, their self-worth rested on the smooth, running of the home as a showcase of their worth. A man who came to read the water meter once told me he preferred not to go just after lunch as the housewives hadn't had time to wash-up. Puzzled as to how washing up affected reading a meter, I put it down to the mysteries of Spanish plumbing and only much later did I realize it was simply that the housewife didn't want the shame of anyone entering the kitchen to find a sink full of dirty dishes which would have been an unbearable slur on her abilities as a housewife.

Everything about Cecilia was unhurried as if she lived on another plane, untouched by the bustle of the big city. It sometimes appeared to me that a hand had plucked her out of the village setting her down casually elsewhere. She had no friends or any social contact apart from the family or relatives. On the other hand, during the summer months in the village she was in her element. She and Juan would take chairs outside the front of the house to enjoy the cool of the evening, along with any members of the family who happened to be there, greeting friends and relatives as they sauntered past, exchanging pleasantries and gossip with other villagers.

Hers was an ordered world running according to a plan, not necessarily hers as planning was never one of her strong points, but a universal plan of what should be, bequeathed through centuries of tradition. She continued to interpret the world through the eyes of another place and another age, simplifying life with unalterable rules which had served to hold things together through times of revolution and strife, wars and conflict, illness and death. She had the fatalism of country folk, forever waiting for some disaster which could be a crop failure, a downpour on harvest day or a sharp frost to kill the spring blossom, all punishment from a nebulous God that could strike at any time. One of her favourite phrases was, "Ya verás...",[26] accompanied by a wagging finger to show that she thought, or perhaps hoped that some fateful consequences would follow any unapproved action.

With no organized activities, no clubs and limits on working, married women often became bored prisoners in their small flats. The fact that a considerable number born in the twenties and thirties were illiterate or semi-literate hindered a life outside the home but like Cecilia many were not rebellious, appreciating what they had gained over the years.

Nevertheless, the fact that women accepted their role didn't mean they were meek; most ruled the home with an iron fist. Cecilia`s supremacy remained unchallenged and for years it had never occurred to her that it might ever be. If she assiduously provided for the daily needs of the family, she had to be obeyed, mollified and admired in her impregnable domestic world. She had acquired the right to rule, after all for 40 years she had been the law, the source of all norms. It never crossed her mind she might be

---

26 You'll see...

wrong. The family accepted her dictates unquestioningly seeing her as something of an oracle and the best of all possible mothers. She was the sturdy anchor for their lives.

Juan was the centre of her life, which was the case for the majority of married women in Spain, not always through choice but unavoidably through circumstances or an ingrained sense of duty. They relied on their husbands for an income: while the women might have cooked the potatoes the men were the only ones who could put them on the table. Cecilia assented to his making any significant decision in their lives, or at least taking responsibility for doing so, whereas she decided on all domestic matters which he in turn would accept. He would never have dreamt of challenging her rights in the domestic realm as this arrangement suited him well enough.

When I first met him he was still wiry and energetic. More intelligent than Cecilia, his wits had been sharpened by his early life in a city at war and from working in a foreign country. Living abroad, the passing years or simply the wish for a quieter life had turned him into a devotee of a Spain with ideas which had much in common with Franco's patriotism, however much he rejected his politics. This country of his was the best. He would sit at table, waxing lyrical about the joys of life in Spain with everything anyone could possibly want: the best wine, the best food and the best people who knew how to live life like no-one else. No matter that he had never visited any other country except France, no nation on earth equalled Spain.

Their children, six children in all including the two eldest who had stayed behind in France, were their reflection in society and each in their own way was deeply influenced by the rapid changes in the family's circumstances. The oldest four, brought up in the simple village life during the harsh years of the fifties, moved from a dictatorship in their early years to freedom in a democracy and two of them also faced a return to a Spain in turmoil. On the other hand, the last two, born in France, spent their early childhood in the softer years of the sixties at a time when the family was prospering. Through all this they were brought up with security, enjoying a stable family life without much extravagance in their formative years. This stability, whatever the drawbacks, was one of the strengths of Spain.

Brought up not to question their parents, they never did, endowing them with an almost supernatural level of perception, all-knowing, unquestionable god-like figures as children were taught to do at the time. The simple fact of being a mother seems to have shrouded women in some strange gown of infallibility, imparting to them a deeper knowledge of life and endowing them with a special aura akin to the Virgin Mary.

The course of their children's lives was set in stone as far as the parents were concerned. They should get a job, preferably one for life. They should marry someone suitable then live as close as possible to their parents.

If their approach to children was practical rather than sentimental, the same can be said for their treatment of the elderly who had a place in the home and were generally shown respect. Cecilia always addressed her father with the formal *usted* rather than the informal *tú*, a mark of this respect or perhaps distance but certainly a reflection of their relationship. Some, who were still strong enough, participated in family life while others were shadowy figures in the background, like characters from the world of Balzac thrown onto the mercy of the family. Maiden aunts laden with jewellery who had failed to catch a man but were too genteel to work were sometimes joined by the family's servants, the country women who had arrived in the forties or fifties to look after generations of children, earning their keep until they became part of the family which cared for them in their final years.

In the eighties it was considered a disgrace to have an old relative, particularly a mother or father in a residential home, which in addition to being few and far between were, in general, dreary and institutionalized. Nuns provided some care with differing levels of comfort for those in need of charity or for anyone with a generous source of income.

Needless to say, caring for parents and parents-in-law was a burden that fell solely on women. Although duty and obligations might be unfashionable concepts nowadays, they helped to keep society together. The price was the limitations on women's lives. When I first came to Spain I met a doctor who took it for granted that his wife, who was also a successful professional, would give up her job to look after his aged mother. That is the way things were and few questioned this role although they might have resented it; apart from anything else the fear of gossip ran deep. Duty, however, was made more bearable if it had its rewards, so the expectation of an inheritance would certainly lighten the task. Cecilia, who looked after both her father and her father-in-law, made no bones about the fact that she expected to receive an earthly recompense, the heavenly version being way too unreliable.

Veneration for old age shared by traditional societies has advantages but at the same time in Spain a desire to uphold this ideal while adapting to urban life created a belief that the autumn years were divorced from everyday life. Having lost their usefulness once they moved to the city, people seemed to slip quickly into an old age without any alternative occupations. The objective of the popular phrase *nuestros mayores*, "our elderly people" was to convey an idea of communal affection yet from my point of view it was closer to condescension and did nothing to solve an impending problem.

As they often did, the Spanish buried their heads in the sand preferring to pay lip service to the wonderful care provided by families rather than face the challenges of the future. With an increasing number of women working and smaller families, looking after elderly people was already becoming more problematic for families in general but especially bewildering for the generations born in the twenties and thirties like Cecilia and Juan who saw the expectations they had held for their final years rapidly vanishing.

Only the grandfathers survived into the eighties, Cecilia's mother, Vicenta, having died in the thirties and María in the sixties. For me at that time both were merely old country folk far-removed from my own grandparents' world of starched shirts, suits and antimacassars but like them, vestiges of an irrelevant past. I never saw either read a newspaper, never heard them participate in a political debate. Many years would pass before I could truly understand what they had stoically endured. They must surely have wondered why anyone would want to travel when they themselves had seen more than they wanted to of the way the world works. If they were limited, it was because of their backgrounds and the way they had had to live. If they could be happy with what they had been given why look for problems? Or as Gregorio would say: Why complicate life?

With the death of María, rebellion died. They were simply swept along by change, accepting whatever life offered them. They had their own aspirations and expectations but back then it never occurred to them to move outside the boundaries that had been set for centuries. It seemed to me that not only the family but the whole of Spanish society was static, mired in structures from the rural past which would never change.

THE RICH AND THE POOR

Understanding Spanish society proved to be no simpler than fitting into the family. If there was any consensus among the Spanish in the early eighties it was in the firm conviction that Spain was a classless society, a merry melting pot of people from all walks of life. There were, I was often told, no social classes and a company director or doctor would happily meet the concierge in the local bar where they would enjoy a beer together to debate the problems of the day. Therefore, it could be concluded that despite economic inequality there could be no classes as such, everyone could meet on equal terms.

This was in marked contrast to their idea of Britain where it was believed, rightly or wrongly, that everything boiled down to class. All evils in society could be blamed on the historical division between the rulers and the working classes in accordance with information gleaned from the romanticized version of 19th century Britain seen on hugely popular TV series such as the first Poldark, early versions of Pride and Prejudice or the Forsyte Saga. It is true there were still considerable economic disparities in Britain when I was growing up back in the sixties and seventies but it was a time when class differences were breaking down. The Spanish, on the other hand, were not only acutely aware of where they stood in society but it was also vitally important to ascertain other people´s status in order to place them exactly where they belonged on the social scale.

One's standing in society was strictly judged on a whole range of criteria: where you lived, how you dressed, how much money you had, if you had a country house and if so where. Lineage carried weight as did the parents' or more precisely the father's profession; being a doctor, judge or belonging to any other respectable profession elevated the standing of the offspring. Then there were family names which meant nothing to me but were of great significance to the Spanish. People from the upper echelons of society expected their name to be recognized. Needless to say, having recently arrived, I never did.

When the concierge and the company director finished their beers each would return to their home, their own private spheres worlds apart. Neither would have contemplated mingling on a deeper level, and if the director's son should decide to marry the concierge's daughter the bonhomie would quickly evaporate. Socializing was skin-deep. Whatever they may have proclaimed, both parties were aware of this, for in Spain no-one was allowed to step out of line lightly. Something of the world of Galdós remained, with its petty jealousies and snobbery.

If classes were not as clearly defined as they were in other European countries it was simply because Spain had just very recently become an industrialized country. Only where industry had developed during the 19th century and early 20th century did a definable working class exist. This was the case particularly in Barcelona, the Basque cities and ports, and to a certain extent in Madrid, the city María and Ramón had arrived in 60 years earlier when the *barrios* or districts were strictly divided according to occupations or social status. This old idea of a divine social order had travelled with the exodus from the countryside in the previous 30 or 40 years. They were the clearly defined divisions of rural societies that some were eager to escape and others were desperate to preserve. Nothing had changed much over the years.

As I have already made clear, immediately after the Civil War Franco did nothing whatsoever to bridge the gulf between social groups therefore, in general, the victorious did well while the defeated fared badly with nothing much between the two extremes. Acquiescence, not equality, was the guiding principle of the regime.

Unsurprisingly, during the war and the dictatorship Franco enjoyed the support of almost everyone with hereditary wealth. People from such old families, rooted in the past, had held the power, money and influence with their estates in the country as well as palatial dwellings in Madrid. Privilege was part and parcel of the game for the good Spaniard and few rejected the position they had been blessed with and most believed rightly so. Their way of life may have been threatened by the turmoil of the thirties, the left-wing governments and finally the Civil War but with Franco's victory it could finally be resumed. Now they enjoyed more privileges than ever before and as long as they conformed, which most were happy to do, protection in high places was guaranteed. Nonetheless money and ancestry weren't everything and there was a place for those *nouveaux riches* who displayed absolute loyalty.

Clever people could profit from the easy financial morals of the time if they were prepared to give unwavering support to the regime. Acceptance of official doctrine which included patriotism, Catholicism and rejection of anything on the left of the political spectrum was all that was required. Next, moving in the right social circles where lucrative contacts could be made was essential. It was definitely not what but who you knew. Franco's hunting parties were legendary and definitely the event to attend for anyone interested in business so much so that they inspired a film. In 1978, the director Luis García Berlanga made the film *La Escopeta Nacional* (The National Shotgun) in which a man finances a hunt in the hopes of fostering the relationships required to win contracts for his products.

The Catholic Church provided further confirmation of status. Everyone's position on this earth was pre-ordained by God therefore anyone destined for a life of ease living in large flats, driving flashy cars and enjoying long holidays was simply benefitting from the hand dealt by the Almighty. In the same way it bestowed a certain grace on the humble, proclaiming that the role allotted to them was lowly but honourable. Or, to put it more bluntly, as far as the church was concerned, anyone born poor should accept that they were destined to remain poor.

These attitudes promoted by the church and the regime came not only from small villages, but perhaps even more so from provincial towns, still firmly anchored in the past, well into the eighties.

In the early years we visited many such towns where the slow pace offered a welcome escape from the bustle of Madrid. One of these was Soria, about 137 miles to the northeast of Madrid with only around 32,000 inhabitants in 1980. Arriving early at a restaurant one Sunday, we were already seated at a central table when the notable families of the city paraded in: women dressed formally and bedecked with jewellery, men in white shirts, suits and ties, little girls in frilly pink dress and boys in suits. As each family entered they did the rounds of the tables greeting all the other families leaving us, with our extremely casual clothes, stranded in a sea of respectability and tradition. Besides being an uncomfortable situation momentarily, I felt as if I had plunged back to an age long gone which I could never be part of even had I wanted to.

Anyone reading novels such as *La Regenta* by Leopoldo Alas, set in the 1880s, would find much in his description of provincial life that was familiar. The story takes place in Vetusta, a fictional town based on Oviedo in the north of Spain, where events are set against a background of gossip, petty rivalries, jealousy, the need to keep up appearances and above all an acute awareness of status. This novel might have been written a hundred years earlier yet it illustrated the atmosphere of the country towns I visited in the early eighties.

Everyone entering the restaurant that day would be from old professions which, as Ramón and María knew from experience, existed in provincial towns rather than in villages. Some of the diners would have been *la crème de la crème* of the society for generations while others would have been sent from Madrid. They were the judges, barristers, lawyers, doctors and perhaps engineers, the upper classes in their secure world, sure of their merits and status. These prestigious jobs in law, engineering or the military provided for a privileged life as well as respectability. Naturally, taking the cloth was less well paid than most others but an equally honourable calling and the glory of anyone serving Christ reflected on the whole family. Moreover, a role in the church brought influence in a Catholic society while promotion to higher things was always on the cards.

Many of these jobs did not entail particularly hard work for those from the right backgrounds, and, if the financial rewards were great, they were merely receiving what they considered to be their due. Many years ago, I taught a notary's children. Notaries, who deal with all official documents such as deeds, powers of attorney and wills, have always been prominent figures in provincial society and very wealthy ones in cities. This particular notary actually worked in Malaga, deemed to be something of a backwater at the time, so it had been decided that his family should live in Madrid where the children could get a better education and, in general, life was more animated. This separation was not too onerous as he worked alternate weeks, flying back to Madrid for his week off and joining the family for a month's holiday in the summer. If he couldn't fly to Madrid his wife would go down alone leaving the children with one of the maids. An enviable style of life with a minimum amount of effort required.

There were other professions which shared equally high esteem. Doctors bestowed a god-like status on themselves with the presumption that no-one else could equal or share their knowledge. Little or no information would be given to the patient in the state system while a request for clarification was considered an affront to their eminence. They were the dispensers of medical care whose duty was to heal the masses not to explain themselves to those with a questionable capacity to understand.

Whilst in theory these jobs were not reserved for the elites, in practice they were since they required contacts and years of study both of which were out of reach for most people until the seventies. Only families with a reasonable acquisitive level could afford to send their children to university when a degree took at least five years, often longer as it was quite usual to repeat the same academic year a few times. For top jobs in the civil service years of studying for the entrance exams followed the completion of a degree, effectively closing them to anyone who could not finance these unpaid years of study. For other jobs, once the necessary qualification had been acquired, a very aptly named "*enchufe*" (a plug) was required which might be a fellow worshiper at the local church, a family member or a family friend who would provide a recommendation for a job in a company or bank.

Stepping out of line was frowned on, and until the late seventies it was hard to move up the social ladder. In a limited world they married into their own group, often to people they had known most of their lives, perhaps in their holiday homes, church or within their parents' circle. Anyone deemed to be from a lower class was never totally accepted. An acquaintance would refer to a sister-in-law disparagingly as the "plumber's daughter" rather than by her name. She would never truly belong.

As women were not expected to work before the seventies, marriage to a man of the right social group was one of their key objectives. Even though they were limited to the home while business, with its intrigue and connivance was reserved for men, they undoubtedly played a significant role behind the scenes and were equally aware of their status.

I taught many good Catholic ladies who insisted they were "*señoras*", ladies, rather than "*mujeres*", common or garden women who might do their own housework and shopping. They arrived, not a blonde hair out of place for they were all blonde, it was the colour to be, denoting superiority possibly because of the time and money required for maintaining it in a country where most people are dark-haired. Being always polished with designer clothes, fur coats and jewellery was not too taxing as they lived privileged lives in large flats with staff to clean, to cook and do everything around the home. Their role was to manage the home, taking care of the moral well-being, keeping the husband content and organizing the social life.

Theirs would seem to be perfect lives yet I got the impression they were bored, that they would have liked to get out more into the world and escape from their golden cages. Many were intelligent no doubt realizing that what they had been brought up to expect could not go on forever and moreover many were active, capable women for whom idleness was not an ideal way to live. The problem was that without further studies or a career, they depended totally on their husbands. I realized that while some were quite happy to enjoy what they had been brought up to believe was their right, others were torn between the advantages of acceptance and the attraction of going against the grain.

Nonetheless, it did seem enviable: the leisured life of a 19th century lady with the mod cons of the 20th century. All that was expected of the lady of the house was to ensure everything ran smoothly, basking in the glow of praise for a well-organized home. One of the group got up early in order to see the children and husband off before returning to bed to let the servants get on with all the donkey work, looking after children, cooking, cleaning, doing the laundry and even ushering in visitors.

Having servants was reasonably accessible for many professional families. Plenty of people were looking for work and wages were low. Allowing a girl in a small village to stay on at school to enjoy a good education was an unaffordable luxury for most parents, therefore young girls from the country regions had few options other than working in the city. They had to be submissive and if they resented their position, which many no doubt did, they rarely complained since there were many more where they came from in the emptying villages or small towns of the impoverished regions. When village life signified hardship and eking out a living, a job as a maid was an improvement while their wages brought relief for the families back home despite being paid a pittance.

In the late seventies and early eighties girls continued to arrive in the cities. Rural poverty still existed although by this time many were looking to escape the narrow confines of the village with its restrictions and lack of opportunity. With sparse educational facilities in rural areas it was little wonder many young girls were eager to try their luck in the city with the hope of eventually finding a better position.

Needless to say, their standing in society was low. A couple of decades earlier, in the forties and fifties, relatively wealthy families would have had at least two maids who were constantly on duty doing almost all the housework and looking after the children. Their days were long and they usually lived in to be available 24 hours and avoid the need for higher wages to cover the costs of renting accommodation. Uniforms, often black dresses and white aprons or overalls, could be bought in specialized shops most of which have now closed down.

The lives of the women I lived among in the peripheral districts when I first arrived had little in common with the ladies of leisure or their servants. Most were immigrants from rural areas all over Spain, perhaps from Cecilia's generation or a little younger. They hovered between two worlds; their origins were in the rural world yet they saw themselves very much as part of the city. Although I did not relate to these urban housewives any more than to the privileged, I could better understand their children, who made up the burgeoning middle-class.

While it was too late for many of them, they were keen to further the prospects of their children. As their lives improved they could allow their children to study at university instead of finding a job to help support the family. In fact, they encouraged them to do so, rejoicing in the fact that their children were now able to benefit from the opportunities they themselves had been denied. I hardly appreciated their achievements at the time, as a higher education was considerably more accessible and obtainable in Britain in the sixties and seventies. The disparity between the two countries was made clear to me when a man, born in the forties, told me of his father's pride when he became a university professor in spite of coming from a family of six children in a remote village. His success, which would have been impossible for his parents with the best will in the world, had required considerable talent and tenacity. This was one among many small incidents which brought home how lucky I had been in Britain in the seventies.

Despite their enthusiasm for education, the emerging middle class continued to favour the old professions which earned recognition in society; to study law, medicine or for some reason journalism, was highly esteemed whereas new-fangled professions did not enjoy the same regard and their value to society or the world of business was yet to be appreciated. The new, confident generation which had benefited from the blossoming economy in the sixties was not always adequately prepared to meet the demands for workers in professions which were emerging despite the worsening economic conditions. Thus, as so often in Spain, the old remained entrenched in people's minds even as society was rapidly transforming especially in the cities.

It is hard to evaluate dispassionately the situation in a country where we have lived all our lives, blinded as we are by friendships, memories, expectation and our own experiences. In a new country, as a mere observer, people's lives can be dissected more clinically, and in this I had the advantage of meeting people from many differing walks of life. Yet they often left me bewildered. It sometimes felt as if I had arrived two generations too soon. I would have to wait for things I could recognize although not for long: society was transforming more quickly than I ever thought possible.

VESTIGES OF THE PAST

There has always been a sense of solidness to Spain, a timeless quality as if nothing had ever altered nor ever would. For me, these perdurable qualities have become identified with Central Spain, the Old and New Castile for it is here that I first encountered them. Immense forests, mountains ranges and plains had seen so much but remained unmoved and unchanged. The inhabitants, old Castilians, believed in themselves, they were proud of their origins, their culture, and their village. If this sense of oldness, of permanence was appealing much remained that I found disconcerting.

After 44 years, memories of the Civil War were still raw, yet deeply hidden, and it was to be some years before Spain could face up to the damage it had inflicted on itself. This may explain why it was not the war which made the greatest impression on me when I first arrived. Along with the old social structures and attachment to the rural past, I saw centuries of isolation, still not completely broken as well as a lingering belief in some ancient glory. But of all this, what was most immediately obvious to me was the pervasion of religion.

Until I arrived in Spain religion had scarcely touched

my life, leaving me unscathed by its obligations and guilt but uncomforted by its reassurance. For those of us not born into religion it is hard to understand the hold it can exercise or how insidiously it can influence. With controversy and bloody conflict long since gone from the Church of England, it had become bland and irrelevant. When it did occasionally intrude on my life it was muted: Christmas carols and hymns in school assemblies, quaint churches and harvest festivals. It didn't impose, neither did it invite opposition or expect undue influence. It was there if it was wanted, something private, generally apart from public life except for occasional archaic state ceremonies.

In Spain, on the other hand, there was no escaping religion. It stretched back through the centuries. It had been key in the fight against the Moors and in the founding of the Spanish state in the late 15th century by the Catholic monarchs. It permeated the very fabric of society and without it Spain would have lost much of its identity. Its power is echoed in the suffocating beauty of its churches and cathedrals, the magnificence of Burgos and Toledo or the stained glass windows of León. It is worth searching out the convents and monasteries dotting the countryside, often set in stunning landscapes or the churches in small villages and provincial towns.

Through the turmoil of centuries, God had been omnipresent in the sublimeness of music and the arts. In the great Andalusian cathedrals, Seville, Malaga and Cadiz, the custom of playing music throughout the day in the 18th century meant new compositions were continually required. Zurbarán, El Greco and many others expressed the religious fervour of their day in wonderful paintings commissioned by the monarch, the nobility or churches, monasteries and convents.

More prosaically, everyday language owes much to religion. A true Catholic would choose names to bestow faith and virtue on a child: Milagros, Dolores, Concepción and Inmaculada from the Immaculate Conception. Anyone speaking Spanish will learn the sayings and proverbs referring to religion, for example to ring the bells and be in Mass[27] or in other words to try to do two incompatible things at the same time. As one would expect, God often pops up, "Birds of a feather, flock together" becomes roughly "God creates them and they themselves gather together"[28].

Religion was not, of course, merely culture and names. It continued to play a role in politics well into the 20th century so that Spanish history cannot be understood without it. With Franco, Catholicism had become a statement of political alliance, a definition of a way of life and proof of conformity. One loved or hated the church, admired or scorned the priests. Throughout the regime, the devoutness of staunch Catholics was matched by the vehemence of the anti-Catholics; the latter a direct result of the former especially among families like Juan's which had supported the Republican cause. Nonetheless, by the eighties rather than the violent anti-clericalism of the

---

27 *Repicar y estar en misa.*

28 *Dios los cría y ellos se juntan.*

thirties disavowal of the church marked a rejection of the regime and all it represented.

Anyone not believing was automatically tarred with the brush of revolution. This link between patriotism, Catholicism and political ideology persisted and would do so for many years in some circles. Not long after I arrived a neighbour inquired if I was Catholic. Educated during the regime she would have known that inhabitants of the north of Europe were likely to be followers of Luther, the demon of the Catholic Church. As she expected, I told her I was not. "So, she replied, you are a communist".

Perhaps her attitude was understandable, after all, Catholicism was a vital qualification for public life. The *Opus Dei*, a most favoured organization for its patriotism and piety established in the 1950s by a Spanish man, Escrivá de Balaguer, came to prominence under Franco's auspices with its members reaching posts of great responsibility. Many were among those technocrats who were called upon to rescue the economy in the sixties.

In one of my first jobs I worked in an Opus Dei centre, although at first I had no idea who they were beyond being told that it was some sort of religious group. Today they conduct themselves more circumspectly but in the eighties they continued to act with confidence bestowed by privilege. I would go to their well-appointed centre where there were meetings rooms, offices and a chapel. The ladies were invited along to a range of classes and courses with the objective of bringing in as many as possible to the organization although most tried to dash off quickly before they were caught. In May, the month of the Virgin Mary, we would troop along to the chapel decorated with flowers to pray instead of learning English. Not only was this extremely boring as I barely understood the rituals and prayers, but later the director refused to pay me considering it a serious affront to expect payment for praying to the Virgin Mary. In general, it was an arduous task to extract any money from the leader. Clearly, Christian charity didn't extend to employees.

They conveyed their doctrine in simplistic messages, by providing slick explanations they reached out to the masses who did not share their understanding of life. They had a parable for everything that posed a threat to society and in particular for new ideas which challenged their concept of the world. At one time I was chosen as a potential convert. I could have been accepted into the fold in a more or less middling position for never having been a Catholic I had never known the truth and was therefore free of the onerous burden of having lapsed. The organizer of the group would give me a lift home aware there was no escape once I was shut up in the car leaving her free to cajole and convince, offering security in this life as well as the next; they look after their own extremely well. Professionals were particularly welcome, while the lowly could enter as servants.

Their fervour and earnestness, their conviction that they were right frightened me. They believed they could and should meddle in others' lives. What I found most unacceptable about the Church in Spain in general was its arrogance and its claim to moral superiority. It did not deserve its self-appointed role of arbitrator in matters of state; after all, it hardly had an unblemished past. How I would have hated life under Franco!

Furthermore, like many other religions it led to hypocrisy. Every Thursday flights left for London with girls from the best Catholic families, in theory off to do a course. As they spoke little English British women were asked to accompany them. On arrival they would disappear into the city to then return on Sunday. These Thursday departures, which became known as the "abortion flights", were no doubt the salvation of many families with a high stake in protecting their reputation.

Cecilia's brand of rural religion couldn't be further from the privileges of these well-placed city dwellers and a far cry from the Opus Dei. She certainly didn't go to church in France and I never knew her to attend mass in Madrid. She did, however, assiduously attend every christening, wedding and funeral, social events with God relegated to second place.

Naturally, as only one religion mattered in Spain, being anti-religion was basically being anti-Catholic. Other religions were the work of the devil all lumped together in one, huge unholy alliance to be shunned. It followed that there was only one true place to worship: in a Catholic church. Men working on the British church attached to the embassy in Madrid were perplexed to be asked to finish the repairs by Christmas. Why finish repairs if Christmas was not celebrated? Celebration of Christmas in their minds was solely for Catholics.

However, not all sections of the church were identified with the regime and tradition. As in many places, the church was a force for good. In the fifties, shanty towns sprung up without any amenities especially along the main train lines. With the help of Jesuits, many of whom were known as *curas obreros* (worker priests), improvements were made to El Pozo del Tío Raimundo, on the outskirts of Madrid raising its inhabitants out of extreme poverty. One of their leaders had once been a staunch follower of Franco but later dedicated his life to supporting the poor workers flocking to the city.

Increasingly towards the end of the dictatorship leading figures in the church were no longer willing to provide unwavering support for the regime and many, most famously the Cardinal Enrique y Tarancón, were to help the country move towards democracy.

At the same time it was becoming increasingly clear that religion no longer played a role in many people's lives, with growing sections of the population viewing the church simply with indifference. The skepticism which was already prevalent in most European countries was steadily taking hold in Spain.

Yet, despite being on the wane, religion continued to influence issues in society. From the official church stance as well as a right-wing point of view, ecology was highly-suspect, redolent of hippies, leather sandals, left-wing politics and revolution. If God had given humankind the earth, it was argued, it was to be treated as anyone saw fit. As usual, the Opus Dei had a useful analogy explaining that if someone lent their flat to a friend, they would want it to be used in whatever way was considered fitting. In other words, as God had given us the Earth we could do whatever we wanted with it. I should have pointed out that destruction in either case was unacceptable but I never did.

In general, ecology was not a prime concern and for people living in the villages it was understandably irrelevant. On a visit to Cecilia and Juan's village during the summer, an old donkey drawn cart occasionally made its way around the village. I presumed that the word "*basura*" (rubbish) scrawled on the back in wobbly painted letters was some village lads playing a joke on a poor farmer but it was actually the local rubbish collection. A weekly round was all that was needed to collect everything the households cast out. Food was home grown or bought in markets, leftovers were fed to the pigs or chickens, paper used to light the fire.

Anyone who has experienced hunger and deprivation in their youth is not usually wasteful. Even in the cities very little prepared food was available in the eighties and most people shopped in local shops and markets. Cecilia would, quite rightly, not have appreciated being told she ought to change her ways and it is hardly surprising that her generation found the concept of ecology hard to grasp. The Spanish didn't appear to have the desire to be constantly buying and discarding. Purchasing only what they needed for a comfortable life, they were more ecological than many modern ecologists who pay lip service to the concept while owning a car and flying wherever they want.

I found this lack of consumerism an attractive quality unlike other remnants from the past which became irritating once the novelty had worn off. Among these was their inability to be punctual. Even though the family had lived in France they kept a strange concept of time: Spanish time, a slow-country time, undefined and elastic. Never having worked out of the home, Cecilia and the older sisters-in-law had no experience of the restriction of a tight schedule.

Going down the road took an inordinate length of time. There were shops to be looked at, trees to be admired, things would be forgotten, someone would need a rest, others a drink, while I got bored and frustrated. Until we bought a country home of our own we would sometimes go to their village house for a few days. It took all day. Things would be missing, people would disappear and reappear and last minute shopping would have to be done. I would turn up ready to leave at the appointed time only to wait for hours on occasions.

It was my time, not only theirs that was dwindling away. They might have been able to wander through life at a village rhythm but, working in the city with all its rush, I had no choice but to do things quickly. In any case this pace of life wasn't something I was used to as in England every trip was run with clockwork precision. We had schedules and plans. We knew beforehand where we were going, when we were leaving and arriving and we were always ready. Our mantra was "tomorrow it's an early start" and it always was. At the crack of dawn, we were all mustered and ready for off. I lived by British middle-class time, a hand-me down from northern evangelic time where every second counted. Slothfulness was one of the cardinal sins, busyness and industry its virtues.

Although I found this casualness hard to accept, there were aspects of the lifestyle which were appealing. In Madrid and everywhere else in Spain there was a plethora of cheap restaurants where we would meet for the set menu. Spanish cuisine is perfect for eating on a budget: simple food with excellent ingredients, and good wine. I still love that smell of coffee tinged with grease. The clatter and cheerfulness were all part of it along with the disregard for hygiene. Everyone happily threw anything unwanted on the floor inside or out leaving bar floors strewn with paper serviettes, cigarette ends and olive stones. People blew smoke and coughed over the open displays of tapas along the bars.

Given the general lax standards, their need to keep their own homes spick and span seemed rather strange. Floors were assiduously swept and mopped but when a huge bluebottle fell into a jug of milk it was allowed to swim around for a while before someone fished it out. They then happily used the milk. In summer, meat and fish dishes were left out for days in the heat, covered in swarms of flies but they must have been immunized from childhood as they never suffered any ill effects. No wonder the Spanish born in the earlier part of the century were hardy, often living to a ripe old age; anyone who survived the rigours of village life and the laissez-faire attitude had a good start in life. This insouciant attitude to hygiene and food controls didn't much matter to anyone until that is, it tipped over into tragedy.

On May 1, 1981 an eight-year-old boy, Jaime Vaquero García, from one of the townships near Madrid which had grown rapidly with the influx of workers in the seventies, was rushed to hospital with all the symptoms of pneumonia. It was too late, he died in his mother's arms before arriving. This would have been a tragic but hardly unusual occurrence if the number of cases hadn't risen rapidly not only in Madrid but throughout the centre of Spain: Ávila, Palencia, Segovia, León, Salamanca and then down to Seville in Andalusia. Jaime was the first official victim of what was first thought to simply be an outbreak of pneumonia until, with daily news of fresh cases, panic spread like wildfire fanned by alarming reports on TV and in newspapers. Nearly all the cases were in the poorer districts on the outskirts of large cities where people with a limited income would buy products from itinerant markets set up one or two days a week. With six other children, life must have been a struggle for Jaime's family. It was a time of unemployment when these markets, with lax controls, offered cheap products such as extra-large bottles of oil, foodstuff in bulk and cheap clothes. If checks existed they were perfunctory and easy to bypass.

I remember feeling only mild concern as we lived a good distance away from it all in the centre of Madrid, an invisible barrier between us and others in their distinct world on the outskirts of the city. Rumours abounded. Strawberries were cited as the most likely cause leaving boxes unsold on the shelves. I wasn't convinced, possibly foolishly, but for us it was "strawberry" spring and we ate kilos of them. Meanwhile, from rumour to rumour 350 people died although unofficially the figure was nearer 4,000. 20,000 were affected altogether, many still bearing the aches and pains today and, in some cases, suffering total dependence.

Finally, it was determined that the most probable cause was rapeseed oil. This type of oil is suitable for human consumption but the batches being sold cheaply in bulk were industrial grade oil unsuitable for culinary uses. As justice is extremely slow in Spain years went by before the culprits were finally brought to trial, and even then the punishment was light. At least it led to more careful health checks for food products as well as ensuring improved investigations of fraud in the future.

Medical care was touched with the same unconcern as food health and safety. The first doctor I visited only weeks after arriving was stretched out, feet on the table, smoking a cigarette. For visits to a specialist there were neither appointments nor an orderly waiting room, only a huge corridor outside the consultation room filled with families, wheelchair, crying children. To get a turn one had to yell "*quién es el último*"?[29] Then spend the next hour or so trying to remember exactly which little old lady in black was immediately in front in the queue. The same system was used in markets and sometimes still is. Ways of cheating the system were developed including sidling up to the counter and pretending to look at something or asking a question. All part of a housewife's skill.

---

29 "Who is last?"

Next in the list of disorganization came public offices. Piles of papers, rubber stamps, delays and conflicting information are clichés but unfortunately true, especially in the early years. I have waited hours to present papers while government clerks disappeared for a coffee break, before being sent to another office for another document, more copies or photos and on and on.

This lack of control, the laxity in everyday life, the antithesis of religion rigour, had long been part of the appeal of Spain and the reason why people like Gerald Brennan came in the fifties and sixties escaping from industrialized Britain. It didn't really matter what one did as long as no political lines were crossed. I once asked what I had to do to pay tax on the money I earned. They laughed: "You don't pay tax here, no-one does", and that was in a bank of all places. Honesty and openness are for a society with strong laws where people are protected and dishonesty has a price. Like religious beliefs they must be ingrained from birth. Morals are hard to afford in a cut-throat world of an impoverished dictatorship. If prospering in the regime required bribery and pulling the right strings, it left no room for the primness of business morals. This attitude, which spilt over into democracy, was to rear its ugly head in years to come.

Acquaintances have claimed that Franco's Spain was one of efficiency and organization. Everything worked, nothing went wrong. Only with their dear leader's demise, at the first touch of democracy did this golden age of organization and efficiency die. It must have met a sudden and violent end as no trace of it remained in the early eighties. Moreover, long before I arrived, religion, laxity, the happy-go-lucky attitude, the cheap restaurants and the poor time-keeping had long been hallmarks of Spain. If they are part of the attraction for the casual visitor there is a downside which became apparent as the novelty wore off.

Faced with so much from a bygone era I found it hard to envisage how change would come. The young, as I was then, do not have the advantages of experiencing transformation. However much they rush through life, they view society if not politics as more static than it ever is. It would not be until many years later that I realized that much of what I saw was not particularly "Spanish", it was simply the remains of the past already being cast off. It was going to be an exciting yet challenging time.

THE TRANSITION

In the late seventies and eighties, Spain once again faced an uncertain future as it plunged into a new era. During this difficult time, the principle challenge was to transform the country from a dictatorship to a democracy which proved to be a highly complex process, much more so than I realized at the time. Establishing a new political system almost from scratch may have had its attractions, but for a country like Spain with its troubled history and scant experience of democracy it was far from being a simple undertaking.

There is often arrogance in the way the people of northern European countries view those in the South. They pride themselves on working harder, being better-organized and generally superior. They consider themselves deserving of everything they have, which whether they realize or not, is a great deal. But recent history as well as their geography has bequeathed a much more tortuous path to the countries in the south. Anyone who criticises Spain as a country of lazy people should go back to times in the past, feel the fear, the fragility, experience the backwardness enforced on large swathes of the population, only then would they comprehend the enormity of the challenges they have faced.

Although to be fair at the time, the Spanish themselves did not appreciate the difficulties that lay before them. Being surrounded by stable, democratic states in Europe was clearly an advantage, although seen from afar, the realities of these countries and systems were somewhat distorted by the wishful thinking of the oppressed. I feel the Spanish believed they could pick and choose what they wanted of democracy, failing to see the extent to which it was flawed and with its own contradictions. If they believed that by starting afresh the problems of other older democracies could be avoided, they were mistaken; it was not a tabula rasa, the past weighed too heavily. Nevertheless, on their side they did have optimism and the will to change.

Each generation had been moulded by dramatic events: the convulsive pre-war, the war, the harsh years of the early dictatorship or the growing dissension in the sixties and seventies. These experiences left a gulf rather than a gap between those born prewar or postwar. Catapulted into this new era, the conservative bank clerk might be the father of a communist activist, the traditional housewife the mother of a staunch feminist. It was mainly the young born after the Civil War who aspired to bring about change. Regardless of their background, they shared aims since even the children of conservative families no longer wanted to be connected with the old regime. They longed for everything they had been denied: fairness, justice, freedom from oppression and from the hold of religion. Young people were joined by other groups such as trade unions, underground political organizations, women's associations and many others. Along with the ideology, they adopted symbols of rebellion: corduroy trousers and jacket, jeans, beards and long hair. Many friends took part in the protests in those heady days after Franco's death.

If this generation of transformation was mine, we had little in common. The rebels couldn't understand my nonchalance about their courage, my lack of appreciation for their revolutionary ideas, my failure to understand that they were trail blazers going where others feared to tread. What for them was bravery seemed to me a naïve, innocent belief that change could be smooth. Besides, I felt that what they were embracing was not new and revolutionary but merely normal and reasonable. Their ideas were hackneyed, the arguments tired and worn. I struggled to understand their "progressiveness" for fighting for things I had long taken for granted. Realism tempers hope with the passing years but few in Spain had had any experience of democracy, I, on the other hand, already jaded, suspected that their longed for future would be inevitably flawed.

The aphorism "it is better to travel in hope than arrive" was particularly apt for Spain at this time. Keeping faith in the future was going to be essential since much remained to be resolved. The most pressing question, from a practical point of view was the form of the new regime. Would Spain be a monarchy? Franco had designated Juan Carlos, the last king's grandson as his heir but few had any confidence in his abilities or his chances of surviving in the role, their view of his future reign earning him the sobriquet of Juan Carlos *El Breve*, (The brief). Naturally, he was not welcomed by groups on the left which had been dreaming of a Republic which would have been the third in Spain's history.

Many of Franco's supporters continued in politics. Most accepted, some willingly others more grudgingly, that they would have to join the democratic band. A number of them, who had been moving closer to the centre of the political spectrum for some years, were well placed to participate in the new government. In fact, the first politician charged with leading the country was Arias Navarro, a close associate of the dictator, who had somberly announced his death on television. He was followed in the post by Adolfo Suárez, an attractive, young politician with a gift for communication who had also risen to prominence in Franco's government. A group of statesmen, again many of whom had enjoyed power under the dictatorship, were charged with drawing up a constitution, a framework for a democratic society, which was approved by a vast majority of Spanish citizens in a referendum, held in 1978. For many people 1979 was the first time they could freely elect their representatives in parliament, the first time for over 40 years that they could freely express their opinions.

The situation, of course, did not transform overnight. The threat of arrest and torture remained. It was impossible to remodel the police and armed forces from one day to the next. Joining certain parties or trade unions continued to be risky, but little by little political associations vilified by the regime were accepted. At the same time, people were losing their fear and members of the opposition were returning, among them the socialists. The PSOE led by a charismatic young leader, Felipe González, had been preparing his return since the 1974 conference at Suresnes in the south of France. It would not be long before he won the elections, becoming the *Presidente*[30] of the government in 1981 with the cry of *por el cambio* [31]. If election slogans are usually banal and empty of any meaning, this one really did ring true.

An important step forward was the legalization of the Communist party and other left-wing groups in 1977, allowing them once again to take part in the national or local governments. Each year a Communist festival was held in a large park to the south of the city, an irresistible gathering with music, dancing and cultural events celebrating the newly recovered freedom. We went in the first few years, not because we were communists but because it was fun and many young people were going.

In general, society was permeated with the aspiration to improve the lives of those who had had fewer opportunities or suffered discrimination under the regime. In spite of feeling a certain amount of skepticism in those early years I applauded this desire to remedy the injustices of the past. On July 3, 1988 crowds gathered in Burgos in the north of Spain for the funeral of Rosa de Lima Manzano

---

30 Equivalent to the Prime Minister in the UK.

31 For change.

who had died in a helicopter crash. Among the mourners were many *gitanos* who had travelled from as far afield as Extremadura to pay their respects to the woman who had put forward a proposal to allow illiterate people to take a driving test adapted to their needs. This included many *gitanos* who, often denied access to education at that time, did not have the reading skills necessary to pass the theoretical exam.

Sometimes, with their eagerness to help the underdog, things went too far, their faith in human nature overcoming realism. The maximum prison sentence was established at twenty years except for very specific cases and prisoners enjoyed many benefits. All crimes prescribed at twenty years except those against humanity, genocide and terrorism causing death. This has meant that, in certain cases a criminal has literally got away with murder. I have heard an apocryphal tale of a man who went to the police to ask them to remove the body of someone he had murdered twenty years earlier as he no longer wanted the corpse in his cellar.

In other areas Spain showed its firm commitment to catching up, after many years of isolation. This in itself was problematic. As it entered into international markets, transformation of the economy was unavoidable and nearly every sector would be affected. In order to create greater competition protectionism had to end and industrial reconversion was inevitable. A number of small private banks were forced to close or merge, which inevitably involved job losses. Unemployment was high in the eighties not for the first or last time by any means.

In spite of improvements in living standards, cities engender higher expectations with all the added costs that that entails. Even with the continuing support from the family, life was tough for many people, much more so than many foreigners living the dream on the coast ever realized. I remember it as a time of struggle, very few new clothes, simple food and little heating even in the depth of winter. Foreign travel was still rare although, of course, the Spanish were lucky to have ample choice for destinations on the coast or in the mountains with more or less guaranteed sun in summer.

Apart from the economy, many other thorny issues needed to be resolved for family, church and class were not all that were left over from the past. Insolvable questions which Ramón and María would have heard about in the thirties remained. Chief among these was the desire for independence in Catalonia, the Basque country and to a lesser extent in Galicia, in the Northwest. Anyone who hoped that immediate answers could be found was to be disappointed.

Furthermore, other inherited structures, organizations and institutions along with the people working in them, could not be simply discarded without setting up replacements. Attitudes in the legal system and in law enforcement dating back to the dictatorship generally continued unchanged over the next few decades, despite being veiled by a veneer of modernity. Pérez Galdós's world of wheeling and dealing was concealed under a façade of concrete and metal so that few knew it still lurked there. For who would want to acknowledge any drawbacks when the country was starting afresh? If this meant that some things were brushed under the carpet so be it. It was a fragile time and drawing a veil over certain practices was probably the only way that the vertiginous political changes could take place. It might not have been the right choice, but at least it paved the way to a stable democracy.

What was most worrying was that, in spite of the strong support for democracy already building up in the latter years of Franco's regime, opposition to renovation remained strong. If many were willing to fight to achieve their aims, others were equally determined that they shouldn't. Spain appeared a peaceful country yet threats were omnipresent; the whole country was living on the edge. Recently arrived, I knew nothing of this, perhaps not many did except, of course, those involved.

Violence against the radical changes was, I suppose, inevitable. A transition from a dictatorship to a wonderland of democracy without a hitch was a fantasy. The early governments were unstable and actions such as the legalization of the communist party stirred apprehension or even dread. Extreme political and social change can be perilous but unlike much of the population who had lived through Spain's past I had no reason to fear violence. Involved in my own life, for a time I could remain blissfully unaware of any threat. All that changed in February 1981.

VIOLENCE AGAINST CHANGE

Remembering feelings and emotions from years gone by without the intrusion of hindsight is not always straightforward. Even so I am sure I had no clear idea of the political precariousness of Spanish society. Everything was suspended in a delicate balance between stability and chaos, the country teetering on the edge of the next tragedy. There are only a handful of countries in the world, among them Britain, which are safe, where life follows a pattern, where people, cocooned and protected, can take risks. In every other country life is lived on the edge of a cliff, clinging on to escape precipitating into the void.

Anyone who lived in fear at that time had every reason to do so. Those who hankered after the good old days of Franco were determined to overthrow the elected governments, with violence if necessary. The general plan was to wreak havoc along the road to democracy by any means available in preparation for the final assault to reinstate a dictatorship. With this objective, the extreme right went into action no sooner had Franco died. One of the most dramatic attacks in the incipient democracy took place before I arrived, in 1977, just two years after Franco's death.

Calle de Atocha is an artery running through the old city leading from one of the main railway stations to the heart of Madrid. It was here that a number of labour lawyers associated with the Communist party and trade unions had set up an office where they worked to support local neighbourhood organizations and workers, both of which had been woefully unprotected under the regime.

On January 24, 1977 a group of armed men burst into the offices looking for the leader of the Transport Union. As he was absent that day, they fired at anyone who happened to be there. Three lawyers, a law student and an administrative assistant were killed while four others were seriously injured, among them Lola González, herself a lawyer and the wife of one of the murdered lawyers. Like the others in the office at the time she paid a heavy price for her struggle for democracy. Pregnant at the time of the attack, she lost the child. But this was not the first tragedy in her life. A previous partner had died several years earlier when he "fell" from a window during a police search. At the time it was reported to be suicide although now it is generally accepted that he was thrown.

The perpetrators of the attack were members of neo-fascist organizations which would have enjoyed protection from the state only two years earlier. So confident were they of their immunity that none of them fled or went into hiding. They were mistaken. After being put on trial they were handed long prison sentences which they only served partially before being released early, which was unfortunately quite normal at the time. If they considered the failure to be granted immunity a betrayal, the effect of the attack on the political situation must have been a bitter disappointment. Instead of inciting violence from the left which would have provided an excuse for further violence, the measured reaction of the Communist and other left-wing parties was proof of their willingness to participate in the governance of the new state. This, in turn, helped to overcome the reluctance of certain sectors to legalize the Communist party. This incident, marked by a plaque on a wall, might have little significance for young people today yet it is a watershed in recent Spanish history, a memorable event for my generation in Spain.

Violence was not solely spurred by politics: it was against any sign of change which went hand in hand with the arrival of democracy. In 1979, a young man was murdered in one of the central parks in Madrid, the Retiro, in the respectable district of Salamanca. In bygone times this park was the king's *retiro* or private retreat, closed to the general public, royalty's haven from the pressures of life and an oasis of calm away from the noise and bustle of the city. Nowadays, it is for everyone in Madrid, a place to stroll and enjoy a little peace. It represents an ageless Madrid varying little as the years roll by, only the tableau vivant of people moving against the background of trees, flowers, boulevards and cooling fountains marks out the passing of the years. While there have always been entertainers drawing crowds of spectators as well as pickpockets, in the early part of the century there were uniformed nannies with their charges and today families with children come to enjoy boating on the lake, games or exhibitions in the glass palace. It is a place of culture, nature, tranquillity and sociability, hardly a place for murder.

Therefore, nobody walking there would have expected to be attacked but this is what happened to a group of young people in September 1979. They were dressed casually in jeans, with beards and long hair like young people all over Europe, except Spain then was not like the rest of Europe. Such attire signified a rejection of the values of the regime with its rigid dress code. In a society which demanded compliance in every way, outward appearance not only marked a failure to conform, it was a sign of rebellion and affiliation to the wrong band.

They were not necessarily left-wing but more likely "free-spirits". If they were unlikely to be right-wing, the young men who attacked them certainly were. Sons of military commanders, supporters of the old regime, they were the guardians of the moral values and saviours of Spain. There was not much room for individuals in their world, or as they would have put it "undesirables".

It was a warning. Probably murder was not the aim but when José Luis Alcazo went to the aid of his friends who were being attacked, he was hit with baseball bats and sticks, dying of his injuries. Two other young men were seriously injured. The punishment for the culprits was lenient. Two of them were given an eleven year sentence, others only months and, as they had no previous criminal record, they were allowed to walk free.

Less than a year later another murder took place and once again there were clear political motivations. Yolanda

González, a young Basque student living and working in Madrid was killed in 1980. One afternoon in February, when two men arrived at her flat claiming to be police it would have been an unwelcome but not unexpected visit for someone belonging to an illegal political organization as she did. The fact that she was not at home when her partner arrived in the evening was again quite normal as they often attended political meetings after work. Only when she failed to return by the following day, did he finally contact the police. They knew nothing. Finally, he was informed that she had been shot and left in a ditch.

The men who had taken her were members of Fuerza Nueva, an extreme right-wing party. The murderers had counted on assistance from members of the police force who had agreed to stand guard outside the building. At first, it was wrongly presumed she formed part of the terrorist group ETA as she was from the Basque country. In fact, the political party she belonged to opposed the terrorists' violent actions.

I remember it well even though I saw it as an isolated incident, which it wasn't. My first reaction was bewilderment that someone should be murdered merely for their political views. I underestimated the deeply embedded fanaticism that went further than mere nostalgia for a past, one I believed had gone forever. It was only much later that journalists claimed that there was a likely connection with the state, the police and the army. By then I had slowly pieced together the puzzle of Spain's past whose tentacles of violence stretched into the present.

It was to take another far more dramatic event before I could begin to understand the depth of the division which persisted in the country. It was one of those moments in life that allow us to see the world in a distinct way, bringing a deeper consciousness of circumstances of which we had been blissfully unaware. Only afterwards can we share other people's fears. February 23, 1981 was one such a day, a watershed in my life. Until then I'd been able to live on the fringe of society, believing it had nothing to do with me.

It started like any other long day. My numerous journeys travelling up and down every day gave me time to read a newspaper avidly following news stories, crimes, robberies and murders as well as gossip. Although I could never remember many of the strange, foreign names, I was becoming familiar with the current issues, opinions, the politicians and their politics. I realized that forming a government was proving to be fraught yet I was not particularly concerned. My interest in the political situation was purely academic.

In the evening I would finish late. On arriving home, exhausted, I would switch on the radio more for company than anything else. Monday, February 23 was no different from any other. An ordinary evening after an ordinary day, I was only half following the debate, one more step in the political manoeuvring, when suddenly something strange happened. There were shouts. Surely I had misunderstood, perhaps tuned into some radio play or drama. Or could it be some kind of joke? Then there were shots. I froze, a rising feeling of panic. There could be no doubt: whatever was happening, it was serious. A commanding voice ordered everyone not to move, with words that changed everything: *quieto todo el mundo!* [32] The phone rang, a call telling me not to go out whatever I did. It was what many had feared for so long: a coup d'état. It was then that it struck home just how delicate the situation was.

As the night progressed, the news became more frightening. When the rebels entered the parliament, television cameras were filming footage to be broadcast later. Although these cameras were shut down, reporters for a radio station were able to leave microphones connected, allowing all the activity inside the parliament to be recorded. The armed rebel guards ordered the deputies to get down on the floor. When the elderly Minister of Defense bravely challenged them he was pushed back roughly. Reports were coming of tanks rumbling down the streets in Valencia. The leader was a General, Milans del Bosch, a name that unfortunately I knew and remembered.

A few months earlier when I had begun a new job, I had met a member of the Milans del Bosch family, a former secretary for one of Franco's ministers when he was the ambassador in London. A close relative of the general, I knew she shared his ideas and ideology. Our meeting was not a pleasant one but when I left the organization for a better job not long after, she was furious. How had someone so far below her dared to leave? A few abusive and slightly deranged phone calls

---

32 Everyone keep still!

left me in no doubt that she was not about to forgive or forget. I would be one of the top on her list for revenge should the coup d'état be successful. So what if the General Milans del Bosch took over? What would happen to me? I was already mapping out my escape. Surely the British Embassy would help us to get out?

If my thoughts were principally about myself, others had far more to fear. Panic was spreading throughout the country. Documents were frantically being destroyed by trade unionists, communists, anarchists, socialists, feminists or anyone else who had used the small window of freedom in the last six years. Now they were afraid. Anything written was incriminatory. No wonder documental evidence for some eras in Spain is thin on the ground. Having destroyed anything that could be used against them, they went into hiding to plan their escape if the troops took over the streets.

A feverish tension gripped the country. Hardly anyone slept. The night was spent glued to the radio, the only source of news left as the rebels quickly took over television studios. It was, as many commented, *la noche de los transistores*[33]. All over Madrid right-wing bands were moving around freely, bursting into cafés and forcing people to sing the fascist anthem "*Cara al Sol*" (Face to the sun). For those first interminable hours the future of the country was in the balance.

Shut away in our homes, we had no way to know exactly what was going on, leaving us to imagine the worst.

---

33 The night of the transistor radios.

In fact, behind the scenes efforts to end the rebellion were frenetic. At nine o'clock one of the leading newspapers, *El País*[34], printed a special edition with the headline, *El Pais, con la Constitución*[35], a play on words using the name of the newspaper. At one o'clock in the morning King Juan Carlos spoke. Dressed in his uniform as head of the armed forces, he declared himself unequivocally against the attempted military take-over. Even so for several hours the situation remained unclear for everyone listening tensely to the news. It was only later that we found out most military leaders had refused to back the insurgents, others remained undecided preferring to wait for the outcome. By midday on February 24th it was all over. The *guardias civiles* left the parliament and returned to their barracks with a promise of immunity for the lower ranks. The leaders were arrested and later put on trial. Those who are alive today are unrepentant: what they did was to save Spain.

Controversy over the attempted coup d'état continues to this day, not over its justification but the extent of official participation. It has always been claimed that agents in civil society who have never been identified and certainly not put on trial, were involved in both the coup d'état and the attack in *Atocha*. This is very likely. In addition, there is ample evidence of international ramifications in these attacks as well as many other thwarted by the security

---

34 The name of the newspaper means "The Country".

35 *El País* here refers to the newspaper and the country. Both supported the constitution.

forces. In particular, it appears that they were orchestrated with the aid of neo-fascist groups particularly from Italy. While condemnation of the attempted coup d'état was strong from most governments including that of Margaret Thatcher, the United States was among those that were more ambivalent at first.

In Spain, there are few doubts that events were orchestrated at high levels. February 1981 was not an isolated incident neither was it totally unexpected. The discontent bubbling below the surface, ready to erupt at any moment, was especially strong in the armed forces. Apparently there were other plots to overthrow the government which were foiled by the security forces. Earlier murders, particularly those of Atocha had shown that right-wing groups with the support of the remnants of the regime felt they could do anything with impunity, even kill.

Milans del Bosch was just one among the many who deeply resented the new government. It was as if the rug had been pulled out from under their feet. They had ruled the country, held sway while people kowtowed to them, they simply would not accept losing it all. For 40 years the leaders under the regime had been safe in the knowledge that they were "right" morally as well as politically.

In these troubled times it wasn't only the extreme right which tried to change the political situation through violence. When the Communists and other left-wing groups turned to Euro communism, a revolutionary group broke away opting to continue using violence rather than politics to achieve their aims. They took their name from one of their first attacks: *Grupo de Resistencia Antifascista Primero de Octubre* [36] or Grapo. Their activities started at the beginning of 1975, a few months before Franco's death, continuing until the early eighties with sporadic actions into the nineties by which time they had murdered more than eighty people. The majority of their victims were members of the police force, politicians, business leaders or members of the legal profession: clearly attacks on the state and its institutions. For finance they raided banks, usually violently, killing anyone who got in the way.

I myself paid less attention to them. Primarily, because the height of their attacks took place before I arrived. The worst took place in May 1979, the *Matanza de la cafetería California 47* [37] in which nine people were killed and sixty one injured. However, unlike other attacks they had carried out, they have always denied responsibility for this one. Secondly, being on the left they featured less in the news than the right-wing groups and after many years of dictatorship they were viewed with slightly more indulgence than their counterparts on the right. Finally, rather than attacking indiscriminately, they tended to target individuals for the symbolism of their professions or kidnapped wealthy individuals to obtain funds. For this reason most people did not consider they posed a direct threat. I do vividly remember the kidnapping of a businessman in 1995 who has never been found and probably never will be despite numerous searches.

---

36 October 1 Anti-fascist Group.

37 Slaughter in the California 47 café.

Fortunately, despite the suffering caused, none of the attacks from either band had the intended effect of destabilization. It soon became clear that only a small minority supported violence, all the vast majority wanted was to move forward peacefully. Senseless violence was actually making the desire for democracy stronger not weaker with a show of unity that made it crystal clear that another dictatorship was unacceptable. I participated in one of the mass marches which took place in many cities after the attempted coup d'état. If it followed the route taken by those far off demonstrations in 1936 and if it was once again the voice of the people, unlike the 1930s, Spain was now part of a modern Europe, making the prospects of success far greater.

Perhaps it was in 1981 with the coup d'état that I began to live less on the margins. I will never be able to understand the unrelenting oppression of the war or post-war years but this attempted coup d'état gave me a fleeting glimpse of what fear could be. For the first time I understood what it was like for people in dictatorships, what it was like to be helpless. Although, if the streets of Madrid and most Spanish cities were safe to walk in even late at night, a sensation of dread and claustrophobia lingered in the country.

Nevertheless, despite the uncertainty, a new country was emerging and the transformation was not only political. Spain was opening up, the colour and vivacity of its culture conjuring up a new identity for a new country.

GOING CRAZY

Notwithstanding any reservations during those early years, watching the country hurtle forward, it was hard not to be swept along with the enthusiasm. Spring in Madrid does not bring a profusion of flowers as it does in England but the first year in Spain, as the chilling winter drew to an end, beautiful flowers blossomed everywhere in the shops, a profusion of pink roses on white fabric, a passing fashion forever fixed in my mind. I could barely afford such luxuries at the time but this one moment of longing somehow symbolized a better future. If these thoughts appear trite compared with the aspirations of a large part of the population, all any of us could do was to wait for what the future would bring.

With the transition underway, much we had taken for granted for years in Britain could finally be theirs. It was not merely a matter of politics, since few were actively involved in the political process apart from enjoying the right to vote for the first time in forty years. Yet through the programmes they watched, discussions in bars and homes, films they enjoyed and books they read, they were participating at least passively. In those first dizzy years, while the new democracy was finding its feet, it was film makers, authors, photographers and musicians who played an important role in cultural change.

The wildest and the bravest were casting off the shackles of 40 years of oppression, sweeping over the dreariness and conformity of Franco's Spain. It would have been impossible for the regime to open up the economy without letting in influences from abroad which, in turn, led to a craving for more. In the late sixties and early seventies young people had admired Europe and America from afar. Music was key, in radio and television programmes and also in concerts. In an official concession to the pressures from society, the Beatles were invited to play in Madrid and Barcelona in 1965. Once again a pop concert played a key role, this time with Spanish groups: a homage to a pop star killed in an accident in February 1980.

This was not about politics but a way of life, about clothes, music and films, in a nutshell everything denied to them: freedom from conflict, freedom to love, freedom to wear what they wanted and freedom to lead their own lives. Through the years they had stored up resentment, a yearning for everything that had been presented to them as wrong, rebellious and iniquitous. Rather than a formal organization this was a group of people expressing themselves without constraint. Those who espoused new ideas, supporting a progressive ideology whether it was political, social or cultural became known as the "*progres*" or progressives.

Big city dwellers were the first to adopt new ideas. In Madrid, "*La Movida*" a cultural movement opened the flood gates to modernity in a whirl of extravagance. If the inhabitants of Madrid are called *gatos* (cats) it is because of the city's vibrant nightlife and at no time was this label more apt than during *La Movida*. An official stamp of approval was given to the movement by the progressive socialist mayor in Madrid and then by other local authorities, usually socialist or communist, as it spread to provincial capitals throughout the country.

Unsurprisingly, in the eighties, there was a clear influence from the punk movement which had come over from London and other European capitals. At the same time, *La Movida* like so much else, owed something to the past. Flamenco singers and dancers, bullfighters, their wives, their children along with Spanish celebrities remained *la crème de la crème* of society gossip. Beloved by Franco for their "Spanishness" if not for their political views which were rarely clearly expressed, their lives wove through the years in gossip magazines and programmes before becoming part of the kitsch world of Almodóvar with its vivid colours, *peinetas*[38] and Castilian villages. Rather than clashing with the present, the past was contributing to the modern.

Some key figures of *La Movida* are famous today, recognized internationally, others have sunk into oblivion but all of them were new for me. Almodóvar was the undisputed leader of the movement, his early successes a herald of his later fame transcending international borders. His films, presenting a polished vision of a garish

---

38 A large decorative comb typical in traditional Spanish dress.

world, smashed all boundaries that had been imposed on Spain. Firstly because the protagonists of his films were usually women, *Las chicas Almodóvar* – Almodóvar's girls, often behaving outrageously. Then because they featured prostitutes and homosexuals, both treated like criminals under Franco's regime, as well as all kinds of sexual deviance. It would be an understatement to say prudery had been cast off, much to the horror of the conservative elements in society.

Every aspect of cultural life was taking on a renewed air of daring and colour, from the ultra bright fashion of Ágatha Ruiz de la Prada to the innovative photography of Ouka Leele. Each influenced the others: the fashion and singers appeared in films, magazines and TV programmes. There was the impression that everyone's objective was to push limits to an extreme.

The prudery and emphasis on sexual morality of Franco's regime had indeed led to the exaggerated excitement of the first taste of forbidden fruits, creating the uninhibitedness of the early years of the transition. Already in the seventies, the rather self-conscious films of the *destape*[39] had been paving the way for a "no holds barred" approach in the cultural world while other films had found ways to get round the censors. If films continued to be advertised with gaudy, hand painted hoardings promising an illusory world of escapism rather than gritty

---

39 These were films that appeared at a time of sexual liberalization. *Destape* literally means "uncovering" although in the case of these popular, light-weight films "stripping off" would probably be a better translation.

realism, cinema was changing. By the eighties, those films favoured by the National Catholic regime peopled with nuns, large families or girls whose main occupation seemed to be singing while trying to catch a husband were banished forever to the *cine de barrio* slot on Saturday afternoon television while new filmmakers were not only innovating but bursting onto the international scene.

Literature was not far behind. When *The Ages of Lulú* by Almudena Grandes was published in 1989 many would say things had gone too far. The story begins with a young teenager embarking on a sexual relationship with a young man, a friend of the family. Try as she might she cannot break free from his hold over her as sexual cruelty is taken to extremes. I didn't read it when it was first published as I had little time to struggle through any book. It was only years later that I discovered how shocking it really was, especially taking into account it had been written only fourteen years after the end of the regime when Spain was only just emerging from a period of prudery and sexual repression.

During those early years sexuality was a new topic to be treated openly albeit somewhat coyly at first. For the last forty years the Spanish had seen foreign lands as a tantalizing world of sexual freedom. If groping on the metro and comments in the street were still the norm it was hardly surprising. The forbidden creates fascination just as much as guilt.

Despite being ruthlessly cut by the censors, foreign films had portrayed an enticing view of the opposite sex, a utopian dream of sexual freedom. It was often the case that rumours about what happened were much more scandalous than the facts. In the famous scene in Gilda, it was claimed that Rita Hayworth removed far more than a mere glove, enough to send men dashing across the Pyrenees. Then once again with the release of films like "Last Tango in Paris" business was booming for cinemas just over the French-Spanish border. A friend told me that the only thing her husband wanted to do after their marriage in the sixties was to spend their honeymoon in France in order to watch pornographic films. Not the best start to married life and little wonder it ended in divorce as soon as that option became available.

Women had much more to gain from these new freedoms than titillating films. After all, they were the ones who had suffered universally under the repression. Now finally, there was a light at the end of the tunnel. Contraception had been banned until 1978, although the falling birth rate suggests that long before this date many women had found ways and means to limit their families. With the introduction of the pill in 1978 women had a reliable method to control the size of their families legally for the first time. I remember reading articles on contraception and other sexual matters in magazines back then which appeared prim in comparison to Cosmopolitan in the seventies in England but looking back I can see how important it was for them. A law partially decriminalizing abortion in certain cases and at certain times was finally passed in 1985, not without considerable opposition from the church.

The right to decide about their own bodies was only the first step. Their legal rights had already been timidly modified at the end of Franco's regime, but they still had a long road to travel. While legal and social advances were essential it was not only a question of new legislation; years of education had left entrenched attitudes against equality which were often shared by women themselves. At the same time, women needed to participate in the workplace in order to gain economic independence.

Other countries in Europe must have seemed like paradise for Spanish women although they were far from perfect. In Britain in the sixties and seventies, girls were still advised that the most suitable professions for them were nurse, teacher or a secretary, and even in the eighties women did not enter the work market on an equal footing with men. Nevertheless, despite having had personal experience of the ubiquity of inequality, for the first few years in Spain I remained totally unaware of the draconian restrictions on women's lives. Every aspect of their existence was controlled. Until 1973 women still needed permission from their husband to be a guardian or to witness a will and until 1975 by law they needed the husband's authorization to buy or sell any large item. Ironically, in the case of electrical appliances like a washing machine, in spite of being the only ones who would ever use them, they were considered incapable of buying them.

Ignorant of all the limitations I was taken aback by small incidents. In 1982, when we applied for a bank card for a joint account, the delivery man stood on the doorstep and resolutely refused to hand it over until my husband was at home and could sign for it. I argued that it was a joint account but he wouldn't budge. We then wrote to the bank which chose to ignore the complaint, most likely because the manager was a man. In fact, until 1981, money earned by a wife legally belonged to the husband who could dispose of it as he wished.

The Constitution in 1978, advocating values of liberty, justice and equality, heralded a promising tomorrow for women who could take up the fight against oppression and inequality brutally cut short in 1936. They were quite capable of doing this; one reason I failed to fully comprehend the concerns of women at the time was because Spanish women never struck me as meek and mild despite the repression they had suffered. Few ever conformed to the ideal woman portrayed by the regime, in fact quite the opposite, they were strong and feisty.

Of course, not all women were affected by the changes in society any more than all men. Anyone newly-arrived in the centre of Madrid at the time of *La Movida* who took an interest in cultural events could be forgiven for thinking that the whole of Spain was joining in with the party, which certainly wasn't the case. Often cultural movements appear more enticing from a distance since they stand out against the monotony of everyday life, providing a handy label to define an era but it is only after time that they filter through society. At the time they pass most people by.

The elderly, who had spent their adult years under the regime, were uncomfortable with the unleashing of so much pent-up feeling. For them, it was simply too much, too late. They might no longer have been fervent Catholics but the dogma drummed into them from childhood by the church and the authorities could not be easily discarded.

According to the teachings of the church homosexuality was wrong, abortion was a sin and marriage was for life. I've heard criticism of widowers who remarried after several years, and the belief persisted that a widow remarrying bordered on adultery.

It wasn't simply that new attitudes were hard to accept: it was difficult for older people to find a place in the new society that was emerging. The job market might have opened up allowing young women who were reasonably well educated to work and gain independence but many middle-aged women lacked any formal qualification and quite a few were illiterate or semi-literate. What is more, it would have taken courage to leave the home where they had been safely ensconced for so long. How could they reconcile women working and earning a living with the ideal of women as the perfect stay-at-home wife and mother only dedicated to the needs of the family? A perennial problem but a particularly thorny one for those brought up with the propaganda of the fifties and sixties. This was the case for Cecilia, who always claimed she would have worked if she had been allowed, yet for her generation working outside the home was never anything more than a fantasy and, as such, none of the dilemmas had to be faced. She could happily pay lip service to progress, knowing it didn't concern her and hoping it never would.

While praising the transition, both Juan and Cecilia hankered for the golden days of yore, the safe simplicity of the past. They happily rejected Franco's regime and all it stood for, yet at the same time they clung to the sentimentality of "Spanishness" that had shaped such a large part of their lives for good or bad. Anyone born, like them, in the late twenties was too young to participate in the brief flowering of democracy in the early thirties but appreciated the secure simplicity of the sixties and seventies, at least for those who accepted the status quo or claimed to do so.

There were also practical obstacles to joining in with the frenzy. In spite of, or possibly because of reform, life could be challenging during the transition. Cultural extravagance was far removed from the thoughts of anyone struggling to make ends meet or unemployed in a country with rising employment and little financial help. In the same way, the lives of country dwellers continued as they always had done, with creeping change over the decades rather than a burst of colour and permissiveness.

Neither did any of this affect my life significantly. Like many people, I was too busy working and tied up with everyday life to get involved in any cultural movement. Working to pay for a flat and managing in another language were quite enough. *La Movida* only featured on the margins of my life, something to read in the Sunday supplements or occasionally watch on the television.

If the changes bypassed large sections of the populations, others simply couldn't cope. Too much freedom too quickly can never be a good thing. Economic difficulties combined with the new permissiveness created their own challenges in the late seventies and eighties. On the outskirts of the city, beyond the new residential estates, shanty towns sprang up with drug "supermarkets", including one of the largest in Europe. Now that films could deal freely with social problems, one of the first films I saw in Spain, "*Deprisa, deprisa*", shone a light on the devastating effects of marginalization and drug use on some of the deprived neighbourhoods of the city.

By the early nineties the drug problem was increasingly affecting the centre of Madrid. Sometimes we would find syringes and papers in the entrance to the flat left by drug addicts who had managed to open the door during the night to find shelter from the cold and the police. When renovation work was being carried out on a building next to the convent where my children went to a small nursery school, a young teenager would be sitting on the ground every morning in the filth behind the flapping tarpaulin, the sleeve of his uniform pulled up to inject heroin, his school bag next to him. He was just one of the many victims of the "opening up" who, judging by the uniform, came from a family with money. Perhaps he was the lost son of the new, successful professionals who had plunged too readily into an uncharted world.

In any case, new is not always synonymous with better and this is not only true for the people. In the rush forward they forgot the richness of their past as they cast off their static world of custom. They abandoned much that was valuable, treating it with disrespect, failing to appreciate its value in their enthusiasm for the whirlwind of urban life. I could applaud the rejection of the recent political past but not the disregard for history. Hundreds of years of culture lay in ruins while history was reduced to lists of dates and facts to be learnt and forgotten. If Spain was fortunate that much of its heritage had been preserved through isolation and the lack of industrialization, it was sad to see that it was now being left, uncared for, to crumble, its treasures falling into rack and ruin. Some of it was perhaps not worth preserving but a large part was buried, undiscovered or disregarded. Some artifacts had always been part of everyday life so that no-one realized their worth: Roman pillars used for seats in a town near Malaga, roman roads and bridges, medieval castles and monasteries disintegrating through the apathy of the institutions charged with their protection. The faded glory of old towns like Toledo, scarred with modern buildings, *El Capricho* of Gaudí in Comillas almost derelict, the best roman ruins outside Rome in Mérida where it was almost impossible to find the sites overgrown with grass. So many places left unmarked, unexplained and forgotten.

Public treasures had been sold to foreign collectors and archeological sites like the Royal Arab site at Medina Azahara barely excavated, never mind studied. Archives were then poorly organized and often unavailable. Museums at that time were soporific: the few visitors would wander around the rows of unlabelled objects in endless glass cabinets like zombies, too bored even to feign interest.

The beautiful countryside often suffered the same fate as the big cities which sucked in the inhabitants of the rural world, to scatter them back only for festivals and summer holidays. With time, the countryside was not only abandoned but treated with a certain disdain. For many it had always been a practical place rather than the Arcadian dream of industrialized countries. Now that they saw themselves as city dwellers it was generally somewhere to be avoided.

When they did venture there, the women tottering in high heels, the men dressed in their Sunday best, they never strayed far from the parked car. The country could be a place to wash the car in a mountain stream and empty the ashtray on the grass verge. Once as we were travelling through a beautiful forest on a bus, the couple in front took out a packed lunch and proceeded to throw all the rubbish out of the window, leaving a trail of packets, cans and plastic bottles among the pine trees bordering the mountain road.

Spain is marked by stark contrasts: the brightness of the too-blue sky against the darkness of the interiors, biting cold followed by oppressive heat, mountains soaring from endless plains. All this has always existed and always will, it is the nature of Spain. On the other hand, the contradictions in the transition were new, packed into a few short years. There was an explosion of colour, the blossoming of a new society against the background of the hidden agonies of the past, modernization against tradition, happy-go-lucky attitudes against claustrophobia and limitation. The craziness of everything new was being imposed on an old stagnating world which continued to meander along under innovation and experiment. Society was reshaping at a vertiginous rate yet deeply ingrained attitudes persisted. It would take time for the country to emerge as a modern country. This then for me was the transition as I knew it: a layer of excitement over the permanence of the past, giving the country a dual face which proved hard for me as a foreigner to fathom.

BEING A FOREIGNER

It was hard to slide smoothly into Spanish society all those years ago. I was used to modern furniture, gardens and greenness, memories of a fading jigsaw puzzle of perfection from my youth whereas Spain often appeared closed and stifling. Society might have been changing yet it had little to do with my ideas of progress and freedom. This might not have mattered if Spanish society had not been one of belonging when, for years, I had belonged nowhere and to no-one. I had made my own way and could continue to do so if I wished, but freedom has its own drawbacks.

Before I went to Spain I had never thought about fitting in. I had lived in other countries where I quickly learnt their ways; therefore, I presumed Spain would be no different. However, I failed to take into account that settling in a place forever is very different from a short visit when life can be lived at a superficial level of laughter and bonhomie, condescension to the idiosyncrasies even a secret scorn. In my case, I knew from the very beginning I had come to stay, that I needed to penetrate to a deeper level. A daunting task given the historic introversion of Spanish society and the turmoil of the moment but equally considering my ignorance of their past, my perplexity in the face of the Spain it was then. I believed then that I would never belong, that I could never wind back to a past I had never even known.

I was lonely, longing to belong but at the same time unwilling to conform, to give up part of myself. I felt I had been dropped onto a stage with the wrong backdrop, adrift on a set peopled with characters that had nothing to do with me. I had long been used to a shifting world whereas in Spain the impression was that almost everyone belonged in one way or another. They had a family, a village, a neighbourhood, they knew their place in the hierarchy of society.

If they had suffered great instability, there were far more certainties of religion and politics; for some these were of the past, for others of the future, both providing them with an immutable identity. The past had been farming the land for generations or later a job and marriage for life, support or opposition to Franco. With the transition came other convictions, either determination to maintain tradition or an enthusiasm for democracy.

What is more, Spain was a closed society which may seem a strange thing to claim when the Spanish have always been considered welcoming, open and friendly and indeed they were up to a point. Nevertheless, away from the coastal areas, in central Spain, in Galicia and the inland provinces in the north and west they were unused to foreigners, viewing them with suspicion. That people would uproot to live in a foreign land for no particular reason was puzzling. "Why have you come?" they asked,

"Don't you get on with your family?" In times gone by, Spain had been an open place only gradually turning inwards over the centuries, engendering a mistrust of foreigners especially in the interior, in old Castile and in the mountains where there were far fewer foreigners than on the plains and plateaus.

People did, of course, come to Spain, often motivated by economic opportunities offered by the country's rich resources. The great bodegas in the south were originally run by English families such as Osborne and Byass which were gradually absorbed into Spanish society. In the 19th century the lack of technical expertise and finance meant foreign companies and engineers were essential for the construction of railways and other civil works. Sometimes they had more lofty aims. Men like George Borrow came to convert the Spanish from Catholicism to Protestantism; some would say bravely others foolishly but always unsuccessfully.

For foreign travellers, the Spanish were from another age. They were to be admired, their lack of modernization bestowing an aura of exoticism, of other worldliness and bucolic bliss as industrialization engulfed much of Europe. If these visitors from other lands appeared eccentric to the Spanish it was because they often were. These dreamers who came looking for the folkloric Spain rarely went to the austere mountain villages, preferring the lure of the south or the ruins of past glories in the cities. The works of romantic painters of the 19th century like Edwin Long and Robert Kemm give an idealized portrayal of the colour of Andalusia not without the occasional sly dig at the priests, while others like Henry Charles Brewer and John Dobbin were drawn to the dilapidated buildings of Toledo, Granada or other old cities.

Writers came too, attracted by the thwarted idealism of Spain's struggling politics. Byron arrived in the 19th century, Gerald Brenan and Laurie Lee in the early 20th, chronicling the otherness of life. It has only been relatively recently, starting in the late sixties that tourists have flooded in to stay for a couple of weeks of sun, sea and cheap wine. Until the mid-eighties relatively few foreigners came to Madrid. Those who did mostly congregated in the centre or in the plush districts to the north. Bankers and business executives came to set up companies in the burgeoning Spanish economy to make up for the lack of expertise and language skills among the Spanish back then. Well paid by their employers, they came with a good standard of living bringing their spouses and families along to enter ready-made social circles.

I fell into none of these categories. I had not come to find work, to escape to another idealized place or as a tourist; I was simply a foreigner. From the beginning it was imperative that I meld into the family, the society and the country but the warmest welcome was reserved for temporary visitors, who did not touch too intimately upon their lives.

In Spanish the word for a foreigner is *un extranjero*, whereas someone not from a village is an outsider or a stranger, *un forastero*, a term used to define anyone from anywhere else, it hardly mattered where, it all boiled down to the same: they didn't belong and they had no obligation towards them. Many years ago, a man from a northern Spanish city came to the mountain village in search of a simpler life, herding sheep and goats and writing poetry. He was tolerated but never accepted, a lost soul, as surely nobody would leave their home unless they had to. For him I was a fellow outsider.

This outlook towards outsiders led to wariness and mistrust, but it also entailed loyalty to their own people which made dealing with them somewhat slippery. To sell an old house or a piece of useless land to a fellow villager would be unacceptable; to sell it to an outsider was perfectly alright or even rather clever. I've known cases where gullible foreigners were plied with produce from the land, apples, cheese, vegetables until they were convinced of the villagers' goodness and honesty. That was the moment to sell. Only when the purchase was completed did they find out there was no possibility of building on a plot of land, converting a farm building or connecting water and electricity, leaving them with a useless property in the middle of nowhere.

These attitudes which had been a characteristic of villages and provincial towns for centuries were exacerbated by the ideology of the regime. If Spain was open to tourists along the coast, much that came from beyond the frontier was to be feared. "Abroad" was a place of immorality, divorce, broken homes, the acceptance of homosexuals and goodness knows what else. Women, books, tantalizing films or pop music, all challenged the precepts of religion and morality.

The Spanish never considered themselves to be under

any obligation to either understand or assimilate foreigners. They rarely travelled, and in the first neighbourhood where we lived a foreigner was mystifying. Others saw us with a mixture of bemusement and consternation. Foreigners did not match the parameters used to place people on their social scale. Being professionals and university graduates we should have been middle-class, our parents had respectable professions, yet we were allowed to wander around alone. We behaved suspiciously with a disregard for any dress code, wearing jeans and scruffy clothes although we weren't visibly revolutionary.

It is normal to view other countries through clichés, some of which may be true. Two opposing views of Britain and the British existed. On one hand there was admiration, ignoring the imperfections: the left looked to the freedom and tolerance of its democracy, the right approved of the tradition, the upper classes, education of Cambridge or Oxford and the ancient culture of Shakespeare. On the other hand, there were misgivings. They were horrified or bemused by British family life. "So, they asked, in Britain can homosexuals marry?" which they couldn't.

If the Spanish had strange ideas about foreigners, foreigners in turn came with their own prejudices and preconceived notions of what the Spanish should be like. Moulded by our environment and family we can only judge others through the lens of our own experiences. Acceptance may be merely a scratch on the surface. We pay lip service to tolerance carried along by illusions of our own trendiness, goodness and adaptability.

What made the strangeness harder to accept was the

fact that going to Spain for a week's holiday was already quite commonplace, after all it was a couple of hours away. If much about it was alien, my own romantic ideas of the universality of the human experience lingered on from the seventies. I could not rid myself of the conviction that we were all, in truth, the same, hoping to find something familiar hidden away as if any differences were merely superficial. I was not the only one. Back then, there was a widely held conviction, particularly among the left, that the working classes were the true inhabitants of any country. When they travelled, they hoped to see a new folkloric world while clinging to the belief that what lay beneath the colourful surface was simply a version of their own world and struggles.

For these people, the real Spaniards would be lurking in the backstreets of the inner city areas. Anyone noisy, rough and ready would somehow be more authentic. A few years after I arrived, I made the fleeting acquaintance of an Englishman who could be described as a middle-class liberal. In Spain for a year with his wife and small child, he had nobly taken on the role of househusband while she worked. Not for them the leafy suburbs in the north. They had, he told me, decided to live in one of the districts in the centre, to the south of the Plaza Mayor, where they were convinced they would get to know the authentic Spanish. This was the same district where Juan's family had lived for those short years in Madrid. In the eighties it was still generally run-down, a place where poorer families dwelled. Some came from the south, others from the coalmining areas in the north, from small villages of the centre or the outlying areas of Madrid. Most had come years before with their families, searching for something better: work and a more comfortable life.

When I met this man by chance a year later in a supermarket, he was a mere shadow of his former self. He had, it seemed, found the true Spanish. Unfortunately they had failed miserably to conform to his preconceived idea of what they should be according to his British scale of values, which had been developed in a world of comfort, freedom, financial security and ease. They were not the happy guitar-strumming, finger snapping, clapping people of the pictures nor a picturesque personification of insouciance; these were people who had to struggle to get by. They were not, he claimed, ecological according to nineties British ecological standards. They were most likely noisy, perhaps not very friendly to a foreigner who spoke little Spanish and who, for them, must have led a bizarre life. The environment that had forged them was tough. They would make no concessions to an outsider. What he saw as his virtue of attempted tolerance was for me patronizing.

The casual visitor is often looking for something original, even quaint. A couple of young lads outside a doughnut shop belonging to a well-known chain expressed their horror that the street had been marred by this import. I suppose they thought that other countries should be kept set in cultural aspic for the occasional British visitor to enjoy while at home they welcomed everything international.

When older friends decided to stay permanently in the

late sixties and the seventies, what proved to be the biggest stumbling block was the most Spanish of all institutions: the family. Whenever Spanish families admitted to their rejection of a foreigner they stressed the enormous effort they had made. In fact many American and British women who married into Spanish families in the sixties and seventies were very lonely. Finding it too hard to be incorporated into the family and with little assistance or social life outside the home, they often left. It was only much later that I realized that in this world of happy families, many, many others were not warmly embraced.

I would have thought that, having lived abroad, Cecilia and Juan would be more open and accepting. In fact it was the opposite, as they were insular and closed in as if they had had enough of foreigners and foreign lands. It was one thing to go to a bar, exchange limited greetings, quite another to accept the unknown into the family. When foreign friends of their children were brought to visit their home, they were made extremely welcome, they would soon be gone. Including them in the family was another matter.

Cecilia in particular made no bones about the fact that she did not want foreigners. She claimed her objections were to the person not the nationality but she was never particularly interested in individuals as such, only what they could be as part of her scheme for life. It is highly unlikely she had ever met many people outside her village circle before going to France. Her life there, cocooned in the home, had little effect on the ingrained convictions she had absorbed in early life; on the contrary, her experience abroad seems to have reinforced her concerns. Then, in addition to her village reticence and the indoctrination of the regime, was her perennial dread of what people might say. A Spanish wife was her ideal and would be welcomed regardless of her character.

Before arriving I already knew one of the French wives in the family was accused of not fitting in, a damning verdict in a society where everything depended on family, although in her case, since she lived in France, her visits were fairly infrequent and therefore not too onerous. It never occurred to me that I would not be accepted either. However, on that very first sweltering July day I was left in no doubt that I was unwelcome. Cecilia simply refused to speak to me. Even so, I didn't immediately reject the possibility of melding into the family. Quite the contrary, for I saw their simplicity, their unwavering values and the lives they had built against all the odds as admirable.

Not being warmly received into the family mattered less to people who had already been in Spain for some years, carried along on a wave of fun until almost unconsciously they had become permanent residents. Interestingly, those who did "accept" the new country with no problem often had stronger links to their own country. They received frequent visits from friends and family and often made trips home. Furthermore, I am aware of the revolution that has taken place over the last forty years, not only in Spain but all over the globe. Nowadays, it is much more straightforward to live in another country whatever the reason. With communications made very much simpler with Skype, cheap flights, WhatsApp messages and email, a firm commitment to the new country is no longer essential. Keeping up with news from the home country is simple, trips back are cheap and many products are available internationally.

Back then Cecilia was sure that I would need them for, in her opinion, no-one could survive unless they had a family. She believed she held all the cards. Plunging into a new life, my only ally was the naivety of youth which led me to believe that I would one day be accepted into the bosom of the family. What I did not realize was that as far as Cecilia was concerned I never would be. She was solid and no-nonsense, built to last, whilst I was a drifting soul. No doubt she took comfort in the hope that one day soon I would somehow disappear, wafted away on a hot, dry summer wind, but I stayed.

FOR BETTER OR FOR WORSE

I got married, or at least I think I did as I barely understood the ceremony, something which didn't seem to matter greatly. It was a dark day for Cecilia. If a girl's principal aim in life was to catch a man, his mother's task was to stop an unsuitable match and in this case she had failed miserably.

Despite the fact that Cecilia's experiences of courting and marriage, like those of most rural women, did not accord with the niceties prescribed by the regime, she unwittingly perpetuated the ideology. No doubt she would have objected to such an assertion yet it was understandable that she did, after all, the regime's principles were in accord with those of the church and the traditional environment in which she had spent her early years.

Cecilia rarely read but, for those who did, the rules for marriage were clearly defined in leaflets and above all in educational material. From the post-war through to the seventies, strategies and pitfalls of romance were explained in books with appropriately coloured covers: blue for boys, pink for girls. The approach may have been coy but the message was crystal clear: formal courtship marked the point of no return. This could cause unhappiness when couples drifted into marriage simply because they were in the same circle; they went to the same church, their fathers worked together or they shared a holiday village. It was the "*novio o novia de toda la vida*", the one and only girlfriend or boyfriend. In the seventies and early eighties, the ideas inculcated by the regime along with advice from Elena Francis' programme held sway and in particular the strong belief that all women were desperately searching for a husband. New ideas on relationships might have been spreading among the under thirties but they proved disconcerting for women like Cecilia who had grown up during the regime. Her generation could not, or would not change at the drop of a hat. Getting married was a big milestone, the step to a higher status for a woman. Success in life was to be wooed before walking triumphantly down the aisle in a cloud of white to live happily ever after with an adoring husband. Failure was to remain single which was a bitter disappointment to the family, although there is no denying a couple of maiden aunts always came in useful around the house.

Finding a suitable partner was equally important for men. If the young man himself was not overly concerned that his future bride satisfied all the criteria, his mother certainly was, since the chosen girl was to bear and bring up the family's children. According to advice given at the time, the future bride had to be demure, reserved and of course, chaste. The emphasis on purity had caused considerable distress among young girls in earlier decades who felt they shouldn't walk down in the aisle in white if they had given away "the greatest gift a woman has". Even in the seventies it was not unheard of for the future family in-law to ask the fiancée if she was a virgin.

Cecilia, therefore, was not alone in having a very clear idea on the desirable qualifications required in a young bride or in her belief that all girls were on the lookout for a husband. If mothers had to be on the alert for girls who might use their feminine wiles to stealthily steal away their sons, none were as bad as foreigners, certainly immoral and definitely not to be trusted. Only one kind of girl would be allowed to travel round Europe on her own.

If a woman travelling on her own was suspicious, a man on his own far from home was easy prey. Whether they were working in another city, had gone abroad or had been called up for military service there would always be manipulative females waiting to snare them. A woman from a known circle, the village, the neighbourhood or the daughter of family friends was always the preferred choice for the mother. Cecilia's eldest son married a French girl who was forgiven for not being Spanish as she was the daughter of a family friend. Besides, she was compliant and adored her mother-in-law, all admirable qualities. With her younger sons, Cecilia was not quite as fortunate, as three married unknown foreigners. Four foreign spouses out of six was an alarming number.

After forty years, an elderly neighbour continued to regret her failure to stop her son ditching his "life-long" fiancée from the village for a new woman he met when doing his military service far away in Andalusia. Whenever I met her on the stairs she would demonstrate with the sweep of a hand how he had been whisked away when he was out of her sight with dire consequences, at least for her. Despite the fact that her daughter-in-law tried to help her when she was elderly and infirm she was never accepted. Forty years is a long time to remain resentful over a disappointing marriage but many managed it.

All this seemed strange to me, used as I was to swinging Britain where at least among the younger generations any constraints had long since gone out of the window, including the belief that only church weddings were acceptable. This could be for religious convictions, to comply with societal demands or for others simply because their lives were always ruled by tradition.

Church weddings had been the sole option approved not only by society but by the state for centuries. Since 1564, when Philip II established the Catholic ceremony as the only legitimate kind of marriage in a Royal Charter, civil marriage had only been possible in two brief periods: from 1870 to 1875, during the First Republic, and from 1931 to 1939, during the Second Republic. After the Civil War, civil marriages were only accepted, which certainly didn't equate to acceptable, for people of different religions or in cases of apostasy. Apart from giving up the Catholic faith, the latter involved renouncing many opportunities to participate in society as non-Catholics were barred from cushy government posts and certain jobs required a marriage certificate issued by a church authority. This therefore was a step very few people were willing to take. By the eighties, when religion was fading, one of the main reasons for a church wedding was to avoid conflict with older generations.

Apart from the religious aspect, weddings were, of course, social as they are almost everywhere. However, in Spain a wedding required the presence of the whole family which included not only parents, brothers and sisters but also numerous cousins and long-lost aunts and uncles. Besides family, the guest list should include work colleagues and particularly the boss. At least there was no divorce back then which simplified matters somewhat. Failure to invite anyone significant caused unforgivable offence, declining an invitation without a good reason even more so.

As well as being social occasions, weddings also had financial benefits, with very clear rules on what should be given. Gifts received had to equal the cost of the reception in order to cover expenses. The aim, on the whole, as many unashamedly admitted was to receive as many presents or as much money as possible out of the event, and in the happy days of cheaper housing there might have been enough to pay a deposit on a house.

We attended a family wedding or two which followed the only kind of ceremony approvable at the time, that is "*como dios manda*"[40], with the bride in white, proof that she was pure even if she rarely was. In the church there was a mixture of social convention and Spanish informality. With no seating arrangements, many guests wandered around and chatted in groups at the back which I found rather disconcerting after the regimented rows of guests surrounded by the sepulchral silence of the English church. Some people, rather sensibly, gave the whole ceremony a

---

40 As God ordains.

miss and just turned up for the reception. After the service, the bride and groom disappeared to some attractive part of the city to be photographed elegantly draped around trees, statues or whatever. In the meantime the rest of the guests waited around or hit the bar. Weddings always seemed to involve an inordinate amount of hanging around.

Many took place in special halls which worked on assembly belt principles. The wedding crowd entered, ate, drank, danced and was thrown out dazed, at the other end. As collecting money was one of the major objectives, there were some strange customs: the groom's tie was cut up and pieces sold and a basket was placed on the tables for envelopes with money even though presents had already been given. Surreptitious attempts at slipping in small amounts of cash were noted and frowned on. It was the custom to go round to visit all the relatives in their homes after the wedding in the hopes of collecting a bit more money.

In comparison our wedding was a muted event. We had already been living together, a fact which was greeted with such a horrified silence in the local supermarket that I wished I had never said anything. Later the shopkeeper felt obliged to apologize although she was still visibly disconcerted. In Britain, my generation had been one of the first to reject marriage as an unnecessary institution, seeing living together as a feasible option and although this was not always approved of, it was in no way scandalous. Now that couples live together quite happily before marriage in both the UK and Spain, it is strange to think how much it mattered, but it did.

For Cecilia the news of our approaching wedding was not welcome. She would have had mixed feelings about a registry office. On one hand, it was the backstreet choice, shabby both literally and metaphorically, strictly for the progressives and shot-gun weddings. It was a sign of rebellion and unconformity, a slur on the family and a rejection of society. On the other hand, and more positively for Cecilia, a registry office wedding with few guests was easier to ignore. I don't remember actually inviting anyone and in any case no one in the family would be offended at not being invited to a non-wedding nor would they feel there was any obligation to attend.

The little effort I put into it was a reflection of its value for me. I wore an ordinary dress, a last minute purchase off the rack in Corte Inglés, one of the few big department stores which existed at the time. I carried a bouquet of white and pink roses because we happened to be walking past a flower shop the day before. We popped down to a registry office among the usual hotchpotch of workshops and newly-built block of flats in a scruffy district whose only claim to fame was as the location of the city's prison.

The ceremony took place in an ordinary office unprepared for any such formality. The desk was covered with piles of papers, the walls encased in tomes of the Civil Code. No chairs were provided, forcing everyone to stand around, fortunately not for long since the whole thing was over in a few minutes. Now foreigners have to bring a sworn interpreter to any official act but then it wasn't deemed necessary although it perhaps should have been since my Spanish was not up to the occasion. It seems I agreed that my husband should marry the registrar. No-one was particularly concerned as the fabled laxity of Spanish bureaucracy persisted at the time.

When it was over and a few photos taken, we went back to our flat for sandwiches. Only now, looking back over the years, have I realized what an excruciating day that surely was for Cecilia in her best hand-knitted two piece: her son marrying a foreigner in a registry office.

As it was unusual then to go abroad for a honeymoon, we went to Galicia in the north of Spain which is an idyllic place, green, quiet, everything Madrid was not. We left from the Estación del Norte, the north station, so called because it was built to connect Madrid to Irún on the Spanish-French border in the north, not for its location since it is actually in the south of the city. As we found our way across the bustling station onto the train packed with people, bundles and old suitcases I could imagine the weary immigrants arriving to work in the city. The clouds of smoke from the steam engines which must have greeted their arrival were all that was missing; otherwise it was much the same.

Although the station was part of the city by the time of mass immigration, in the early 19th century this area was in the country. Anyone who has seen Goya's painting of "*Los fusilamientos del tres de Mayo*" which hangs in the Prado will be looking at the same site. On May 2, 1808 the Spanish rose against Napoleon's troops in the centre of the city. The rebellion was crushed and the following day the leaders were taken out to what was then the countryside to be shot. This is one of the famous works of the many in which Goya depicted the horrors of war.

Just over fifty years later, in a very different era, a temporary station was built on the same site and in 1882 the present station was finally opened. The construction was symbolic of all that was wrong with the Spanish economy in the 19th century. The introduction of railways arrived late and, without the necessary technological know-how, capital had to be used to bring technology and experts from other countries, mainly France or Britain.

Like most buildings in the area, the station was shelled during the Civil War, leaving it in an unacceptable state for Himmler's visit in 1940 until it was hastily bedecked with the same fascist symbols used to decorate the streets. The addition of a red carpet laid on the platform provided the perfect setting for this reception which caused considerable concern among the Allies.

By the time of our wedding it was almost as dismal and chaotic as in those post civil war years: hardly a fitting place to make a new start. We took the night train to Galicia, in the northwest of Spain, at that time still a largely undeveloped region. Its rugged Atlantic coastline is dotted with fishing villages while inland there are mountains and forests. For all its beauty, like so much of Spain, it was a harsh place for those who had to make a living from the land or sea. Therefore, I could understand that if leaving their homeland was painful for the emigrants, staying would have been even harder.

When we came back to Madrid, any joy evaporated. Compared with the tranquility of Galicia it appeared dirtier, noisier and more chaotic than before. At the time, I didn't see life in the city as being forever even if marriage was. There was no divorce which must have made life extremely hard when reality struck, especially for women. According to the manuals, the key requisites for a happy married life were smiling, submission, forbearance and patience from the young wife. In this way she could win the love of her mother-in-law. If they should live together, she should not aspire to be the decision maker or keep her husband all to herself. Moreover, it was her duty to accept that her mother-in-law was always right in any conflict. Not quite my idea.

Divorce was finally introduced in 1981, causing an uproar. Needless to say, the new law was met with vehement opposition from the Church, an attitude which was not totally coherent for, despite divorce being illegal during Franco's regime, with a generous quantity of money and appropriate connections it was possible to obtain an annulment. Even so, the Church and many conservative groups could never agree to something they had been brought up to dread, seeing it as a sign that society was on the verge of moral collapse. As usual the Opus Dei had an appropriate metaphor. Divorce was as dangerous as a burning building they explained, thus they who knew the truth, were obliged to warn us not to enter. Naturally, the progressive groups saw it as a step forward, an end to a considerable amount of hypocrisy.

Whatever the opinion on divorce, it carried a stigma for many years especially among older people, not only because it was against church doctrine but also because it went against the concept of an immutable family. If it was marginally acceptable to people of Cecilia and

Juan's generation it was simply because they were utterly convinced that it would only affect "other" people. Except of course, it did affect them, and indeed many other people.

The first divorce in the family was not wholly unwelcome. After a few tumultuous years the marriage between the youngest son and his foreign wife came to an equally tumultuous end. A few years later there was a second divorce. This was a shock: the wife was after all Spanish to the core, they had got married in a church, she regularly attended Cecilia's Sunday lunches and they had their child baptised. By the time of the last divorce in the early 2000s, times had changed dramatically. Even so, when the law came in they would never have envisaged three divorces out of six marriages.

When we married, however, a divorce law was still in the future. For the moment I was irrevocably part of a tight-knit family but as far as I was concerned life continued much as before.

GETTING BY

Sometimes it seems the world was an easier, less complicated place when I was young perhaps in part because we made it so or it may simply be that that is how we prefer to remember it. With time, memories may mellow but, born in the post-war years, growing up in the hippy era and then the oil crisis of the seventies, I do think we accepted jobs simply to scrape by and life in cold, scruffy flats more readily. Yet, although we were used to less, it is true we lived in an era when the future offered greater certainty. We looked forward to ever increasing wealth, a better place to live in peace and prosperity. For that two things were essential for us: a job and a home to call our own.

When I arrived in Spain I was lucky that the demand for English was high. Since the main language taught in schools had always been French, few people spoke English. Therefore, when they suddenly needed to learn, language schools sprung up everywhere, often in dark and unsuitable flats in the centre with creaking floors and little light. Like mushrooms, they appeared one day, disappeared the next. The first one I taught at was owned by a man who had to decide what to do with an inheritance. It was a toss-up between a bar and a language school, the latter winning as it would involve shorter hours.

Hours for teachers were long, the pay poor but it was enough to manage on and even save a little. We started at the crack of dawn before the students began work and finished late in the evening, travelling around all day. Public transport was decrepit with cramped boiling carriages, some with wooden slats for flooring. Weeks were one long blur of interminable stairs, cranky escalators, throngs of people, metro stations, offices and banks. Only the centre of the city was adequately served by the metro, the new dormitory towns outside the city boundary were not catered for at all, leaving vivid memories of travelling to outlying districts, bouncing along on buses across tracts of desolate, windswept waste ground. It was a time of weariness, endless coffees in bars strewn with paper and cigarette ends, keeping going with the thought that one day life would be better.

Much remained of the laid-back attitude that foreigners had come to expect of Spain. In the absence of an efficient bureaucracy it was possible to get away with almost anything. In particular the relaxed approach to paying tax and social security made saving easier. Rents were relatively high but since life was generally cheap, with a complete ban on all luxuries, we scraped together enough to pay a deposit on a flat. As mortgages were extremely hard to come by even with a steady income, it was customary to pay a deposit with promissory notes for the remaining amount to be paid to the owner periodically.

New buildings had the advantage of financing through the construction company which offered the possibility to pay off the debt gradually over several years.

With demands for housing, estates had sprung up on the outskirts of Madrid or beyond, often lacking proper amenities, lighting or roads, but cluttered with piles of bricks as if the builders were intending to return and finish the job one day but never did. Some were better than others. The divide between the north for the better off and the south for the less wealthy persisted, nevertheless they both represented something similar: the confirmation of achievement and hope for a better future, offering a new style of life and a symbol of modernity, as Spain shed the past and moved to the future.

The majority of new-builds were flats but there were an increasing number of houses, huddled together, tall and thin with rooms on four floors as if the Spanish could not quite bring themselves to spread out despite the large areas of land available. There were shared pools and sometimes other communal areas, made for large families to spend long, summer days outside together. If a new nuclear way of life was on offer, in many ways it echoed an earlier more communal style of life.

Most people still worked in the centre. Big business had its own district, a slick commercial centre in the northern part of the city constructed in the 1960s. Flashy buildings, boulevards, clubs in the basements, restaurants: everything for modern business and entertainment all with a hint of sleaziness. For foreign bankers and business people this was the face of modern Spain, unexpected yet pleasing. It gave the visitor an impression of Madrid as a young, vibrant city which it was in a way.

The old centre, on the other hand, had been forsaken, decaying over time, left to the old or the less well-off who could afford nothing else. It was from another age. The ugly modern buildings built to fill the gaps left by the wartime bombing jarred against the dilapidated elegance of the 19th century streets. Old shops continued to sell an array of articles of clothing that had disappeared from Britain years ago: cotton bloomers along with other practical clothing, woollen waistcoats and warm undergarments while slightly risqué wear was piled up in dusty boxes, only accessible using a ladder. These were ancient family businesses where old shopkeepers knew exactly what their customers required as they spread the goods out on the wooden counter polished with years of use. There were no supermarkets as self-service seemed an alien concept among the local shopkeepers who had owned their shop for generations.

We stayed in the centre because, despite being rundown, it was convenient, accessible and besides, it was all we could afford. At the time many people expressed surprise that we should do this.

Finding a flat was far more time-consuming than it is nowadays. Every weekend we trawled through the property columns in newspapers, learning the jargon while we searched for the cheapest. With no photos available, numerous phone calls had to be made about light, noise, the number of rooms and layout. Questions had to be very specific, whereas the answers were invariably vague. Tiny streets then had to be located on a printed map.

In looking for a flat, I discovered another city, one that intrigued rather than appealed. Many buildings in former wealthy districts had once been grand blocks bearing witness to the transient glory of the city in the late 19th and early 20th century when it aspired to emulate other capitals, especially Paris. Street names harked back even further, with names of great Spanish artists like Velázquez and Goya, designed to reflect the achievements of a bygone era and triumphs long gone. These crumbling mausoleums in the district of Salamanca were the relics of a way of life that had vanished by the fifties or sixties. Many had long lain empty, or at least those we visited, for the well preserved were far beyond our means. There was no longer any particular attraction in the shabbiness of the derelict buildings, their former elegance covered in grime from the incessant traffic.

We spent all our free time wandering around these rambling properties, up wooden staircases, down endless corridors losing ourselves in the maze of rooms, one leading off another, where privacy was not given or expected. Each building threw together those who were to be forever worlds apart: the privileged eternally confident of their rights and the downtrodden growingly resentful of the wrongs.

When Juan lived in Madrid in those turbulent years before the war, they would have been the hub of life for the wealthy, closed to families like his or maybe glimpsed at a distance. Nonetheless, while they enjoyed their comfortable lives, supported by a bevy of cheap servants from the country, they must have been aware of the brewing storm. When their lives came crashing down, those who had not escaped in time would, like Juan, have spent the war years in the city but unlike his family which was out on the streets participating in the war efforts, the owners would have been cowering in fear waiting for the knock on the door, the walk along the street and then the shot in the head. Forced to stay, they would have spent their days desperately praying to go unnoticed whereas a short time ago they had been eager to be seen. During those few years of the war Madrid belonged to the servants.

By the time we visited in the eighties, all this had been forgotten. These flats had been languishing empty for decades, abandoned by the owners who could no longer be bothered with them now that they had moved on to another life somewhere more prestigious. I found these relics of a gone-by era fascinating, but we realized the renovation would be too costly and we needed somewhere to live immediately.

After much searching, we finally bought a flat at the top of a block in the run-down part of the centre. The "attic" floor was not considered especially desirable. Nearly all old buildings were arranged as a mini-cosmos of society in reverse, with the bottom at the top so to speak. In the past, at a time when the streets were not filled with cars, the spacious dwelling on the first floor with a view of the street was reserved for the owner, whereas sisters and brothers might be given the next floor and so on. The higher the floor, the smaller the space allotted for each flat up to the tiny attics on the top floor. These were icy in winter when temperatures dropped below 0° and sweltering in summer with no air conditioning when life without fridges and freezers must have been unbearable. Nowadays, with the noise of incessant traffic, pollution, the lack of light and the ubiquity of lifts, the situation has reversed and the attic flats are in great demand but this was not the case in the eighties.

It was a cosy flat with beams and a fireplace, and views across to the Guadarrama Mountains. We could look out over the roofs of Madrid with their terracotta tiles, running with rain in autumn, covered with hoar frost or sprinkled with snow in winter and beneath them thousands of lights, secret places where other people lived. When I shut the front door I was sheltered from the city, protected from its noise and chaos. There were, however, the neighbours to contend with.

As communal living is the norm in Spain it is well-regulated. In theory the statutes of each *comunidad* set down the rights and obligations of the owners as well as decision-making procedures, but in practice it was ruled just as much by age-old friendships and enmities whose origins were lost in the mists of time. At least once a year the assortment of neighbours gathers together to deal with any problems and decide on building work that needs to be done. As leaseholds are not normal for housing in Spain the owners themselves make decisions about repairs, decorating, alterations and any other matter. The arguments can be ferocious. When an agreement is miraculously reached, all the owners pay for work in communal areas, depending on the coefficient of ownership. Naturally everyone objects.

The inhabitants were nearly all elderly widows, the offspring of people who had bought the flat just before or soon after the Civil War. Most had never worked. They knew everything about the building, its inhabitants, their sins and hidden secrets. Some of them had a view of the staircase from the windows and net curtains would twitch whenever anyone went up or down. They kept their status, clinging onto this fading world, blissfully unaware of the new one emerging. The daughter of the owner of a tile factory in Extremadura in the spacious first floor opposite the owner of a cake shop who nearly lost everything in the Civil War, then lesser beings on the higher floors: the wife of a taxi driver, the concierge who let his flat, and finally us. They helped and hated each other in equal measure, yet the feeling of community could not hide away the loneliness, rejection and despair of any big city that was creeping in behind closed doors.

They all had stories to tell about the building. The occupants had their quirks like anywhere else, and old feuds simmered on, tales of madness and greed, alienation and loneliness, minor characters in some drama from the 19th century worthy of Pérez Galdós or Dickens. The woman on the fourth floor staggering up the stairs after a little more alcohol than was good for her would wax lyrical about the time she played on the communal terrace or out in the streets before they were taken over by cars. But more often than not the stories were of the other occupants.

Often at night wailing would float up from the third floor where a strange, old woman lived. Rumour had it, her twisted face was the result of a botched facelift in the early days of plastic surgery; for this or some other reason people disliked her. One night someone tipped a large paella on the floor outside her front door. Whether they were fed-up with the moaning during the night or it was vengeance for some distant slight, it must be a uniquely Spanish method of revenge.

As she had no children, she had employed a married couple to look after her in her final years. Far savvier than her, they persuaded her to bequeath them half the flat in her will in exchange for their devoted service for the rest of her life, typical in Spain at that time. The other half was to be left to nuns in a nearby convent. Once she had signed in their favour their interest in her rapidly waned. She had become a burden, an annoyance to be borne until they could take over the property. As she sunk further into madness, they slipped away. Whenever she sat in the doorway shouting, neighbours would try to help her or phone the absent carers to come back and look after her. They never did.

When she died, the carers bought out the nuns for a song dividing the flat into smaller units which they then let for exorbitant sums as rents soared in the nineties and early 2000s before the crash. The tenants were always complaining, the plumbing was badly done and water leaked into the flat below, which meant the owners were constantly embroiled in legal battles with all and sundry. This was not something that bothered them unduly as they lived off the wrangling as much as the rent. It was all part of the deal.

Two women, Carmen, the wife of a taxi driver and Petra, a widow, lived in adjacent flats on the fourth floor. Unfortunately they hated each other, after many years of living cheek by jowl. One summer afternoon Petra shut herself in the bathroom, wrapped herself in plastic and opened a bottle of gas. Soon, with open windows, the smell of gas pervaded the whole stairwell and the fire brigade was called just in time to rescue her although it was clearly not what she had wanted. When Carmen had friends round not long after, she could be heard complaining loudly that the whole building could have been blown up, which was quite true. This was too much for Petra to take; not only had she failed in her endeavour but she had to listen to her enemy's comments, so she decided to join in, pointing out that that was what she would have liked to do. On they went all afternoon shouting at each other loudly through the open windows.

Several years after we moved in, it was decided that the exterior walls needed to be re-plastered. The work got off to a flying start late one autumn when scaffolding was put up with tarpaulins completely covering the windows on one side of the flat. The chosen builders set to work with great gusto, sometimes bashing right through the wall. At this point the architect supervising the work decided that, as she was unhappy with the builders, they should go but they refused. Long months of stalemate ensued. By stuffing newspaper into the walls, we kept out the worst of the cold and wind but the tarpaulin kept out the light as well as the weather. This went on all winter until eventually the problem was solved and in spring we welcomed back the light and a proper wall.

The flat had its inconveniences. Living on the top floor without a lift we had to carry everything up 10 flights of stairs: shopping, suitcases and above all children. Many people in the old centre had done the same for years without complaining. I am no longer convinced by the British argument that flats are problematic for families. Living in a flat is perfectly feasible with children, moreover the communal areas are well maintained on the whole, noisy residents are condemned and problems sorted out one way or another.

Imperceptibly during those first years, my views on how things should be, changed. I accepted my life was unlikely to ever be in a detached, forever home. Anyway, I loved being perched up above the city and it was truly a community for all its weirdness. Purchasing this flat meant more than merely having a place to live: it was a symbol, something final, a decision made.

THE PASSING YEARS

Time passed. As the weeks, months and years rolled by imperceptibly, I grew accustomed to different ways. What had been strange became normal, the bizarre, customary. Chickens had heads and feet and didn't always come in polystyrene packets. I could find alternatives for things I needed. I grated lumps of fresh suet with blood and membrane. In the shops I shouted *"quién es el último?"*[41], defending my place against the fiercest of Spanish housewives. Christmas, less glittery, came and dragged on until January 6th. There were things I occasionally craved: cream filled Easter eggs, biscuits, exotic spices, nonetheless, what I missed most were the changing seasons.

Living in the countryside in Britain, the unfolding of seasons formed the background to my life. Each has its own defined character, yet one blurred gently into the next. Early spring came with snowdrops, winter aconites and forsythia, signs of hope after the winter. As a child I would look for the first shy violets under a hedgerow, then celandines, cowslips and buttercups. I loved the

---

41 Who is last in the queue?

lushness of summer, the unpredictability of the weather, then the mellowness of autumn, the arum lilies, the smell of decaying leaves, the melancholy. Even winter, however dismal, had its own character.

For years I would feel a longing for the countryside where I was brought up. Could it be that for country children it's more difficult to accept other countries? While cities everywhere are fast becoming the same, the countryside with its native flora and fauna can never lose its identity. Madrid boasts many parks but, however beautiful, they lack the haphazardness of nature. There are years in the region of Madrid when spring and autumn go by unnoticed. Winter passes abruptly into summer while the heat lingers on into October. There are fewer golden leaves or decay, the winter chilliness arrives from one day to the next.

Gradually the bleakness of the first years softened. I rarely went back to England. It was too expensive, and besides I had no particular place to go. Since English newspapers, the main source of news, were an expensive treat and phone calls rare, I was losing touch with political life. As Britain was becoming more shadowy, a memory of what it had been fifteen years earlier, I realized Spain had imperceptibly recreated itself into a more modern country.

Sometimes I wondered if it was me or the country that was changing. Perhaps it was both. Our actions and thoughts are conditioned by time and place more than we like to believe. My opinions were gradually adjusting to my environment. Ideas and beliefs that had seemed alien now appeared less so. I could appreciate the rhythm of life, the lack of many excesses which were the hallmark of Britain. I understood better the challenges that Spain faced.

At the same time the country was rapidly shedding more of its past, making it easier for me to accept. It seemed as if a century of social change in Britain had been packed into a few years so that Spain in the nineties was quite distinct from the country of the seventies. By the nineties the Spanish were traveling abroad for tourism or to study languages in increasing numbers. Two international events, the Olympic Games in Barcelona and the Universal Exhibition in Seville, were successfully organized in 1992. The latter, with the theme of "The discovery of America", lasted six months, bringing people from all over the world and transforming the city. It boosted the transport system with a new central railway station, an extension to the airport and most importantly the first AVE, a high speed train which would later run to other major cities.

Change was inevitable. Religion was rapidly losing its hold although strangely I had become used to its presence. I was offended by too overt attacks on the church, by drawings or jokes that were not appropriate. Even so, the influence of the church was weakening, as well as its dictates on how to live which, for some people, was a change which complicated rather than simplified life. Society in general was very different; things that had shocked a mere fifteen years ago, like divorce, were becoming acceptable. In 1995, *Pepa y Pepe,* the first Spanish sitcom, portraying a rather chaotic working-class family, appeared as a change from the stilted comedies of the seventies and eighties. The younger generation of women both in the cities and in the rural environment were beginning to organize themselves for business and leisure.

All this had repercussions on family life. This was brought home to me recently when I visited blocks of flats in a small town near Madrid. Those built in the eighties were designed for communal living with large rooms on the ground floor for family gatherings. Here the extended family would set up tables to enjoy lunches together, as Cecilia and Juan loved to do in their village house. However, those built just over ten years later were intended for a very different style of life. They had a communal pool, always welcome in the hot summer, but apart from that, all they shared was the entrance hall. These were clearly designed for small families with one or two children who would eventually want to spend their free time in their own flat after a busy week.

This new state of affairs was easier for the young to cope with than for the older generation. Although Cecilia was not old by today's standards, the society of her youth was receding more quickly than she would have wished. Her reaction was to cling more tightly to tradition, hoping perhaps the changes swirling around her would never affect her family life. She was not alone. For those born in the pre-war period, their later years would be a disappointment. They had dutifully respected and cared for their parents, now they expected to be looked after in their children's homes without taking into account that with working women and small flats this was nigh on impossible. Juan and Cecilia were always waiting for the family to come, sitting at home in front of the TV, doing bits of knitting, strolling around the neighbourhood, filling time.

It was in the nineties that I noticed people were more open about the drawbacks of their own family lives, having lost the fear of societal reprobation. I found it easier to fit into the new style of life now it was more relaxing. What is more, with a family our lives were changing just as rapidly as the country was.

THE WRONG CHILDREN

As far as Cecilia was concerned marriage was merely a first step and one which, with the imminent introduction of divorce, could easily be undone. Children, on the other hand, were the final straw, stamping a seal on a relationship that could never be broken. She would have claimed that children were always welcome. After all, enormous broods of children glowing with happiness were a mark of Mediterranean countries, part and parcel of the laid-back relaxed life, unlike those born into the starchy families of the north with their distance, authoritarianism and restrained love.

Yet neither recently nor in the past have children always symbolized joy in Spain. For centuries a large family was one of the exigencies of rural life. Many hands were needed to till the land and support parents in their old age especially as the scarcity of food and lack of medical treatment meant the death rate among children was very high.

With the strict ban on contraceptives during Franco's regime, families continued to be large in spite of the rapid movement to the towns. The regime positively encouraged these families, not with financial support but with publicity and prizes. They would appear on television, proud parents of around twenty children who received a pat on the back and a moment to bask in the glory of doing their bit for the *patria*[42] but nothing much else. In the absence of financial aid, the reality of urban life tempered the concept of "the more the merrier". Having hoards of children in the country with the large houses and open spaces is one thing, but in a small city flat it is quite another. Therefore, by the final years of the regime there had been a marked drop in the birth rate which has caused concern in some quarters ever since.

Young people brought up in large families were averse to repeating the experience, deciding to have only one or two children, partly because women could go out to work, partly because the economy was unstable, and perhaps more than anything else, because their own lives had shown them the drawbacks. Asked on a call-in radio programme in the nineties whether it was selfish to have fewer children, the participants clearly believed it was not. The majority, brought up in big families, expressed their desire for a style of life that had been denied to them as children due to the number of siblings. They explained that the size of the family had meant shared rooms, no holidays and fewer opportunities in education, in other words it required sacrifices that most parents did not want their own children to endure. They realized that they could give their children a better chance in life if there were fewer of them.

---

42 The word for homeland or simply country but with strong connotations of patriotism.

Such a programme could never have been broadcast while Franco and the Catholic Church held sway. Not only were children encouraged, family life was sacred. An unhappy mother or childhood was an unacceptable blot on the image of domestic bliss, something to be brushed under the carpet. In this utopian society dysfunctional families simply didn't exist, anomalies were never acknowledged. In spite of the stability of family life, this was, of course, simply not true.

Yet few people would have admitted this. Despite most children growing up happily in an extended family, I have heard disturbing tales of childhood, especially in staunchly religious families. So what of children who were unhappy in their families? What of children who had not been welcome? As with any thorny issue during the dictatorship or the early years of democracy, the solution was quite simple: there was no problem. Whether they suffered from poverty and isolation in rural Spain, or in the rigid, traditional families, it was all behind closed doors. In 1942 Camilo José Cela[43], published his first novel *La familia de Pascual Duarte*, a portrayal of a brutal upbringing in Extremadura. The narrator tells his story while awaiting execution for a murder, although as the son of unloving parents, an alcoholic father and illiterate mother, his circumstances had already condemned him at birth.

One of the most wretched generations of children were those born, like Juan, in the twenties and thirties.

---

43 Spanish author and winner of a Nobel Prize for literature.

Although few talked about it, they would always remain the victims of the Civil War. It is only now that I realize that many people who have passed through my life were these children. The vanquished and the vanished, given a life-sentence for something they had never done, second class citizens for many years. They would generally be unskilled workers for, whatever their abilities, few of them would have had a chance of a decent education. Some who grew up knowing that the body of a parent lay undiscovered in a ditch, accepted early on that silence was the only option. It was, therefore, only rarely that I came to know their stories.

One man who must have been born not long before the Civil War did tell me something of his life. He was the owner of a small junk shop where he spent his days among dusty piles of second-hand furniture. It would be generous to call it a shop. It was more of a large storage space packed with mounds of furniture. At the time junk was not common or popular since families that had owned nothing much until the sixties, were eager to furnish their flats with modern furniture and not with other people's casts off when they moved to the city. Moreover, moneyed families would cling on to their heavy old furniture even when it was no longer wanted, giving their flats a claustrophobic feel while making a true junk shop hard to find.

I noticed this man had a prodigious memory, an enormous capacity for calculating large lists of figures, a wide knowledge and well-argued points of view. We chatted as we hauled out items from the enormous piles of furniture. After a time, he told me he was an orphan of the war, brought up by nuns. He had never tried to find out who his parents were, probably an impossible task as records were destroyed, often intentionally. I would imagine they were intellectuals, killed or executed leaving a child who had no future, a child of the defeated who, almost fifty years later, would be among his heaps of rickety furniture because anything else had been taken from him. The last time I saw him he told me that he was seriously ill and was leaving his business. He was resigned to his imminent death just as he had been resigned to a life which could have been very different had he been born at a more benevolent time.

Without records, situations such as his were hard to unravel. In the nineties a television programme "*Quién sabe dónde?*"[44] helped people find missing family, some from the Civil War period. There were children who had been lost during evacuations or during bombings, children given into the care of family or friends who wrangled over them in later years or children who simply vanished into thin air.

Loss of family and war were not the only reason for misery among children. In recent years, when many scandals of sexual abuse in the church have been emerging in countries like Ireland and the USA, surprisingly in a country like Spain where the church controlled a large part of young people's lives it has only been very recently that discussions have been instigated on investigating past

---

44 "*Who knows where*"

abuses. For many years victims felt they would not be believed.

Whatever the church's record of sexual abuse may have been, its influence, along with those theories of Vallejo-Nájera which had proved so useful for Franco after the war, would linger on after the regime had fallen. Mistreatment of children reverberated through the years, leaving stains on society which can be covered up but never erased, affecting people I have met, people whose stories I have read, or who appear on the TV, all blighted by a dangerous mix of ignorance, fear and indoctrination. Institutions have not always been quick to accept their responsibility.

Only relatively recently have stories of cruelty and discrimination begun to trickle out. Books have appeared narrating the inhumanity of Franco's regime towards children, for, as ever, the Spanish prefer to cover things up, leaving their ideals untarnished. They have been reluctant to sully the idea of the happy family and the perfect mother or they preferred to believe the dictatorship wasn't so bad after all. Views on the right kind of parents and upbringing were so deeply ingrained in some minds that they continued to hold sway well into democracy which became clear when a scandal hit the headlines in 2012. This incident which involved the cases of children stolen from their families at birth was finally taken up by the legal system somewhat grudgingly.

In a private clinic, until the eighties, children were being taken away from mothers who were deemed to be "unsuitable", whether because they were unmarried, in an adulterous relationship or possibly foreigners. Sometimes one twin would be removed. Suspiciously, all were informed that the child had died after a normal birth. Some were shown the body of a child which they didn't believe was theirs. In other cases the body had vanished.

It turned out that most of these children had, in fact, been adopted and the papers were signed by María Gómez Valbuena or Sor María, a nun who would tell the adoptive parents that the birth mother lacked the means to bring them up. When some of the mothers found their child with considerable difficulty, legal proceedings were started. The victims were dismayed when Sor María died in January 2013 before she could be proven guilty. Obviously, on her death any charges against her had to be dropped. Most of these children will never be reunited with their birth parents and might never even know the circumstances of their adoption.

It would be comforting to believe that, as fervent Catholics, she and her accomplices acted purely from the conviction that they were doing what was best for the child, except the adoptive family had to pay. From what is known, payment was for the days in an incubator or the mother's costs, not for the adoption procedure. Nevertheless, if money was exchanged it seems that, yet again, religion had simply become a convenient excuse for unethical behaviour.

If these cases were relatively rare by the eighties, attitudes to childbirth and children retained much from the past. Antenatal classes were an innovation at the time. They were held in an enormous hall by a pioneering midwife whose first question was to find out who was unmarried. As the information provided was rudimentary, I read literature from British organizations such as the CNT, a mistake since their demands and complaints bore little resemblance to anything I would experience. My first child was born near Christmas and, after a couple of days, everyone left the hospital for their own world, shutting themselves off in their own little boxes of comfort and family. The services available to support British mothers did not exist in Spain. Caring for children continued to be the domain of women as it had been for centuries, with the assumptions that everyone would have some other female member of the family, a mother, aunt or grandmother readily available to give a hand. The first months were a challenge. A British book suggested snowdrops on the breakfast table to brighten life but there were none. In a winter jungle of concrete, even grass is in short supply.

The issue of working mothers was only one among many arising in the transition which were not dealt with at the time. Debates on radio and television programmes, focusing almost exclusively on ideology, failed to address practical matters. What should be done with children? It reminded me of Britain in the sixties, when the question was around the right or wrong rather than dealing with the practicalities, but in Spain it was new and exciting for the progressives. Needless to say, Spanish women had worked in many occupations for centuries: on the land, as servants, sewing, washing for other people but now they were in new professions in banks, offices and shops, often far from home and with rigid timetables. The controversy over childcare exists everywhere of course, and probably always will, but what I found hard to understand was their unwillingness to acknowledge it and their reluctance to accept that even positive changes stemming from democracy such as women's rights posed problems that could not be solved with a magic wand.

The situation was, and still is, complicated in Spain by the extremely long working hours. Nowadays, there is often a very long break at midday which extends the working day especially for most people in big cities who don't have time to return home for lunch. Never having worked out of the home, many women of Cecilia's generation thought it was straightforward. Apart from anything else they were taken in by adverts giving the impression that anyone could look after the home and children as well as working full-time. With a whoosh of the right furniture polish and the purchase of an effective brand of soap powder all was perfect.

To make matter worse, my children were not welcome for even though Cecilia might have had little interest in history, she did know they, like so many others, were the wrong children. Old ideas die hard in a conservative society, passed almost imperceptibly through sermons, a word here or there, or an item in the media. The key question was how I would care for the children who belonged to their family following the male line. I was simply there to look after any children, and as grandmother, Cecilia was there to guide the whole process.

With her new status of grandmother would come respect as well as acknowledgement of her authoritative opinions. Whereas women in Britain had turned to books and magazines for childcare, in Spain methods of bringing up children, passed down from generation to generation, were rarely reassessed, probably as it was unnecessary in a static environment. Although many of Cecilia's views were swiftly becoming outdated, I decided early on that arguing about the finer points of child rearing would serve no useful purpose. Penelope Leach stood no chance against centuries of tradition, folklore and the Catholic Church and above all, Cecilia's unshakeable conviction that she was right and always would be.

For Juan and Cecilia, cold autumn evenings relaxing around a log fire in their village house were just the place to wax lyrical about the good old days, expounding on theories about this and that. The third favourite subject after gossiping about other family members, and the joys of Spain, could be called "how to". They were the ultimate authorities on everything that happened in life and above all on anything concerning the family and children.

Childcare was based on a simple creed of what should or shouldn't be done. They had to be bounced up and down and cajoled. Baby carriers were barbaric; hats should be worn at all times. For some reason, carrying them around was a serious mistake, whereas meat was essential. If these simple rules were followed, they almost brought themselves up and were still expected to do so. Few educational activities were organized although it is true that filling days with plasticene, colouring books and the myriad of activities available to children in Britain was unnecessary when they were surrounded by an exciting natural environment that they could discover, relatively free from danger.

Nevertheless, discipline was important and, in general, parents were often surprisingly strict. It was very much spare the rod and spare the child which Juan and Cecilia claimed was the secret to their success in bringing up a family. In fact, relatively few families had problems with children brought up in the 60s and 70s. They were rarely spoilt as luxuries were unaffordable in most homes, and, with a mother solely devoted to their care, the home provided a stable base.

Paradoxically, the British were condemned as parents for their strictness and severe punishments. Once again BBC dramas, good though they might have been, must take a certain amount of the blame for suggesting to the often impressionable Spanish that all British beat their children when they were not ignoring them or packing them off to some dismal boarding school on a windswept moor. If children appeared at all, they had aloof parents who handed them over to forbidding nannies. In certain quarters there was the presumption that I would treat children cruelly. Actually, the view of the British parents as cold, uncaring, stern disciplinarians could not have been further from the atmosphere of the swinging sixties, the permissiveness that was already permeating society and which, from my point of view, was going too far.

Furthermore, not being Catholic appeared to entail a lack of maternal instinct since devoted motherhood was all part and parcel of the Catholic doctrine, elevating the status of "mother" above all else. I was once asked earnestly how I could be a good mother if I was not a Catholic. This view gave rise to the belief that the British did not love their children as much as the Spanish, as if maternal love was a genetic characteristic. Upbringing is a reflection of a society at any given time. If children during Franco's regime almost always had someone to care for them, what is changeable is not the amount of love but the environment.

In the seventies and eighties provision for childcare continued to be thin on the ground. In my case, the only nursery school available nearby for us was one run by nuns in a convent which extended over a very large plot between two streets. The younger children were under the care of two nuns who believed firm discipline and indoctrination into the faith were the best way to start life. Only later did I find out that one punishment for the littlest children involved kneeling in front of a picture of the Virgin Mary to pray for her to bestow more docile behavior. In general church schools had the knack of combining punishment with religiosity; another favoured punishment guaranteed to rectify the most wayward behaviour consisted of holding out both arms at the side with a bible balanced on each palm. Having been brought up in a Montessori fairyland I was horrified, although I must admit that the only lasting damage seems to be an aversion to any kind of religion. Older children in the same nursery school were taught by a wonderful nun, gentle and understanding whose formal, old-fashioned approach gave them a good start in life.

Schools and in particular those run by nuns and monks were firmly anchored in another age. Having been promoted by the regime, religious schools were plentiful in the eighties whereas places in state primary and secondary schools were insufficient to meet demand. Therefore, subsidies had to be given to religious schools so that they would take more students. Often parents preferred a Catholic school anyway because they were thought to offer a higher standard of education, although a syllabus which included memorizing passages from the bible and psalms might be edifying for the soul but was useless in the modern world. We opted for the state system despite its poor reputation. State schools were, I was told, intended for the poor who couldn't afford anything else. They did indeed have the advantage of being free except that all materials had to be purchased, and by the nineties they were becoming trendy among the non-religious who preferred a secular education.

In most schools until recently, rote learning has been the order of the day. Kings, queens, rivers, dates and formulas, everything has to be learnt by heart and churned out in exams which serve as an excellent preparation for all the exams required for jobs in the public sector: wasted years of learning, regurgitating and forgetting. Although I accepted the system somewhat reluctantly, in the end it doesn't seem to have had done any harm. Nevertheless, there is growing awareness that a major overhaul is required for education to meet the demands of a modern country.

If the education system was designed for a time in the past, equally Cecilia's ways of bringing up children could never be mine. Just as the world of Dickens and the Forsyte Saga had long since gone in Britain, her country ways were no longer valid in the city: urban life evolves more rapidly and has its own demands and expectations. Many years later, when my children were already older, I remember hearing that courses were arranged for grandparents to teach them new ways of dealing with children, which was a timid admission that the old village ways were over and that successful childcare was not an inherited national characteristic.

Even so, I was in no way unhappy that my children were brought up in Spain, quite the contrary as there were many advantages. The continuing strength of the family in general made life more stable, sheltering them longer. Furthermore, with fewer material possessions expected, they were less influenced by consumerism. All in all, it was a more innocent place where they could be children longer.

On holiday in Britain, I remember seeing some pre-adolescent magazines suggesting ways the children could escape their families unless it was a rainy afternoon in which they advised going to the cinema with parents, where the disadvantage was putting up with them, but the advantage was that they would pay. My children found this bewildering as they were always quite happy to go out with us, and tea with Granny was seen as quite an acceptable reason for not going out with friends.

One of the drawbacks for Spanish families was managing in city centre flats which are usually small. Houses with gardens are rare, parks often at some distance. The long summer holidays don't make a parent's task any easier. Planned so that country children could give a helping hand during the hectic summer months on farms or for children in the south to avoid trailing to school in the hottest months, they have been slightly shortened now, but in the eighties, if children had passed all their exams they would finish in mid-June, not returning to school until mid-September and then only half a day for two weeks. Three months in a small flat up ten flights of stairs with the oppressive heat, no garden and increasing boredom was daunting.

THE ENDLESS PLAINS

Escaping from the city in the summer heat became a necessity rather than a luxury with children. From the rain and fog of England, endless sun seems like utopia but it is not, it is hell. English summers evoke memories of mown grass, broad beans, raspberries, soft rains and gentleness while those in central Spain bring dryness and relentless heat. I enjoyed the first few summers in Spain and it was only as the years passed by that I found them hard to bear with no relief from sleepless nights or the energy sapping heat until merely thinking required too much effort. Tall, concrete buildings in the city centres trap the smell of car fumes along with the heat. There is no escape. Anyone who can leaves the cities.

In the past the rich went to the north, to the mountains outside Madrid or the coast, trailing servants and children to popular mountain villages and towns like Navacerrada and San Lorenzo de El Escorial, or coastal resorts in the north such as Santander. The migrants, who, from the 19th century onwards, had moved en masse to the cities, would go back to the place of their birth. In the 1980s most people still had an old house in a village where they themselves could go or at least send the children to spend the summer with the extended family, thus providing respite from the restrictions of the city. There they had space to play freely, and sultry evenings were spent staying out late. Moreover the old houses, constructed for the climate, are spacious and cool.

For centuries the use of local materials gave each region its own character: granite in the family's village in the mountains, whitewash for the white villages of Andalusia, slate for the "black" villages in the north of Madrid or adobe and bricks in the centre of Spain. Traditional materials were the best method to combat the heat, cold, rain and snow and besides, for the majority of villagers, nothing else was available or affordable. Since the sixties, many villages, especially those near big cities have become gentrified, not with chocolate box prettiness but sadly marred by shoddy structures built with few regulations. Town planning is haphazard in Spain. As permission to build is granted by the local mayor and council, a chat in a bar is often sufficient with disastrous results. Only looking at the photos of urban monstrosities in a book about traditional villages in Castilla y León, written by architects with an interest in preservation, was enough to understand why they felt desperate. If for the moment they are fighting a losing battle, there is a burgeoning interest in protecting picturesque villages which will hopefully be done while many conserve their essence.

In many cases their deterioration has not been through an unwillingness to preserve them but because they had been shut off for years down unbeaten tracks, along narrow, winding country roads or in the mountains far from any towns which meant that, despite their undeniable charm, nobody wants to live there. The abandoned village is part of Spanish culture, even appearing in literature, notably in *The Yellow Rain* by Julio Llamazares which gives a dramatic account of the last man in a mountain village, living with the ghosts of the past after his few remaining relatives had moved to a neighbouring town.

Numerous places can provide nothing to compare with the lure of the cities: no large shops, no internet connection, no entertainment or social life. Usually people have left voluntarily, although at other times they may have been forced out. In the 1960s the regime drew up a hydraulic plan to meet the growing demand for water with little concern for the villages which were to be flooded to make way for the new reservoirs. In particularly dry summers these villages reappear with the houses, streets, church and cemeteries all eerily reflected in the receding water. The villagers return to remember their early lives, their parents' sorrow at being uprooted, to mourn the part of their identity which was washed away as the waters flooded in.

We could have gone back to spend each summer in the family's village in the mountains but we were reluctant to be caught up in the web of relatives and past scores, so instead we bought a semi-ruined cottage far away on the plains to the northwest of Madrid where we could be ourselves without the encumbrance of past generations. The village we chose had other advantages as it was easy to reach and more importantly, it was cheap. Homes in the country, a luxury for many people in Britain, are relatively normal in

Spain. Whilst there is a great demand for housing in urban areas which has pushed up prices, this is not the case in the country, especially at a distance from any city.

In the early nineties when we bought, according to the villagers buying a derelict house was a strange thing to do. The one we chose with its thick walls and small deeply set windows is always cool in the shady interior, even with searing heat in the streets, and at night, except at the hottest times of the summer, cool breezes fan across the vast plains providing a chance to sleep. It is exactly like those described by Laurie Lee as he travelled through the area immediately before the outbreak of the war. Constructed in rows each had a piece of land behind which would include outbuildings, a well and perhaps a fig tree and vines.

The houses were designed for livestock as well as people. Most had a separate entrance for animals, ours didn't. At the end of each day animals had to be taken through the stable-type door, along the cobbled corridor leading through the house to an outbuilding at the back where they could be kept safe. For years the kitchen, with its huge chimney, had only been used to smoke chorizo, *morcilla*[45] and hams leaving the walls, beams and ceiling so darkened by smoke that it was hard to see much except for an interesting collection of dead animals, birds and insects, and bits of fat hanging from strings. In a corner, a large sink was built up over a brick alcove where a fire would be lit to heat water.

---

45 A type of blood sausage.

The houses and the old bar opposite had collapsed and were slowly crumbling into a pile of beams, adobe, weeds and rubbish. Owned by people in the next village, they would neither build on it nor sell it and probably never will. Although this often happens in the villages, nothing is ever done about it even though it affects the preservation of the rural environment. The owners could be waiting for prices to go up or they might simply enjoy their claim to land ownership. Often, through inheritance, a property is owned by numerous people who have never been able to agree on what to do with it. With time some have died or are scattered across the globe totally unaware it exists. For whatever reason, for the moment only rats and cats fight out their battles in the tangle of wood and rubble.

Everyone in the village seemed to have lived in our house at some time or other. Houses, like the village people, have a history which anyone worth their salt in the village could reel off. A dwelling of some kind had stood on the same spot in the centre of the village for centuries although when we bought it, it had lain empty for years, used only as a dumping ground for old bottles, earthenware pots and farm equipment and even ancient medicine bottles, a treasure trove of everyday objects. Outside there was a cartwheel, an old wooden plough and a grinding stone. It is built of adobe, wood and bricks, an organic structure, changing gradually over time with neighbours taking pieces of the land, bits being added on or removed to suit whoever lived there. In summer it is peaceful, redolent of wood and oldness, with enormous beams which must have been cut in a bygone age when trees grew thickly over most of the land.

A huge ceramic pot, a *tinaja*, stands in the entrance probably intended to hold water although as there are vineyards, it could well have been used for wine. For us it was part of the charm, for the villagers a chance to air their opinion. They would lean on the half-door and enquire when we were going to get rid of it. Only years later did they accept that it was there to stay. Old things held no appeal for the villagers, they saw the past as it really was: hard, uncomfortable and inconvenient. We might never see eye to eye on the charms of country houses but the first summers in the house did strip me of any romantic notions of returning to the country.

Many people consider the region to the northwest of Madrid beyond the Guadarrama mountain range unattractive. I can understand why, for when I travelled down on the first day I arrived in Spain I saw a monotonous expanse of land unbroken by either fences or hedges. With time, however, its appeal grows. It has its own gentle charm with welcome expansiveness after the choking city. We go in summer when poppies and cornflowers in late spring give way to the bready smell of dry wheat. The emptiness is waiting to be filled with romance and it was. Doctor Zhivago was filmed here in the sixties. I first saw it in a tiny cinema with a woman behind giving a running commentary. "Ah look, she exclaimed knowingly, the Urals". But they weren't, the train was travelling across the Castilian plains, the snow-capped mountains in the distance were the Guadarrama range.

The flatness of the land facilitates communications with better road and later rail connections. Unlike Juan and Cecilia's village, which was cut off from many events for centuries, at the height of the Spanish Empire the central plateau formed the background to much of Spain's early history. Apart from anything else it was the route between the principal cities of the time so there would be a constant traffic of dignitaries travelling through. Alfonso VIII, king of Castile died in the village itself in 1214, admittedly unintentionally as he was taken ill during a journey. Married to Leonor Plantagenet, a daughter of Henry II of England, he is famous for winning a decisive battle against the Moors at Navas de Tolosa in 1212, a date all Spanish children used to know.

In the 15th century, Isabel of Castile, a key figure in Spanish history, was born nearby in Madrigal and spent her adolescence in the castle of the nearest town to the village, Arévalo. Although it is a small provincial town today, it was a major city in the 15th century chosen by the king to hold court. When Isabel married Fernando of Aragon they became known as the Catholic Monarchs with their union eventually leading to the unification of a large part of today's Spain.

If it enjoyed greater significance than the mountain villages in early modern history, it was more seriously affected by the decline of Spain which began in the 18th century. Apart from anything else the court, which had been itinerary until 1561, was based permanently in the capital, Madrid, where all political activities took place. In addition, many of the industrial activities in the area were shrinking. Disease ravaged the population and then in the early 19th century the French under Napoleon invaded.

Further devastation was caused by the *Carlist* wars not long after. Fought principally in the north, there were incursions further south. George Borrow recounts an incident when a Carlist chieftain made an inroad into this part of Castile, sacking Arévalo, invading a neighbouring village and devastating the area.

Despite the disaster of these centuries, the region has one advantage: the land is perfect for intensive farming. If arable land is scarce in much of the country, here it is plentiful, so by the end of the 19th century it had become the bread basket of Spain providing flour for the expanding cities.

Nowadays, with a far more tranquil situation, the villagers' chief topic of conversation is local news and events: burning fields, tractor accidents and the frequent droughts. If the old villagers add their own anecdotes about the days when the village was overflowing with people, one thing they rarely mention explicitly is the Civil War. These were the areas of poorly paid agricultural workers and large landowners, where people must have joined the conflict, many dying or sentenced to death yet there is nothing to record their fate.

Whenever I visit English villages I like to spend time looking at the memorials to the fallen in the two World Wars. If tangible recognition of loss was seen as a way to unite the nation, a form of communal mourning, monuments of a Civil War would serve no such purpose. If squares or streets were named after the victors and statues erected, they served to divide not unite so the majority were removed with the consolidation of democracy. Some, however, remain. On the way to the village we go past a monument to *Onésimo Redondo*[46] standing at the entrance to a roadside hamlet of adobe houses, uncared for and overrun by weeds. For some time I saw it as merely a wistful whim, unaware of his significance at the outbreak of the war. It was only later that I learnt that he had been an early hope of the nationalist side, his death in July 1936 a harbinger of the slaughter and that the word *presente* engraved across the monument was the cry of the rebels. The illegible graffiti scrawled across its surface almost obliterating the fascist arrows could have been a mark of respect or disdain. The blood red poppies a better memorial to the death and suffering that was to come; his and of so many others.

It is tradition rather than memorials which draws people together. Friendships, family ties and festivals, are all part of their identity, providing a nexus between generations. The phrase "*Viva la quinta de 1964*" can still be seen daubed on the walls. This was the draft or call up for that year which might have been written after a few too many drinks or in the early morning as they were leaving. The lads off to do military service would have grown up together, going to school, taking first communion until they decided to leave but even then they would meet every summer and for the festivals.

---

46 One of the founders of the fascist Falange movement.

Although I had been in Spain some time I was surprised how ready people were to help, any misfortune would be shared by the whole village. It is said people living on the plains are, like the landscape, more open than those living in the mountains and in this village at least it is true. They are generous and supportive. They welcome strangers, they are proud of their village. Whenever I am alone there, I always feel safe.

By the time we arrived, life in the village was less demanding, especially with subsidies from the EU. Moreover, modern farm equipment had come to this area much earlier than to the mountain regions, as the large landholdings and higher profits allowed the purchase of tractors and combine harvesters to work quickly on the flat fields. Nevertheless, village life does not usually lead to innovation; it leads to acceptance, to continuing more or less as they had done for centuries. The people are, in general, conservative.

With only a brief visit, it is all too easy to idealize village life. With time I could understand the desire to leave. It wasn't primarily the hardship, it was the claustrophobia. If life events brought people together there could be no secrets. Before the days of mobiles, we had to use the only pay phone in the village in a woman's home. Village telephone operator was a good job, providing never-ending gossip, and in this case it was strategically placed in the corridor so conversations could be heard wherever she happened to be in the house, then any news could be relayed around the village. I was glad I had other languages apart from Spanish to speak to the family and friends back in Madrid.

As far as gossip is concerned, few villages were any different. Cecilia was always involved in some quarrel or other. There was a brother she no longer spoke to and a long-standing feud with the neighbours which involved a wall and a piece of garden although the exact details were long since lost. Generally, most gossip was merely idle tittle-tattle to pass the time and lend a little excitement to life. However, in other more remote places it could be much more dramatic. Unsettled scores dragged on through the years: disputes over land, a bride scorned, slights from the past and quarrels about inheritances were all kept alive from one generation to the next until the origins were lost in time. This rancour for real or perceived actions would smoulder on then one day they burst out to shatter lives of neighbours and families.

One of the worst cases, which became known as *Caso de Puerto Hurraco,* took place in August 1990 in a small village in Extremadura, a region in the southwest of Spain. It all began in 1967, many years before the tragic outcome, with a border dispute between two families, the Cabanillas and the Izquierdos. At the same time there was a story of unrequited love. Amadeo Cabanillas refused to marry Luciana Izquierdo even though they were supposed to be in love. Not long after, one of Luciana's brothers, Jerónimo Izquierdo, killed Amadeo Cabanillas as revenge for jilting his sister. He was tried and handed a sentence of 14 years.

While he was in prison his mother died in a house fire which, according to the police, was accidental. Nonetheless, Jerónimo once again blamed the Cabanillas family and when he had served his sentence he attempted to murder

Antonio, Amadeo's brother. He failed but was sent to a psychiatric hospital where he died a short time after.

Now the two remaining Izquierdo brothers were bent on revenge, above all for the death of their mother. On the evening of August 26, 1990 they donned their hunting gear, grabbed their rifles and set out for an alley in the village with the intention of killing as many of the Cabanillas family as they possibly could. Their first victims were members of the family, then they began to shoot indiscriminately finally killing nine people, among them two sisters aged thirteen and fourteen. They had fled into the olive groves of the nearby hills with the intention of returning to continue with the killing spree when they were found and arrested. Both died in prison, Antonio committing suicide in 2010.

Like their brother many years earlier, the two sisters were sent to a psychiatric hospital which they never left. Many people were convinced that Luciana, still bitter from her rejection, had instigated the crime in 1990 but there was no proof. With the death of both sisters in 2005, Luciana at 77 and Angela 64, a feud which started in 1967 or possibly even earlier ended after almost 40 years.

This rather complicated story illustrates the darker side of rural Spain with hostility over land borders or love that could poison life from one generation to the next. In villages cut off by time and distance insignificant events can become all-consuming, leading to a tragic finale. Surely such a tale is worthy of a play by Lorca who captured the tensions in Spanish society at an earlier date. Fortunately, any quarrels in most villages are minor.

In any case, when I became aware of any conflicts in our peaceful village the tensions didn't really bother me. I was never part of them.

Only very recently have we felt we truly belonged in this village, even though the children were very small when we first arrived. I have never minded as it was an excuse to do whatever I wanted. In the early nineties it was considered slightly eccentric for a woman to cycle round the fields on her own or to choose to be in the house alone. That has all changed now partly because most villagers have lived in Madrid and partly because they are more connected to the outside world. If the women in villages go to church it is mainly for the opportunity to dress in their finery. Normally, they wear trousers, ride their bikes to a neighbouring village for Pilates classes, have their own cars and are *au fait* with the Internet, especially when it comes to prices of houses anyone is trying to sell. No detail of village life escapes them and that is one thing that has not changed and probably never will.

I still love to go. I arrive in a rush, exhausted and then as the days go by I relax and tension drains away. I enjoy the life with the peace, the pace, the sounds and smells of the warm season. Nonetheless as summer lingers on into early September I become restless. Nothing is expected, there is nothing particular to do and nowhere to go. After a time, as monotony sets in, the will to change seeps away, I long to get back to city life, not to the noise and contamination but the choice, the hustle and bustle, the buzz that cities emit. I go back renewed to face the city where news is more urgent and things happen. However much I would like to I can never detach myself from world events for long.

A THREAT TO PEACE

With the consolidation of democracy in the late eighties and nineties the danger of another coup d'état steadily diminished yet, with terrorist attacks from the Basque separatist group ETA becoming all too common, the streets of Spanish cities were once again threatened by people who refused to accept democracy. Although the majority of attacks took place in the Basque country, the terrorists made their presence felt in other big cities particularly the capital. In a relatively small city like Madrid it was almost impossible for the acts of terrorism not to touch everyone's life in one way or another. Because sounds travel across roof tops, in our flat we would hear the distant boom of a bomb in the morning, the wail of sirens as ambulances rushed to try to save the victims. For most of them it was already too late. Despite road blocks being set up which caused total chaos in the already chaotic traffic, the criminals were hardly ever caught, at least not immediately. The disruption caused was annoying, yet nothing compared with the feeling of sadness for the innocent victims and their families along with a sensation of helplessness.

If some justification for an armed struggle could have been found in 1958 when the group was founded under the repressive dictatorship, any rationale for their existence had long since gone. Euskadi (the Basque country) and Catalonia are just two of the seventeen *comunidades autónomas* which make up Spain. With the implementation of democracy each of these regions was granted a statute of autonomy setting down the way they would be governed and granting ample powers for decision making. All the autonomous communities were to have a parliament with elected deputies and a president as well as a tax office to work in coordination with the central government. Each is responsible for its own local police force and education, cultural and health services. Moreover, some communities have a second official language, such as Euskera in the Basque country and Catalan in Catalonia, and knowledge of these languages, along with Castilian Spanish, is a requisite for access to public posts in these regions. Therefore, an inability to speak them effectively limits the possibility for "outsiders" to work in these communities. In most other regions of Spain which only use Castilian Spanish there is no such limitation.

By the late seventies, support for ETA was falling away among the general public. Whatever they might have claimed, by providing the opportunity to decide by peaceful means, democracy had effectively deprived them of their *raison d'être*. Therefore, they targeted the armed forces or the Civil Guard in the hope of provoking a rash response which would have plunged the country into turmoil or, even better for them, would have led to the installation of an authoritarian government thus providing them with the perfect excuse for recourse to brutal tactics. For the same reason, many of ETA's attacks were aimed precisely at public figures in the military, political or media world who supported conciliatory rather than hard-line policies. Quite clearly compromise and debate did not suit the terrorists' agenda which is why the eighties and nineties, when society was becoming more settled, were to be the cruellest years.

In July 1986 in Madrid a van was blown up, killing 12 of the Guardia Civil. In December 1987 the Civil Guard were once more the victims when their headquarters in Zaragoza were targeted with 11 fatalities. Other victims were citizens going about their everyday lives, passers-by, shoppers, children and families. In June 1987 one of the worst attacks on a hypermarket in Barcelona left 21 dead and many injured. In the Basque country itself tensions were high, especially in small provincial towns where the separatist parties governed. People fled into exile in other Spanish cities or abroad. Death threats were used to force businesses to pay a "revolutionary" tax to finance the organization. Anyone opposing the violence through politics or journalism knew that they were placing themselves in extreme danger and if they harboured any doubts bodies of the victims were often left in the street as an example of what could happen. Police, not wanting to be the next body blown to bits by a car bomb, carefully hid their identity behind face masks when making arrests. It was a reign of terror.

Fortunately for me, my first encounter with an attack was only casual. In 1986, I was going to visit my parents-in-law only to find road blocks had been set up on all the roads leading out of Madrid after a bomb had gone off that morning. When I arrived I discovered that the terrorists had used a car which Juan had only recently sold. Cars laden with explosive which were used in the attacks were either stolen or purchased under a false identity. The police had visited them early in the morning so it was fortunate he had sold it legally and all papers were in order. A scrap of paper with an address and travel instructions had been found in the wreckage and the police needed to know if it was his. Juan and Cecilia seemed strangely unmoved by all this as if it was an everyday event yet even such a distant connection affected me. A car I had often travelled in blown to pieces taking with it innocent victims. It wasn't the last time terrorism touched my life.

My closest brush with ETA was on February 6, 1992. Surprisingly, I had heard nothing unusual early in the morning. I might have been running down the stairs or walking along some alley. My children and I would walk through the old city every day, past the small door which led into the convent of the enclosed order. How fortunate they were at times to be shut away from the world! We would go past the town hall, down narrow streets and finally pass through a little square, *Cruz Verde* (Green Cross). Dating back to medieval times, it took its name from the symbol marking the sites used by the Inquisition for its executions. In later times it had become more peaceful. With a fountain constructed in the 19th century and surrounded by cobbled streets and 18th century buildings, it is an ideal meeting place with street cafes and restaurants nearby. Before arriving there, one of my children would run down a steep, narrow street leading into the square to wait for me next to a car usually parked at the side of the street.

That Friday in February was an ordinary day. I had planned to go earlier but changed my mind at the last minute. This spur of the moment decision for no particular reason, which I like to think of as a premonition, was probably simply luck but it saved our lives. As usual a car had been parked on the pavement but this time full of explosives ready for its victims, who used to drive past everyday on their way to their headquarters.

As I turned the last corner, the square had gone leaving only a scene of utter destruction. What was spread before me bore no resemblance to the scenes as they are in newspapers or on television: the bodies, already covered, twisted metal, windows blown out with glass and debris covering the floor. Five innocent men dead. Five families senselessly destroyed forever. Sixteen buildings damaged. It had happened only fifteen minutes before.

The scene replayed itself in my head incessantly during the next few days. Obsessive thoughts of what could have happened if we had left a few minutes earlier, what if she had run joyfully down the hill and stopped by the car. The terrorists would have cursed to see a small child, they might even have hesitated for a second, not through compassion for they had none but they knew killing a child brought bad publicity, something they could ill afford.

A plaque has now been added in memory of the victims recording another bloody episode in the history of the square, one which, in the 20th century, should never have disturbed its peace.

Bombs and shootings were not the only methods the terrorists used: kidnapping was a way of pressurizing the government into accepting their demands. José Antonio Ortega Lara, a prison officer, was kidnapped as he returned from work in January 1996 then held for 532 days in appalling conditions. After spending almost one and a half years in a damp underground chamber with no windows and a single light bulb, he had fixed a date to kill himself. He was given only fruit and vegetables and had lost such a huge amount of weight that he was nothing more than a skeleton when he was finally freed by the police. Suffering from post-traumatic stress, he was given early retirement soon after. Even though the terrorists had not succeeded in forcing the government to accept their demands, this was not the end of kidnappings.

If there was ever a risk that the public would become accustomed to violent deaths, the case of Miguel Angel Blanco changed that forever. It was the second weekend in July 1997, a few days after the police had freed José Antonio Ortega Lara from the secret hideaway. The release of their captive had enraged the terrorist group who, with the prospect of losing face, planned a dramatic operation to show they were the ones who held all the cards. I was spending that weekend in the country house, still ramshackle and dilapidated. Without television or newspapers I could momentarily escape the outside world until that is, news of the latest kidnapping shattered the monotony of summer.

Nobody in the whole country could have ignored the drama which began on Thursday, July 10. Miguel Angel Blanco Garrido, who worked for a consulting company, lived in a small town in the province of Vizcaya, in the Basque country. At the same time, he was on the town council, a post he had only accepted unwillingly in the absence of any other candidate. Politicians whatever their level had been assassinated so anyone taking office knew they were running a risk. Even worse, Miguel Angel belonged to a centre right party, the *Partido Popular* or People's party which was opposed to Basque independence and therefore one of ETA's principle enemies. Nevertheless, once he was on the council he courageously spoke out against members of *Herri Batasuna*, the extreme Basque group and political arm of ETA.

Despite his awareness of the risk, he couldn't have known that on July 9 three members of ETA tried to find him on his usual route to his office, unsuccessfully as that day he had gone by car. The following day he was on his way to catch the train back to work after lunch when, at 3.30 in the afternoon, he was bundled into the boot of a car near the local train station. At 6.30 a communiqué from the terrorist organization informed the government that they had until 16.00 on Saturday afternoon to move ETA prisoners closer to the Basque country or Miguel Angel would be murdered. They knew perfectly well this blackmail could never be accepted by the government.

From that moment, life in Spain was in suspense. Given the ruthlessness of the organization, no-one doubted that the deadline was to be taken seriously. I found myself pacing the room, thinking of him and the indescribable agony of his family, trying to believe that they would not carry out their threat, hoping that the police would find him in time yet knowing it was an impossible task. In the stillness of the house, thin beams of sun filtered through the cobwebs draped across windows and festooning the beams, the gloom aggravating rather than alleviating the intense July heat. Nothing moved in the oppresive air. Time ticked by inexorably in the hot dark interior. Nearly forty eight hours passing second by second. Millions of others all over Spain shared the feeling of helplessness, of wanting to do something to prevent the inevitable. The time given for his death was 4 o' clock on Saturday, July 12.

The deadline came and went. Silence. I refused to listen to the news as if not knowing would change the outcome. It didn't. He was found by two men walking on a common. He had been made to kneel with his hands tied behind his back before being shot twice in the head and left for dead. It is still not known where he was kept for those two days but it was probably in a flat belonging to sympathizers of ETA. He was still alive but died on July 13 in hospital. A shock wave ran through the whole country. It is hard to imagine anyone so inured to violence that they would go ahead with a cold-bloodied murder having known all along that their demands would never be met.

The tragedy of Miguel Angel marked a turning point. With his murder, ETA had become nothing more than a band of killers for the majority of people. Only the most fanatical could claim such acts had any pretensions whatsoever to being political. The end was in sight, attitudes had changed, passive anger turned into action as Spanish society as a whole increasingly rejected the band's methods. The population, weary of senseless violence, rose up organizing massive demonstrations in many cities after his death. Groups such as the *Foro de Ermua,* the Ermua forum, named after the town where he lived and the *Fundación Miguel Ángel Blanco* were set up to lead the movement against violent groups. Furthermore, his cold-blooded murder shocked not only Spain but leaders throughout the world, including the Pope and the French president. Finally, the Spanish government could count on support from foreign powers which had not always been the case.

Before deciding to cooperate, the French had provided a sanctuary for the terrorists for many years. It was all too easy for them to mount an attack before disappearing across the border beyond the reach of the Spanish police. Belgium refused to extradite members of ETA even when their part in murders had been proven. If the lack of support from abroad complicated the fight against ETA, in no way did it justify the reaction of certain politicians in the government at that time who adopted a strategy known as *la Guerra sucia*[47] against ETA, a dark episode in Spanish history. Among the many undercover groups fighting against ETA, mainly anti-communist or with links to the former regime, the one that stands out was the GAL which operated between 1983 and 1987. Its activities, including

---

47 The dirty war.

murders and kidnappings, were organized clandestinely by certain state authorities using mercenaries. The objective was to force France to deal with the terrorists hiding out on French soil. Nobody killed or kidnapped by the GAL was given a fair trial and it is known that some were definitely innocent. The Marey case was one of many. In 1983 Segundo Marey was kidnapped and held for ten days by mercenaries with collaboration from members of the police force, in the mistaken belief that he was a member of ETA. He was not, he was an ordinary citizen. In 1998 ex-ministers and high officials were condemned for the kidnapping as well as for other actions carried out by the GAL. It has always been claimed that the *Presidente*[48] of the government, Felipe González, was involved but this was never proven nor was he ever brought to trial. With the dissolution of the GAL, France did start to take a more active role in the struggle against ETA which was the only positive outcome of a very murky and shameful affair.

While some politicians resorted to terror, unlike ETA the state was slow to use propaganda, another powerful tool. Why did many people readily swallow the propaganda devised by a terrorist group whose very nature took away any obligation to tell the truth? Organizations or political groups, unfettered by any controls, are adept at promoting their interests, often more so than most governments. Language is one of their most powerful weapons as any separatist group is well aware. Words such as "oppression" and "freedom" are worth their weight in gold coming with

---

48 The equivalent of Prime Minister in Britain.

a guarantee to sway the readership of the liberal press abroad. Only someone not living with the bombs and destruction, not following the inhumane kidnapping, not facing the senseless death could have shared the generous definitions of ETA as Basque "freedom fighters". What "freedom" were they fighting for and from whom? As I have already said, in the 1978 Constitution they had been given ample powers for their own governance. For anyone interested it would not take long to verify the truth of this although the answers would not have bestowed the same self-righteous glow that could be gained from supporting the down-trodden against an omnipotent oppressor.

It was not David against Goliath for ETA had power with its ability to strike randomly, inflicting damage on democratic institutions and, through innocent citizens, society as a whole. I would never dispute the right to work towards independence if any action taken is peaceful and legitimate. I would, however, question their motives: economic gain is usually far more of an incentive for separatist groups than they would ever care to admit.

Now, thankfully ETA has disappeared for good. After Miguel Angel's death they did continue but the tide was turning against them. Through the years, there were several attempts at negotiations by governments on the political left and right. With the attacks on the Twin towers in 2001 and in Madrid in 2004, terrorism could no longer be tinged with an aura of romanticism. ETA itself hastened to disown the attacks in Madrid. In 2006 ETA agreed to a ceasefire which was broken with an attack at Madrid's airport in December of that year, nevertheless efforts towards a peaceful solution continued. Parliament voted to initiate a peace process not without considerable dissension, and in October 2011 the terrorist group laid down its arms although it wasn't until May 2018 that they finally announced their disbandment.

830 deaths, thousands of injured and endless suffering had achieved nothing in over forty years. It was all ultimately pointless.

BOOM AND CRASH

With a house in the countryside, a flat in Madrid and my own family, life was quite settled as the 20th century drew to a close. What's more, now that it had much in common with other European countries I was more in step with Spain. As the new millennium approached, it became clear how dramatically the country had transformed. Trust in politics in the early eighties had given way to a belief that the economy was the solution. It was indeed booming.

Anyone born in the 1970s, who had never known life under the dictatorship, could forge ahead unencumbered by the past. Their parents or grandparents, having benefitted from improved living standards, were now in a position to help them and they were thriving. It was a generation which exuded confidence. A higher percentage than ever had studied at university, new types of job were available and with improved language skills greater opportunities were opening up. Whereas foreign companies had been forced to bring in their employees from abroad in the eighties, there were now plenty of suitable applicants in Spain. The future looked bright. Adverts, picking up on this, proclaimed their products were for the *"Joven pero sobradamente cualificado.*[49]

If there was a feeling of optimism once again, all was not well. Unemployment remained high and salaries, although improving, were definitely not good. Someone coined the term *"mileurista"* for those earning nothing more than around a thousand euros a month. This would not have been too bad if the house market had not been booming with ever increasing prices and rents. It was, however, because of the housing market that Spain was enjoying such spectacular growth.

Rather than being a new trend, faith in real estate was a continuation of village life where anyone with property, be it houses or land, was king. The advice often given was "put your money in bricks" and they did. People were buying properties right, left and centre. Flats which had been sold off-plan before they were completed were already resold at a much higher price or rented out before construction on the next block had begun. People with a flat in the centre bought an expensive house in the suburbs. The elderly man and woman who cleaned the entrance proudly told me they owned six small flats, all with mortgages. Like them, people would buy multiple properties with hefty mortgages they could barely afford, convinced prices could only rise. Sometimes they would purchase two at the same time, planning to sell one in order to pay off the mortgage on the other in the future thus leaving them debt free. What had started as a search

---

49 Young but highly qualified.

for security became a frenzy fueled by greed more than anything else.

Needless to say, prices soared as they did around the world. Old flats we could barely afford twenty years earlier were now unaffordable for most people, including us. Repayment was over 30 or 40 years, meaning the buyer was burdened with a debt into retirement. This in no way acted as a deterrent. Young people, convinced by reports and rumour that prices could never drop, believed their only option was to buy straightaway taking on a crippling debt.

Juan and Cecilia, now in their very late seventies, joined in the fun. Having been happily settled in their flat for many years, in 2007 at the very worst moment, they suddenly announced that they had put down a deposit on a new home in an anonymous block on a windswept common. It boasted a communal swimming pool despite the fact neither of them could swim and had no intention of learning. By this time it was already clear that the days of the property boom were numbered but they would not be dissuaded. Ignoring the tears and supplication from the family, they insisted on going through with the purchase since matters such as this were never open to discussion with children, however old they might be. Parents were to be obeyed, not questioned. They should have listened. When Juan sold the flat several years later after Cecilia's death it had lost nearly 50% of its value.

If the situation in cities verged on madness, the coast, where the market was fuelled to a large extent by foreigners, was crazier. The attraction of having a place in the sun was more enticing when it could be considered as a financial investment. It mattered little that the legality as well as the quality of these newly built homes were often dubious.

Other businesses flourished alongside the housing boom. Beautiful but impractical hand-me-down antiques had no place in small, modern apartments or the rambling old flats in the centre now subdivided to suit single professionals. Timeless furnishings, rarely replaced, inevitably gave way to the ubiquitous flat-pack and IKEA designs. Throughout these years, skips for building rubble lined the streets offering a treasure trove of cast-off furniture.

Revenue from municipal sales taxes and building licenses boosted the coffers of town councils and if this windfall was not enough, cash was willingly lent. All this meant that the level of public as well as private building soared to the glory of the town or more particularly, of the mayor and his councillors. Some of these developments were positive. Historic sites were being developed and museums built or improved, encouraging tourism to Spain's rich cultural areas rather than just to the coast. In Mérida, a spectacular museum was designed to display its Roman treasures while another was opened in the royal Arab city of Medina Azahara, outside Córdoba, as excavations were uncovering more of this unique historical site.

Nevertheless, there were more worrying developments. In small towns, airports, huge sports centres and galleries were being constructed, many of which have never been used or even completed. They were mainly vanity projects and have remained deserted and derelict, white elephants draining the city's finances until many have finally had to be closed down. But that was still in the future, for the time being nobody cared as long as money was king.

All this building work created an enormous demand for labour so for the first time foreigners flooded in to take jobs the Spanish couldn't or wouldn't accept. Workers came from South and Central America, Morocco and the EU, in particular Romania. As many South Americans were the grandchildren or great grandchildren of those immigrants who had left in the early 20th century or during the post-war period, obtaining Spanish nationality was straightforward. Furthermore, being Spanish speakers they found it relatively easy to fit into society although they faced their own challenges. Women would come alone leaving their children behind with the grandparents until they were in a position to provide for them. Often, the children were sent for when they were adolescents, an age when it was hard to slot into the rigid educational system which requires detailed knowledge of Spanish history and geography. Moreover, the academic year in South America runs from January to December not September to July so, unintentionally, they were entering school in the middle of the academic year. All this set up a whole generation for failure, especially those who arrived in the late 90s and early 2000s. Many never realized their potential, leaving school without qualifications.

Receiving an influx of immigrants was a new experience for Spain. The array of customs and accents enriched life as well as helping to open up of the country. At first they were welcomed with open arms as the Spanish recalled their own difficulties in adjusting to another country during their time abroad. With time their sympathies waned. Soon the newcomers began to be unfavourably compared with the Spanish experiences abroad. Their claim that Spanish immigrants had had to work hard, receiving no help unlike those recently arrived in Spain, was unfair as scant aid if any was available and most worked extremely hard for low wages.

It would have been a good time for everyone with only one tragic blot: the terrorist attacks on stations to the southeast of the city which left the whole country deeply shocked.

It was a Tuesday in March, a few days before the general elections. Early in the morning I was walking along the Paseo de la Castellana, the main artery running through the city from north to south. In the past it was the district where the wealthy had their palaces and dynastic homes, now it belongs to the rich of today, banks, embassies and financial entities. A wide tree-lined boulevard with space for cafes and kiosks, it is always busy. Throughout the day and well into the night traffic hurtles up and down, but that day, March 11, 2004, it was eerily empty. No people rushing to work, no cars until one lone ambulance dashed down sirens wailing, shattering the silence. That was how I knew that something had happened, something very serious.

I put on the radio as soon as I got home. The news was bad. The attack had been on local trains coming into one of the main stations, Atocha. Four trains had been targeted, at that time in the morning all packed with commuters from the working class areas to the southeast of the city. Rumours attributed it to ETA at first even though, in all their years of activity, the group had never carried out an attack on this scale. The death toll was a grim reminder that Spain was now an international country. The victims came from Eastern Europe, South and Central America as well as one or two people from African countries. The rest of the 193 deaths and many of the 2,050 injured were Spanish.

If the tragedy for the seriously injured and families of the victims will last forever, in the immediate future the attack altered the course of Spanish politics. The PP, the ruling party, had enthusiastically supported Bush and Blair in the alliance for an attack on Iraq despite opposition from 90% of the population who took part in a mass protest demonstration against the invasion. Realizing that any admission that Islamist extremists had perpetrated the attack would definitely not have helped their cause in the elections the following Sunday, they insisted it was ETA despite mounting evidence to the contrary. It did no good, the socialists won anyway. Later research purported to prove that the attacks were not a reaction to the war but had been planned earlier, partly because Spain was seen as an easy target.

Despite this dark moment for Spain, the optimistic mood was to continue for a few more years. With the victory of the socialist party, new social initiatives were envisaged promising seismic transformations for the new millennium. For the first time, benefits were to be provided for families who were caring for anyone who was seriously ill or disabled. If intentions were good, implementation was hampered by the deteriorating economic situation and slow bureaucracy. Others went ahead successfully.

Already in the nineties some regions had allowed same sex couples to register their relationship in a civil register when, in 2005, a law permitting same sex marriages was passed. Spain was only the third country in the world to legalize this type of marriage. Considering that, under Franco, homosexuals had been treated like criminals, often spending time in prison, the law was a measure of how far society had come in only thirty years. What with divorce, abortion and same sex marriages Franco would be turning in his icy grave in El Valle de los Caídos, as it was still called then. The law was received with opposition from a number of sectors. Besides objections from the Church which were to be expected, the right-wing People's Party was reluctant to give its approval no doubt worried about upsetting its more traditional voters although, as younger generations of voters held more liberal views on social issues, they soon softened their stance. At a later date, one of the leading members of the party married his male partner with many of his parliamentary colleagues attending the wedding.

With new progressive social measures and a booming economy, Spain was definitely moving forward fast. It seemed nothing could go wrong. Of course, it did, badly.

The worldwide financial crisis hit Spain hard in 2008. Stable jobs more or less disappeared in a puff of smoke.

The 1,000 euro salary which had received such criticism suddenly seemed pretty good. Unemployment, forever the scourge of Spain, was once again extremely high, leaving people unable to pay the huge debts they had taken on to buy one or more properties.

The pre-crisis policies adopted by banks had hardly helped. Instead of warning about the risk of overstretching, they had been actively encouraging people to take on considerable debts. Among those affected were many vulnerable groups including newly arrived immigrants who had been proud to have their own home in their adopted country. With a desire to help out they would put their own flat as a guarantee for several other families, something which banks should never have allowed for it meant that if one person fell into arrears others automatically lost their property even though they had kept up with payments.

Once the crisis, as it was aptly called in Spain, hit, the banks were ruthless. While sympathy for anyone who had bought various properties was thin on the ground, to see people losing their only home was heart-breaking. Anyone who missed only three payments risked having to hand back their property to the bank. If this wasn't bad enough, once the bank had repossessed it, it was sold for far less than the purchase price. Therefore, when hefty legal fees and costs were added on, the total was often much higher than the original amount borrowed, making it impossible to ever clear the debt. To make matters worse it was family homes that were often lost. Elderly people who had lent only a small sum to their children using their own home as a guarantee found themselves homeless. Unlike the crash of 1929 when it was investors who were driven to despair, those bearing the brunt this time were people who had always scraped by, while the leaders of the financial sectors continued to enjoy generous bonuses.

Mortgages were not the only problem. For years the local bank manager was regarded as almost a friend who could always be trusted to look after the best interests of his customers; another notion from the past which was soon to be shattered. Some banks had been aggressively selling a complex instrument, *preferentes,* with conditions that were incomprehensible to anyone without some financial expertise. The scandal broke when people tried to cash in the investment which proved virtually impossible. At first, only those who could show they were incapable of understanding the intricacies of the investment due to illiteracy or Alzheimer, for example, could claim although after many years most people managed to recover at least part of their savings through the tortuous Spanish legal system.

As the crisis deepened, families were called on to help out. Children, now with their own young children, went back to live with their parents, crammed into tiny flats with only 2 bedrooms: children in one, grandparents in another and parents in the living room on a sofa bed. Meager pensions had to be eked out to feed the whole family. The jewellery business, where one of Juan and Cecilia's sons had been working, floundered. There was no money for jewellery and, in any case, it was only the older generation who wanted to have hands laden with showy gold rings. What he saw as a few months' well-deserved holiday quickly turned into years with very little hope of a job. His partner had a small income from part-time work but despite having a son, as they were not married, officially he had no family responsibilities and received nothing once his unemployment benefits had ended. With a scant income they had no choice but to rely on the family.

Luckily, their families were in a position to help. For other families with very little or no income the situation was desperate thus, yet again, for many people the only option was to go abroad where their skills were in demand and salaries higher. They were following in the footsteps of their grandparents and great grandparents, except that they were not unskilled workers but often highly trained professionals. The generation that had proudly been "highly qualified" had become bitterly disappointed and probably more realistic. Not all of them could get good jobs at first. In northern European countries, the MacDonald's worker, the hotel cleaner or the shop assistant with a dicey accent could well be an architect or a scientist.

Many did well. Those who went to work in Britain commented that not only was it easy to find work but that once in a job promotion was rapid for those who worked well. This made a return to Spain problematic since anyone who had enjoyed a good position abroad was aware they would have to accept a lower salary and limited prospects in Spain where unemployment remained high and salaries comparatively low. Furthermore, promotion within a profession is extremely slow and in many institutions impossible.

When Spain and other Southern European countries were hard hit in 2008, people in Northern Europe liked to believe this crisis was entirely their fault. They were lazy enjoying siestas and a life in the sun. I saw interviews with British people regretting the need to return to Britain to earn some money as they loved "the Spanish way of life" which, for them, consisted of lying around the pool sipping ice-cold beer. *Ojalá!*, if only..., as the Spanish would say. Many British people would be surprised to learn that the majority of Spanish people do not spend their lives on a permanent holiday in the sun but working in big cities, getting up at the crack of dawn and arriving home late in the evening. A working day with a long lunch break was convenient in the past when cities were small and homes were often within walking distance of the workplace allowing workers to go home to enjoy lunch prepared by the stay-at-home wife and perhaps a siesta after. Nowadays, when most people have to commute to work, a long lunch hour means a long day which is not popular.

Although most criticism of Spain is unjust, it is true the country had one endemic problem: corruption. This was not a new phenomenon. From the late 19th century, corruption had been rife in the country fiefdoms of the *caciques,* the local lords with a finger in every pie whose power Primo de Rivera had attempted to curtail in the 1920s without success. It affected all political groups. Immediately before the Civil War, in 1935, the socialist party was rocked by corruption. After the war, it continued unchecked. Men such as Juan March Ordinas, who started his business life smuggling tobacco, used deals on the very edge of legality to make a fortune and the regime was more than happy to turn a blind eye if they could rely on unwavering support.

The arrival of democracy brought no acknowledgement of any dishonest dealings. Not only were there other more pressing matters to deal with but many of those who should have instigated change were themselves benefitting. The money obtained unlawfully, through misappropriation, bribery, embezzlement and other fiscal crimes was used for personal gain or to finance political parties which boiled down to much the same as power is linked to money, especially in a corrupt system. One of the first cases to come to light was the *Caso Filesa* in the 1990s, when members of the socialist party were tried for illegally obtaining funds for the party. The cynical would say this was one of the first because, with less practice than the right, the socialists had never fully mastered the art of subterfuge.

Rather than receiving thanks early whistle-blowers were ostracized or castigated making it more advantageous to join in than take risks to end the corruption. One of the early cases, the scandal in Marbella that broke in 2006, involved huge sums of money and had been going on for years. This city, which has always attracted the rich and famous, was a prime example of the wantonness of political life although, if the house of an ex-councillor shown on television is anything to go by, money certainly can't buy class. In the Catalan parliament, reference had been made years earlier to the practice of pocketing a surcharge of 3% of any works contract without provoking much of a reaction. It was an accepted practice. Mayors and councillors, trade unionists, bankers, builders and public utility companies were involved to name but a few. It couldn't have happened without the complicity of people from local and state institutions.

It was the press that brought the scale of the scandal to public attention. Every day the headlines were screeching corruption and the judiciary was forced to become involved. Unravelling the threads of some cases which reach out internationally and particularly into tax havens abroad has been time-consuming and laborious. Each new case involved higher sums which, after a while, failed to have any meaning for me. Why, I wondered, would anyone want such enormous quantities of money?

Apart from being a huge drain on the public coffers it eroded trust in authorities. Each case of corruption appeared more scandalous as the repercussions of the crash continued to reverberate through society. The anger of anyone living at poverty level was justified when their elected representatives were frittering away public funds. By the second decade of the twenty first century, the optimism of the transition had long since evaporated taking with it the remnants of the naive faith in politics and the certainty of never-ending economic improvement. All that was left in its place was a growing sense of disenchantment. The fact that the economic crisis was global did nothing to prevent politicians receiving all the blame, part of which they undoubtedly deserved.

Cecilia and Juan were among those who had only seen Spain improve for many decades and, in spite of their early lives, they were unprepared for the new circumstances. They had come to believe that their children's future would always be better; it was hard to accept that one of their children was unemployed and to realize that their grandchildren would have a struggle ahead. Their last years were spent in a society far removed from their early village lives. It was one they no longer understood.

DYING

If the manner in which we are born and die help us to define a society, Spain's history of untimely death from poverty and disease, war and rebellion, tells its own story. Its significance is revealed in exhibitions of Spain's past with death at all age from waxen children cradled in their parents' arms surrounded by family and flowers to villages filled with black-clad women. Death held a morbid fascination for the photographer as if by immortalizing it, it could be tamed. Photos of the people's heroes served for communal grief or perhaps distraction from weightier matters: Manolete in 1947 and Francisco Rivera, *Paquirri,* in 1984, dying in the bullring in an irresistible blend of tragedy and romance. Death served as a warning in unsettled times, the rebels executed in uprisings, ETA's victims left on pavements for hours, symbols of the fate of anyone who went against the grain. In war, it provided propaganda for either side as well as a powerful call to foreigners.

Death was a constant companion in Juan and Cecilia's early lives. The death of her mother and two baby brothers were not the only ones Cecilia suffered, as there would have been many other deaths among the young in the village, especially in the cold winter months. In the city, Juan would have passed ravaged corpses lying on the streets everywhere and everyday in wartime Madrid. At an early age, extended families along with inadequate medical care bred a familiarity with dying that has been lost in modern societies.

Those who survived conflicts, disease and poverty were the tough ones who often lived to a ripe old age. Ramón's death in 1985 was the first in the family I experienced. When he died after a fall in Madrid in November, he was taken to be buried in the village churchyard. Four years later, one sweltering night, Gregorio passed away where he had been born 89 years before. Most of the family was there to spend the summer as he lay in his final agony on the metal bed in the August heat. Yet even dying on his own ground could not ease his death. In the late evening groans echoed through the stillness while a hush fell over the rest of the house. The villagers, his friends, relatives and acquaintances came with whispered enquires about his health. The sense of waiting, respect and quiet sorrow were palpable.

He died at 3 am in the room where he had lived, slept and joked with the family. Arriving before dawn broke, the undertakers worked swiftly to empty the room of its sparse furniture. Then chairs were arranged around the wall in the bare room, the simple bed was replaced by a glass-topped coffin on a stand where he would lie in state waiting for his visitors. It was not long before they came.

Teenagers, who saw the funeral car when they were returning from a night out, told their parents the news.

Before the sun had risen people came along to pay their respects. First, the men called in on their way to work in the fields, later as the tolling of the church bells marked his passing, the women came bringing their knitting and embroidery to chat around the coffin as if his death was of no consequence. All the while he lay there silently, listening to the womenfolk gossiping about this and that, just as he must have done so often. Life went on. Death was merely the next stage; a continuation not an end.

I once heard a story of a village in Toledo where the elderly women all dressed in black, their sparse white hair drawn back in a bun sat outside in summer in a row, knitting. When asked what they were doing they chorused, "Waiting for death". There must be worse ways to spend a summer afternoon. It was the natural order of things. If death brought sorrow, if the tolling bells were a reminder of the fragility of life, it bound the village together in communal mourning and compassion. It was to be expected, not feared.

After the deaths of the grandfathers there were others of course: friends' parents and neighbours. I went to packed churches where everyone who had known the person in their life went along especially if they belonged to certain professions or if they regularly attended church. Some deaths were lonelier. The woman on the fourth floor in our building finally succeeded in her quest to end her life. This time the other neighbours noticed no smell of gas but after her daughters had been phoning for days without an answer, they called the police. When they arrived with firemen and ambulances, it was already too late. Once it was ascertained that there was no hope, a policewoman was stationed at the door.

When I went down to present my condolences, the neighbour's daughter was inside the flat along a corridor, I was outside, between us was the policewoman leaning on the door jamb furiously chewing gum. She clearly had no intention of letting me in or letting the daughter out, forcing me to shout my message of condolences along the corridor as if I was merely asking about a sock that had fallen off the washing line, the cigarette ends left on the stairs or the walls that needed painting. I was shocked by the casual way officialdom treated death, not only in this case but in other reported incidents. Police training then appears to have omitted the part about dealing with the bereaved. The policewomen's attitude stripped away the little dignity that was left to someone dying on the kitchen floor connected to a gas pipe.

Inevitably urbanization has altered death. Deprived of its communality, with naturalness and familiarity gone, nothing yet had emerged to replace the quiet compassion of the village. Cecilia's death, the next in the close family, had none of the closeness of her birth, nor of fading gently into eternal village life. Her decline was long, years of sinking into incoherence with all the indignities of old age. I hardly visited; old doubts persisted.

As her health failed, Juan struggled with her care alone at home. Their children could offer little help as they lived far away, they worked or had their own children to look after. Finally, when she suffered a massive stroke one Christmas time, he could no longer manage and she was admitted to hospital. She clung onto life for four more months, never regaining consciousness. Care on the public health service, excellent but with limitations, was coming to an end. She was about to be moved to a private clinic, which would be expensive, when she slipped quietly out of this life, alone in a sanitized hospital.

Burials or cremations are held immediately, usually the next day. I suppose originally because bodies could not be kept long in the heat, and, besides, arranging burials in a village was relatively straightforward. The mass for the departed soul, which was more important than the burial, was celebrated at a later date when any absent relatives would have had time to arrive. Nowadays, at least in the cities, companies deal with every aspect of death, competitively selling their services, offering everything: an all-inclusive package tour to the next world. Cecilia's body lay in a coffin lined with white satiny material, the set face framed with an exuberance of red roses. Everyone was invited to walk past the body for a final farewell, a chance to kiss the cold cheeks one last time. I declined.

This was the first part of the ceremony held in a room near the hospital. With the family scattered, very few people attended. Relatives that would gather one ceremony after another when I first arrived had been dropping off, dying, moving away or simply forgetting about distant relatives they hardly ever saw. We stood around outside in the pale spring sun in desultory groups, exchanging family gossip and news from the last few years.

After a time, we all drove across the usual wind-swept plains around the city to a crematorium near a small town to the north of Madrid. The building, some way outside the town, was efficient and pleasant enough. A room was provided where a few words could be said about the deceased but as nobody wanted to only Juan followed the coffin inside. Meanwhile, everyone else wandered around the small garden commenting on how warm it was for the time of year with the flowers already out, that we didn't often meet and that we should try to do so more often. The ashes were presented and that was it. No service, no homage or final tearful goodbye, we drove back into Madrid with the urn and the relevant documents.

Two days later, a small party gathered to take her ashes to be scattered around the village, which to all intents and purposes she had never left. It seems fitting that she is there with her ancestors, forever in the place that decided her destiny the day she was born, lying in winter at the foot of the icy mountains, in summer among the fig trees and vines. Life would go on and she could rest peacefully.

Despite not always being the happiest of marriages, theirs had lasted over sixty years, leaving a large gap in Juan's life. After the first months when he was understandably disorientated, facing everything she had left behind, he needed to tackle the question of how to spend his remaining years with a freedom he had never before enjoyed. If the life he had forged for himself had not always fulfilled its promise, suddenly the future offered opportunities he had missed.

Not long after her death, now in his mid-eighties he joined a computer course. Quickly getting to grips with this new skill, for the first time in years he made friends of his own although we knew little of this until he announced he had met a woman who lived in a distant town. Thinking back I'm not sure that he told anyone before he was off one day to start anew in Gandía, a town on the coast far from that small mountain village. After all, life was for living, moving forward, changing. He had learnt that early on. He would live with other people of his age reminiscing about times gone by, playing *petanca*[50] or chatting with his contemporaries in seafront bars. If this caused a certain disconcertion among the family, he himself would never have imagined those final years in another town, with strangers, far from the family. To cap it all, living together without being married, but what had once been scandalous was now quite acceptable.

Mentally he was still very much on the ball, whereas his partner found bureaucracy difficult; he, on the other hand, was becoming physically frail and needed someone to care for him. It was good that they could be together although the family did not quite agree. Finding someone else so soon after bereavement was still frowned upon. Rather hypocritically, this only appeared to apply to the older generations as the young were happy to divorce and quickly embark on a new relationship.

He bought a large flat in the new town hoping the family would spend time with them. Despite his ready acceptance of new customs, he himself clung to some of the conventions of the past, failing to accept that old loyalty and duty had died with modern ways. With the

---

50 French bowls, also played in Spain.

sanctity of family broken, his children and grandchildren rarely visited. As far as they were concerned, he was gone not only from Madrid but from their lives. It was a great disappointment for him.

He died suddenly at the age of 90. Only a few years earlier it was a death he would never have dreamt of, far removed from the village with only his partner by his side. A mere handful of people went to the funeral, not that he would have minded in the least. He was not one for ceremonies.

It is never easy to tie up a life. Cecilia's gold and jewellery, the collection marking the milestones of her life, had been given to his partner, in a final travesty against the decorum of another age. The house in the village had gone years ago, and the flat Juan and Cecilia bought in 2007 was sold at a great loss. The rest was to be divided between the children.

The laws on inheritance, far more rigid than in Britain, are a reflection of a rural society, intended to protect the family's land and thereby, their income. On marriage it was customary for parents with the means to give their children a piece of land either to farm or, like Juan and Cecilia, to build themselves a home. The children would then generally work with the parents who would remain in the family home when their working days were done. Guaranteed care in old age, which few in villages and small towns would question, was part of an arrangement which was mutually beneficial for all parties.

The system remains very much the same. By law the deceased's estate, which in the case of a couple is half the assets, is divided into three parts. One third is to be shared in equal parts between the "compulsory" heirs who are the closest family members, usually the children but not the remaining spouse. The second third is apportioned between the same people but not necessarily in equal parts and the final third can be freely allocated.

What happens if the children die before the parents? In this case the estate reverts to the parents who, having lost someone who should have cared for them would need it for their old age. This system makes perfect sense in the rural environment but less so in the city where most parents don't or can't give their children much. Moreover, older generations usually have their own pensions whereas younger ones are struggling to pay a mortgage and raise a family. It means that, should one of a couple die after they have worked hard for several years to buy a flat or to save, half of the money or property would pass not to the surviving spouse but to the deceased's parents. Then, on the death of the latter, the estate would pass to their surviving children. It was with some dismay that I discovered this before we had children, realizing that if I were widowed I would have to hand over half of the property we had bought although I could still have kept the usufruct[51] as is customary.

The fact that the law lays down the order of inheritance clearly cannot put a stop to wheeling

---

51 This legal instrument is often used in Spain. One person is the owner of the property but others may have the usufruct which grants the right to use the asset but also the obligation to pay all costs.

and dealing while, at the same time divorce and remarriage have introduced further complications. Even so dissension is still kept behind closed doors. Occasionally reports appear of old people thrown out of their flat by their own family which leads to much hand-wringing and lamentation. The reporter condemns the heartlessness and ingratitude towards the aged person, cast out and unloved, the ultimate rejection in the twilight years, but as the drama unfolds, hints appear that things might not be quite as they seem, whispers suggest that there might be hidden stories from years gone by of favouritism and playing the system. The family is unavailable for comment, unwilling to admit to the world that the illusions of the happy family have dwindled with the passing years.

Cecilia, through inheritance, reached out with a hand from beyond the grave. Seventy years ago she had had the responsibility of running a family thrust upon her and that is what she had always done; she had no intention of letting go even at the end. You were loved and appreciated by a third or a half of a quarter of their worldly good, no more and no less. Sadly, it left the family that they had so valued split, dismayed and unhappy.

For me all this was unimportant, which is not to say that her passing did not leave me with conflicting emotions. Even though I sympathized with the family, her slow death caused me no great sorrow. Rather than regret I felt release and perhaps, for one fleeting moment, triumph. She had always wished me somewhere else, now she was gone and I had stayed.

It was too late to tell her anything, she would never have listened anyway. But what would I like to say to her if she were before me now? That I never came to challenge her life, that all I wanted was to be happy. When she died, she took with her her rigid and immobile world of the past. If limitations were the price of stability bringing comfort, even as they stultified initiative, she had accepted. I can see how I threatened her ideals and she was right that I did not fit in because I could never do so on her terms. It was never a question of who was right or wrong; it was simply that we came from worlds apart. For years, she was doggedly clinging to a rapidly fading world whereas I was floundering in a society that appeared backward. Just as I desperately wished it would change, she hoped equally fervently it never would.

Now they have both gone, they have taken with them the old world of war, adversity and suffering. They had accepted it was their lot with stoicism. Catastrophes were what they expected, what caused them greater disappointment were the gradual, almost imperceptible changes: the anonymity of the city, the breaking up of the family and foreign influences creeping in. All this was unwelcome, an intrusion against the pre-ordained life of their youth sending the delusion of the "happily ever after" up in smoke. Yet on balance, life treated them quite well. The hardship of their early years had given them the strength to face the rest of their lives as well as gratitude for what they had finally achieved. They took good things offered rather than brooding over unfairness and injustice. Early deprivation had left them content with the material possessions they had, not constantly hankering after more.

With their deaths their hold over my life was loosened, nevertheless, as I have become older the advantages of their world have become clearer. I understand now what they wanted to keep and I am aware of the relevance of years gone by. What they appreciated lives on, diluted in each generation, but making Spain all it is today. For my part, I have come to realize that the past was theirs; it could never have been mine.

REMEMBERING

When Juan and Cecilia died they took with them their memories of the war and post-war. Few people with first-hand experience of these bitter years remain, leaving the conflict as well as the dictatorship relegated to the history books, exhibitions and films. With age I have realized how events that were once distant and irrelevant can draw closer and I understand why these few need to remember.

If the war was pushed to the background during the transition, it gradually crept back through the eighties and nineties, at first in timid exhibitions, later with a plethora of documentaries and books. Of course, the victors would see no point in remembering while for others improvements at the end of the regime had helped to assuage their pain, yet some could never forget and wanted society to acknowledge all they had been through before time ran out.

For the latter and their families there had been nearly forty years of waiting, silence and fear during the dictatorship. Grief had always been inwards, gnawing away through the years, unexpressed and unacknowledged. Close family members had died while others had been used as forced labour or had been imprisoned without a trial. Those who survived against the odds were forced to silently suffer the consequences of their experiences. In the eighties and nineties there were widows, widowers and children who had borne not only loss but also ostracism for many years. Often they had been left wondering about the fate of relatives dragged out of their home never to be seen again, or of those who had failed to return from fighting in the conflict. Unable to accept that their dear ones lay in anonymous ditches beside a road or in communal pits, they wished to mourn their dead, to lay them to rest with the respectful burial they would have wanted.

A few years ago we visited Cartagena, a coastal city in the southeast which has always been an important naval port. Held by the Republicans until almost the end of the war, during the frequent bombardments the population needed to seek refuge. A cave high up on a cliff above the city, which served as an air-raid shelter, now houses a museum of life in the city during the conflict. As well as the usual objects and photos, there were contemporary news reels bearing witness to the desperation of the population. By the end of the war, as towns and cities along the coast fell, the sea was the only way out. When the port was surrendered to the Nationals many had no choice but to flee by boat.

While we were there an elderly man approached the staff at the desk to ask if anyone could give him information about film footage being shown. Who owned it? Where could he find more details? He explained that he had seen his sister in his mother's arms in a boat. At a later date she had died, he didn't say how but it might have been in an attack, or from starvation or disease which were all too common. Although I didn't stay to find out if they could help him, it touched me that, despite the many years gone by, he had not forgotten his dead sister. I could imagine how it had always affected him, this pain of loss weaving through the decades.

Like numerous other ordinary people he had lived with a gaping hole in his life until, with the implementation of democracy, families finally began to appear on television in documentaries, interviews and news items, talking about their lives and experiences. They were keen to tell their stories and fulfill the promises made to their mothers, fathers or grandparents that they would do everything they could to find their missing relatives.

If nothing had been done during the early years of democracy, it was because a certain reluctance to stir muddy water persisted. Many people believed it was advisable to move forward rather than dwell on the divisions of the past. Moreover, it was a delicate time when too much investigation carried the risk of opening up old wounds thereby unsettling the fragile political situation. This would explain why in 1977 an Amnesty Act was passed with the objective of fomenting social reconciliation and why it was decided that government officials should be allowed to continue in their roles, as it would have been unwise to upset anyone in a position of authority. Later, the first socialist government, already grappling with the Herculean task of establishing a democracy, did nothing and from 1996 right-wing governments saw few advantages in dragging up memories of the conflict and no doubt the majority of their voters agreed. Besides, much time had gone by since the crimes were committed, and Franco had issued a general pardon for all war crimes in 1969. Nevertheless, despite all this in the early 21st century remembrance was an issue that needed to be tackled and solved definitively.

It was a complex question which required the utmost care, therefore it was not until 2007, thirty two years after Franco's death, that a law was passed under a socialist government with the objective of resolving the grievances and injustices of the Civil War and the dictatorship. It was about close relatives, and if at the time trade unionists or political parties were mentioned, it was only in passing. Most people were not seeking revenge or retribution, they simply wished for remembrance and recognition, raising their relatives out of the anonymity of a communal grave. Despite the expense, this did not seem too much to ask.

I believe it was correct that the law should be concerned with people rather than politics or revenge, yet, impunity for certain individuals was hard for the victims to swallow. One such case was a man nicknamed Billy *el niño*, Billy the kid who, according to his victims, had derived pleasure from the cruelty of torture up until the end of the dictatorship. Not only had he managed to escape punishment but he received promotions and awards during the democracy which increased his pension. A movement was underway to deprive him of his privileges when he died in the Covid pandemic, depriving those who had suffered at his hands of any chance of justice.

Another concern was the existence of place names from Franco's era even at this late date. Finding new place names for one reason or another is almost a national hobby for if some heroes are to be remembered, others must be obliterated. The problem was the list of suspects was drawn up hastily without adequate scrutiny of the history. A plaque in memory of nuns was destroyed although they could hardly be guilty of any wrongdoing during the conflict since they had been dragged out of their convent and murdered before the war broke out. This particular memorial was restored at considerable expense.

Another victim of the purge was a statue of Franco's brother, which would have been reasonable had it not been intended to honour his prowess as an aviator, not his role in the war. To make matters worse he had been a leading Republican until he realized it was expedient to go over to his brother's side. He died not long after in an accident amid rumours of assassination which were never proven. What were his motives for changing sides? Could he be blamed for his actions? War and conflict raise many questions, right and wrong are rarely clear-cut.

Although his family had suffered under the regime, Juan was always more pragmatic than emotional. The street where he lived for many years, named after General Fanjul, one of the National generals killed at the outbreak of war, was renamed after a local train station. By that time Juan had already left but I doubt he would have agreed since time and familiarity had taken away any relation to past events.

One burning question that remained to be resolved was the fate of the huge memorial built with the sacrifice of many men including Ramón: El Valle de los Caídos. Although it continued to be financed by the state after the implementation of democracy, its upkeep was in the hands of a religious order whose abbot was openly sympathetic to the former dictator. Every year on November 20, the date of Franco's death, far right groups organized a ceremony in honour of both Franco and Jose Antonio Primo de Rivera, the founder of the fascist group the *Falange*. They would meet on the huge esplanade in front of the monument dressed in the *Falange* uniforms with a navy blue shirt, waving the National flag with its black eagle. In the early years of democracy they then drove around Madrid horns blowing and flags flying from car windows. The introduction of the Law of Historic Memory put an end to this performance which had already lost most of its power and appeal. Even so, for the time being nothing could be done to prevent the memorial from serving as a place of pilgrimage for the extreme right.

It was precisely because of its symbolism for certain sectors that many people deemed it unacceptable that the dictator should continue to lie in state in the centre of the magnificent building. When plans to remedy this situation were broached, debate was fiery. On one hand there was Franco' s family, the prior, his monks and most right-wing parties, on the other the government, left-wing parties and associations for the Republican victims of the war. Most ordinary people were more interested in other pressing concerns in their daily lives.

Once it had been decided that Franco's body should be removed, the next question was what to do with him. His final resting place had to be somewhere that could never be turned into a shrine. At the same time the family had to be reasonably satisfied since they had been threatening legal action despite knowing opposition to his removal was futile. In the end a solution was found which was more or less acceptable for all parties. The ceremony to move the body was to be private nevertheless representatives from the government attended. There was a certain amount of pomp to pacify Franco's supporters now they had been forced to accept defeat, and the whole thing was broadcast on television. I heard the helicopter as he was flown out of his mausoleum to be interred in a private chapel where he could not be worshiped by anyone except the close family. With him the vestiges of another era were carried away forever.

There has been talk of removing the cross, the huge stone structure erected above the mausoleum and basilica. I hope it remains. Towering up between the mountains, it is visible for miles silhouetted against the sky. Recognizable to me at a time when little else was, it symbolizes not religion or the dictatorship but my early years when we escaped from the city to the mountains. What is more, erasing a building cannot cancel out the past. The best thing to do would be to make it into a museum of the war since none exists as far as I know.

The war ended over 80 years ago, the dictatorship almost 50. Like Juan, anyone old enough to remember would now be over ninety. Many people no doubt regretted their actions but they did what they believed was correct in the circumstances at that time. Now they are no longer soldiers, they are grandparents, great-grandparents or more likely dead.

History is complex and cannot be brought down to a common denominator to neatly comply with the political correctness of the day. We can only learn from history if we are willing to examine events with an unbiased mind and to accept their complexities. Facts can always be found to suit a preformed narrative, presenting them to give a cardboard cutout while any event reduced solely to memory does not represent a historically balanced account unless there is an open search for what really happened. This is why history should be a field for historians. At the same time evaluation of the rights or wrongs is for moral philosophers, not politicians. Whatever the problems in Spain today, they have little in common with the situation in 1936, therefore it would be well for politicians to dwell less on the events and more on the dangers of intolerance and intransigence.

SPAIN TODAY

What of Spain today? What remains of the country I arrived in over forty years ago? In many ways, very little. Of this I am happy, despite occasionally remembering those early years with nostalgia. Names which were once familiar now only appear in obituaries or history books. Adolfo Suárez, the first leader of democracy, died a few years ago receiving a late acknowledgment for his part in the transition. "Do you know who he was?" a young girl asked me. "My father told me about him".

The influence of religion over politics has dwindled over the years although I sometimes wonder if the diminishing numbers who lived through the years of enforced Catholicism can ever completely shake off its tentacles. Rejection of the principles so long indoctrinated must bring guilt or at least unease. Nevertheless, it is no longer a case of either blind faith or vehement rejection nor does it feature much in policy-making except possibly for the extremes of the political spectrum which cling to ideologies of the past. Inevitably, the demise of religion has taken away simple answers, moral guidelines and the sense of duty.

The craziness of the early transition has been tempered by time. Celebrities from the *Movida* have cast off their wild ways to become established figures on the cultural scene, receiving awards, recognition and of course, money. If most rebels of the seventies long since gave up their militancy, it could be because their dreams of a perfect polity did not turn out as they hoped or because life took them along an easier path. Many of the brave students of the sixties and early seventies have been successful in their careers and are the owners of flats and houses. Some, however, have not lost the will to fight for their rights and are out on the streets once again, demonstrating against pension reforms. As grandparents they can recount their tales of struggle to a young generation who most likely will have little in common with their early lives. These new generations, convinced they are pioneers in politics, are greatly influenced by the past.

In 2011, a movement which became known as the 15M[52] began following the publication of the book, *Indignez-vous!* by Stéphane Hessel the previous year. It was not unique to Spain although it might have been stronger here than in other countries. On my way to work I would walk through the emblematic Puerta del Sol and the surrounding streets and squares where groups of young people with dreadlocks and casual clothes were sitting on the ground, piles of books next to them as they earnestly solved the world's problems. A reminder of a half-forgotten time when I too had all the solutions.

---

52 This movement started with a demonstration on May 15, hence the name.

Podemos, a new party with an ideology in many ways close to that of the old Communist party, emerged from these gatherings. Fuelled by the generalized discontent with measures of austerity after the crisis, it was going to rid Spain of corruption, sweeping away any remnant of the past to leave equality and hope. Theirs would be a brave new world of solidarity, a beacon of brotherhood or rather sorority as feminism has always been a central policy. Once again young people raised the standard of progressive politics and radical reform. It was not surprising that this optimist new voice in a sea of decay appealed mainly to the young. The founders, almost all from the department of political sciences in one of the leading universities in Madrid, understood the power of modern media in a way that the old parties never had. Students were happy to help, spending hours on twitter, replying to comments and defending the party.

Observing them reminded me of the past rather than a new future. They were critical of the transition yet, despite being unhindered by the obstacles faced in the inchoate democracy, they themselves had objectives that were unlikely ever to be reached. They were obsessed with the Catholic Church, no doubt influenced by their parents, for no justification could be found in the declining power of Catholicism. Where they differed radically from their parents' generation was that they risked nothing, on the contrary, by entering politics they had secured for themselves cushy jobs for years to come.

Podemos shared a crusade against corruption with another new party, *Ciudadanos,* founded earlier in 2006.

Both made much of their probity yet neither had existed when corruption was almost a way of life in the union of politics and business. Obviously, their anti-corruption stance was admirable and certainly influenced the political ethos in Spain, however, it was the press rather than the new political parties which deserve a large part of the credit for uncovering cases of corruption.

An extreme right-wing party, *Vox,* took longer to emerge possibly because it was a reminder of the forty year dictatorship. Nevertheless, after a faltering start, its chance came with the rise of Catalan separatism which provided them with an opportunity to follow in Franco's footsteps as the champions of Spanish unity. This was the only ideology they shared with *Ciudadanos,* which was founded in Catalonia as an anti-separatist party. Vox's policies unashamedly harked back to another era before the arrival of immigrants, the erosion of the church's power and homosexual marriage among, in their view, other aberrations in modern Spain.

With time even the new parties have become almost indistinguishable from the old and risk being absorbed or disappearing. Their original eagerness to reach agreements, their idealism and their faith in the power of politics to find solutions, all reminiscent of the transition, have quickly evaporated leaving the usual disagreements, bickering and accusations. Of course none has managed to solve the problems brought by the transformations in society thus leaving issues that the Spanish felt would never affect them still to be tackled. What to do with children of working parents? How can elderly parents be cared for with most women working and often absent from the home most of the day? What should be done to reduce the number of unemployed? How can families best be supported?

If problems remain, dramatic changes which were seen as a threat to the very fabric of Spanish society have been rapidly assimilated. Divorce and abortion, once so feared by the church and the conservative parties, have become an accepted part of life. Not only has the prophesized cataclysm never materialized but instead the shame attached to marital problems has disappeared at least in the cities. Equally, the rejection of foreigners in the family has gone. Recently a young British woman marrying into a Spanish family told me her future husband was an only child of divorced parents. His mother lived alone leaving him solely responsible for her as she had no-one else. How different from the large families when I arrived, where acceptance was conditional and they held all the cards!

The low birthrate, hard to imagine in the fifties and sixties, is unlikely to change in the near future with the limited financial aid and support available. In the run up to Christmas there used to be jokes about putting up with the *cuñado,* the brother-in-law. In recent years the joke has been that there is no *cuñado*. With smaller and smaller families few people have a brother or even less an "in-law". The hordes of cousins, aunts and uncles have gone and relations within the extended family are more relaxed and casual. Last year we went back to that restaurant in Soria where we had eaten among the formal families of the eighties many years ago. Once again the food and service were excellent, the décor was very much the same but now it was full of people like us: casually dressed young couples, small families each at their own table, each in their own world.

The family I entered on arriving has been no exception to this transformation. They meet from time to time but their lives have diverged. They live at greater distances from each other on the outskirts of the city and their hectic lives leave little time for their own nuclear families, never mind the array of relatives. Since the family house in the village was sold, there is no longer a shared dwelling to bring them together.

Juan and Cecilia had not been back to their village for some years before their deaths but if they had they would have found it dramatically altered. It is still beautiful with the mountains, the river, the olive and oak trees, and stone houses, yet the inhabitants have little in common with the villagers of the past. Many newcomers have adopted a hippy lifestyle producing ecological soap, other hand-crafted products and ecological gardening.

Ironically, many of these are activities Cecilia would recognize except that they are carried out by earnest young people with university degrees who, never having known the old ways, consider themselves to be pioneers. Some have been drawn by the beauty of nature and the simplicity, others wished to escape city life which has become too expensive and hectic. They are the grandchildren or great grandchildren of the children taken to the cities many years ago, who looked on the village as a place for weekends, not somewhere to settle. Their ancestors would look askance at a large part of their lives: the men folk caring for the babies, doing the cooking, the women tending the land. Yoga, an irreligious activity, would certainly not meet with their approval. The young children will have golden memories of freedom rather than of toil and discomfort. It is unlikely, however, that they will ever acquire the stoicism of earlier generations.

If this particular village has been able to reinvent itself with the help of improved connections, others have not shared the same happy fate. Vast expanses of the countryside in the interior of the country have emptied with the demise of villages, making it hard for the traveller to believe that only sixty years ago it was a predominantly agrarian society. These sparsely populated inland regions are sometimes referred to as "*la España Profunda*", literally "deep Spain", although "dark" might be a better translation with its connotations of ignorance and backwardness. With the exception of the summer months, only a handful of very elderly folk remain in some villages waiting for the weekly visit of the priest or mobile shop. While Spain tussles with remembrance of the Civil War, it has cast off its rural past lightly without a thought despite all that it had signified for the concept of "Spanishness".

The reasons people no longer want to live in the country are quite clear. Often there are no services, internet or shops for the most basic purchases while doctors, let alone hospitals, may be at a considerable distance. Houses are in a state of disrepair with little or no heating. In many cases access is via a narrow, winding road and, after heavy snowfalls, some of the mountain villages are cut-off for a large part of the winter leaving the inhabitants isolated and vulnerable. One key problem is that, for decades, these areas have held little interest for most authorities, foremost among them politicians. If they receive desultory interest even at election times, it is hardly surprising as there are few votes to be won. Furthermore, any solution would involve a long-term plan which would not bear fruit in time for the politicians to reap the benefits.

Nevertheless, various institutions have expressed an interest in reviving the rural world and there is considerable potential. New means of communication and better services for tourism as well as the development of agro-food industries would provide Spain with a much-needed source of income. Besides, life in villages could appeal to people struggling in cities which are becoming increasingly expensive and crowded.

Madrid might be more costly but it has improved beyond recognition, evolving without my realizing it. Finally, it has become the modern capital it aspired to be at the end of the nineteenth century. Through the years the old elegance had re-emerged, the icing-sugar houses in pastel shades have been renovated, polluted streets cleared of traffic and trees planted, making it brighter and cleaner. Streets that once endured war and revolution are now threatened by nothing more sinister than speculation as well as town planning, or rather the lack of it.

Like all cities, it is still divided into districts but not according to those sweeping plans at the end of the 19th century. If each district has its own character, they are certainly not the ones projected originally. Nowadays some are favoured by the LGBTQ+ community, others attract bohemians, young professionals or families. The centre is the place to be for anyone who can afford to live there.

Were María and Ramón to return they would barely recognize their old haunts. La Latina is trendy, or as an estate agent would say "sought after". A multicultural district, it is full of bars, nightlife and tourists. The old *rastro* or flea market which they must have often visited has been taken over by Chinese shops which sell just about anything anyone would want. They wouldn't believe that the old iron market of San Miguel is a place for visitors, that the products they would buy everyday are admired, that the colourful language of the shopkeeper and the filthy floor have been replaced by exotic languages and cleanliness, a show piece for what Spain can do. Through all this the nuns live on across the road as they have always done, selling sweetmeats oblivious to all that has gone on around them. It is good to know some things never change.

If their Madrid has gone, so has mine or at least the one I knew when I first arrived. I wonder now if it really was so stagnating, disorganized and chaotic and why I needed so desperately to escape. The grimy station I left on my honeymoon which had so forcefully represented the past is now unrecognizable. As well as being a busy station with fast, efficient trains carrying commuters to and from the pleasant suburbs in the north, it is a bright shopping centre offering a new consumer life with Starbucks, Zara, cafés and cinemas.

My own neighbourhood has evolved from a place where elderly people lived their whole lives to a shabby, run-down area for drug addicts and then to a desirable residential area for young professionals. Driven out by rising costs or the death of the owners, the old traditional shops that would let us take items and pay later have all closed, soon reopening as trendy bars and boutiques. It might appear to be an improvement yet the effects of modernization on people's lives have not always been positive. The squabbling widows are long gone, taking with them the communal spirit of the blocks of flats. One of the flats was temporarily taken over by squatters, a serious problem throughout Spain which the government appears unwilling to solve. Others have become holiday rentals, never very good for the upkeep of the building.

I hardly know who people are when I pass them on the stairway. The elderly women carrying shopping up flights of steps have been replaced by tourists lugging suitcases, looking forward to a weekend of heavy drinking and vomiting on the stairs. Flats are rented to students on an Erasmus year who mistakenly think that the Spanish are impervious to noise at any time of the night, a view not shared by the residents who must get up early in the morning to go off to work.

If city life has taken its toll on the laidback country way of life, it is true that the Spanish attitude in general remains more relaxed as if some rules are never quite to be obeyed, however, this is not always the case by any means. Woe betide any foreigner who persists in believing that anything goes in Spain. Tax has to be paid on assets anywhere in the world and control is relentless, no-one, not even the ex-king can avoid investigation for tax evasion. Even while regretting the laxity of the past, and who doesn't occasionally resent the tax collector, improvements requiring finance make everyday life infinitely better. The health service is excellent with an appointment system and modern installations. Transport within the city and greater Madrid area is fast and frequent.

Legislation has, of course, driven progress to make life safer and pleasanter. People still meet in bars, cleaner now but just as noisy. Strict standards of hygiene are observed with tapas along the bar carefully covered so no-one could blow smoke over them as they used to. In any case, smoking, once so widespread, has now been banned in most public places. While accepting that it is better, it leaves a touch of regret, I still half hope to find the hazy, smoked-filled rooms, the realm of poets, writers and artists which George Borrow or Laurie Lee might have visited.

It took Spain some years to embrace ecology but even now it has never reached the dizzying heights of waste and consumerism many other countries have achieved. Neither has it taken on fast food the way the British have; the Spanish don't appear to have an irresistible need to devour large quantities of food in public at any time or in any place which means public transport is cleaner and less smelly.

Progress can be slow. Spain has some way to go before it manages to commercialize every aspect of its history and a large part of its cultural heritage remains to be exploited.

Someone who recently worked in *Patrimonio Nacional*[53] described it as "stagnated". Spain, or at least anything run by the state such as palaces, castles, museums, is officially closed on Mondays for the hapless tourist, which is good for the workers but not so good for the tourist industry. It is as if they would like to virtuously separate the cultural from the commercial. It always amazes me that they have often failed to realize that the best place for the gift shop is the area everyone is obliged to walk through on the way out.

Problems persist, they always will. The thorny question of independence for Catalonia or the Basque country is a recurrent issue in politics. With unemployment, the aspirations of many immigrants and young people have come to nothing. Nevertheless, Spain is much better now than it was forty years ago. For generations it was an effort to move forward, to leave the old Spain behind yet in this rapidly evolving society the immobility of rural life seems far away. Its emergence into the new world has been painful and somewhat erratic but in the end it has been largely successful.

---

53 The state department responsible for the preservation and promotion of Spain's cultural heritage.

EPILOGUE

I always knew that whatever I wrote could never be lighthearted, of olive groves or laughter. Neither could it have been a faithful reflection of how the Spanish saw themselves for that is not what I observed, nor what I experienced. More than many other countries, Spain continues to be ruled by clichés. We have the merry Spaniards, the country bumpkins, the friendly neighbours more than willing to throw over a bag of figs or a carafe of olive oil. They buy drinks in the bar, slap each other on the back as the children run happily around their feet. They are the builders who never turn up for work on time, people who pay no tax, the insouciant southerners living off hard-earned cash from northern Europe. The picaresque lives on. Should there be any clouds across the azure sky in this carefree place, help will always be available from the ubiquitous family while fruits ripen, wine flows and the sun beats down.

This Spain has never existed, at least not for me. It is a figment of the imagination, wishful thinking for anyone dreaming of an escape to a place in the sun. For them Spain is beaches, sand and sun, whereas I know more of the mountain ranges, the empty plains and high plateaus.

Spain for me has never been a place of eternal holidays. I always noticed the biting cold as much as the warmth of the sun, the darkness as much as the light.

I could only write of a country which has struggled for centuries to find its way and continues to face inherited challenges. If I ever doubted it, I have seen that history inevitably shapes a country and its people, yet at the same time I have realized how quickly things can change. Spain has been forced to move from a rural to a modern economy, from dictatorship to democracy, everything that happened in other countries over centuries was compressed into a short time. It has survived revolution, war and dictatorship, striving to catch up with other European countries, casting off centuries of backwardness and isolation to emerge as a settled democracy.

Modern amenities have transformed places which meant hardship to past generations. Nowadays we can share the route King Alfonso XIII took in *Las Hurdes* almost a hundred years ago, visiting the simple room with a wooden bed, a mattress, a wash basin and a crucifix where he spent the night. Afterwards, we can admire the impressive scenery before returning to the comfort of our own time. With this glimpse of the past I am reminded of how far Spain has come not only from these penurious war years but also from the time of my arrival. I've seen the old world vanish and a new one emerge, hope and optimism then disillusionment, the rocky path towards democracy. I acknowledge, however, that if Spain is different now, so am I.

Thinking back to my first years in Spain, I remember how far away everything was, how different, strange and impenetrable. When I arrived I neatly separated the present from the past as the young so easily do, I no longer can. With age the past becomes more relevant, not less. At the same time, I realize that if the young people of today were taken back into that society they would find it no easier to fit in than I did. I, on the other hand, like the Spanish of my generation, have lived through many changes. I have travelled along with them gradually catching up with their past as I shed my own. This is my world now and to a certain extent I have adopted its past.

Nonetheless, I know that, despite absorbing some of their identity, I will never be Spanish. Anyone who claims they can lightly reject their own nationality are turning it into something tangible, with flags and past glories, when nationality can be simply memories of childhood and youth. It is the smells of rainy days and melting tar, misty mornings and autumn hoar frost on rosehips and privet hedges, ancient hedgerows and bluebell woods, unchanging things of nature along with the softness of the land and the unique architecture of the past. These things will always be with me.

If I should ever go back, I wonder if I would understand Britain. Friends warn me it is not the same, they tell me it has changed for the worse and I fear it has moved much further into rootlessness and consumerism. It would be an unknown land just as Spain in the eighties was for me. Yet, if it has left me behind I don't particularly mind for I prefer the older more stable world with one foot in the past and the other in the present.

Looking through this collection of memories of events and experiences, I realize that on occasions it appears gloomy; photos, however, tell another tale. I am struck by the happiness, the joy of life in the family, friends and children in them, my own private life where I would let nothing intrude. Besides, I do not dwell on the past and, moreover, never having been an idealist or expecting perfection I have rarely been disappointed.

I also believe that discontent had its advantages, leading as it does to a search for explanations. The background to my early years in Spain was, in equal measure, dismaying yet intriguing. Had I been delighted with everything I saw, I would never have delved below the surface to understand more deeply. I'm aware this has led to my own opinions but then any country is not one but many, our interpretation depending on our own experiences and prejudices. Living abroad has taught me that journalists, correspondents or travel writers have, like everyone else, their own biases. It is wise to treat their views with scepticism as well as interest.

Almost 50 years have passed since that misty day in November when I heard of Franco's death. For Spain as well as for me, that moment is long gone. Yet sometimes I wish I could go back to that time, start afresh. If I could see that grainy black and white film of the Civil War once again, I would know the places and the people. The men fighting could be the old men in the villages chatting on park benches, the young girls with them would be aged grandmothers. I would judge them more benevolently for all they had been through.

Many times I have travelled the same route I took on that first journey through Spain, but there is little to remind me of that stifling day one July. Not only are the trains fast and efficient, almost always running on time, the people are not the same. They no longer share food or even speak. In fact there is little time for these civilities since even the longest journeys only take a couple of hours. They sit separately in comfortable seats booked well in advance, eating sandwiches in plastic wrappers from the bar, reading or watching the film that is being shown. They are concerned with their own lives, not the people in the next seats. But what for me is more important is that the landscape I travel through is no longer of an unknown country. Not only do I understand its present, I can fill the emptiness and remoteness with the past.

It is summer once again now, with the same heat, the same dry landscape and the sleepless nights but the bewilderment and loneliness have faded into a memory. That journey belongs to someone else in another time, another place. When I came, it was never meant to be for good and sometimes I wonder if I would have stayed knowing then what I know now. Probably not, but I'm glad I did.

This book is printed on paper from sustainable sources managed under the Forest Stewardship Council (FSC) scheme.

It has been printed in the UK to reduce transportation miles and their impact upon the environment.

For every new title that Troubador publishes, we plant a tree to offset CO_2, partnering with the More Trees scheme.

For more about how Troubador offsets its environmental impact, see www.troubador.co.uk/sustainability-and-community